A CAPTIVE OF WAR

Solon Hyde

A Captive Of War

By
Solon Hyde
*Hospital Steward 17th Regiment
Ohio Volunteer Infantry*

*Edited and with a Preface by
Neil Thompson*

 Burd Steet Press

First Printing, 1900
Second Revised Edition, 1996, with supplemental materials

Second Printing by
Burd Street Press
Shippensburg, PA 17257 USA

This Burd Street Press publication
was printed by
Beidel Printing House, Inc.
63 West Burd Street
Shippensburg, PA 17257 USA

In respect for the scholarship contained herein, the acid-free paper used in this book meets the guidelines for permanence and durability of the Committee on Production Guidelines for Book Longevity of the Council on Library Resources.

For a complete list of available publications
please write
Burd Street Press
Division of White Mane Publishing Company, Inc.
P.O Box 152
Shippensburg, PA 17257 USA

Library of Congress Cataloging-in-Publication Data

Hyde, Solon.
      A captive of war / by Solon Hyde : [introduction by Neil
Thompson].
            p.   cm.
      Originally published: New York : McClure, Phillips & Co.,
1900. With new introd.
        ISBN 1-57249-010-1 (acid-free paper)
        1. Hyde, Solon. 2. United States--History--Civil War, 1861–1865--
Prisoners and prisons, Confederate 3. United States--History-
-Civil War, 1861–1865--Personal narratives. 4. Prisoners of war--
United States--Biography. I. Title.
E611.H96   1996
973.7'71--dc20   96-6270
                                                          CIP

PRINTED IN THE UNITED STATES OF AMERICA

To
Miss CLARA BARTON
Whose Life Work
Has been to minister to the bettering
Of the Condition of the unfortunate in
War, Pestilence and Famine,
This book is respectfully inscribed
As a tribute of appreciation
By the
AUTHOR

Columbus, Ohio

CONTENTS

PREFACE

When I was a small boy, my grandmother used to tell me stories about her father, a man with the peculiar sounding name of Solon Hyde. She'd say he served in the Civil War as a hospital steward in an Ohio regiment, helping wounded and sick soldiers as best he could. She told me he'd been captured at a place called Chicka-something in Georgia, and that he spent the next eighteen months in five different rebel prisons including one terrible place called Andersonville. She told me her mother, Czarina, spent those eighteen months in anguish, not knowing what had become of her beloved, the man she would marry after the war. She told me Solon barely survived the ordeal, returning home a virtual skeleton. She said he lived the rest of his life with scurvy scars on his legs. I remember wondering what scurvy scars looked like. And she told me he'd written a book about his experiences that I should read. He had titled it *A Captive of War*.

It wasn't until long after she was gone and the one and only family copy of the book had been entrusted to my older sister that I finally heeded my grandmother's advice and read it. I had become a Civil War hobbyist myself by that time, reading whatever I could find of histories, biographies, and diaries. I thought it was about time I availed myself of my great-grandfather's own story.

Two things struck me immediately. First of all, Solon wrote his story well, even eloquently at times. He described the events of his captivity with remarkable detail, wit, insight, and compassion. Although he blamed the leaders of the Confederacy for the harsh treatment Union prisoners received, a controversial if understandable bias on his part, still he could be tough on his own side too. He freely condemned Union soldiers who preyed on fellow prisoners, he decried hypocrisy and puffery no matter what uniform it wore, and he remarked many times on the courtesies extended him by Southerners.

Secondly, *A Captive of War* is a good tale. It begins with Solon's capture at Chickamauga, Georgia, September 20, 1863, and ends with exchange in Wilmington, North Carolina, February 27, 1865. In between he was kept within Richmond's Libby and Pemberton prisons, then moved to Danville from where he escaped. Once recaptured, he was sent on to Andersonville for a six-month stay. He finished his captivity at Salisbury, North Carolina.

Like many men of his age, Solon viewed the conflict as a religious and moral battleground. As such, his opinions were strongly held, uncompromising and frankly, on occasion, wrong. His claim that Confederate captives did not suffer the same deprivations in Yankee prisons as his Union brethren did in Dixie is ridiculous. (History tells us more Confederates died in captivity than did Union soldiers, although it is true that the rate of death was higher among captive Federals.) Likewise, he has nothing but contempt for the beleaguered Andersonville Commandant, Captain Henry Wirz, or for Nathan Bedford Forrest, whom he meets along the way. Jefferson Davis, Robert Toombs, and Alexander Stephens don't fare much better in his estimation. And yet in a remarkable passage he blames General U. S. Grant, more than any other man, for the captive Yankees' predicament, because of Grant's adamant refusal to exchange prisoners.

All in all, as my grandmother tried to tell me some forty years ago, *A Captive of War* is a story worth reading.

> Neil Thompson
> Great-grandson of Solon Hyde,
> Hospital Steward, 17th Ohio
> Volunteer Infantry

The Bare Facts

Solon Hyde, twenty-two, enlisted September 5, 1861, into Company K of the 17th Ohio Volunteer Infantry. He was assigned to duty as a hospital steward and as such participated in the battles of Mill Springs, Perryville, Stone's River, Hoover's Gap, and Chickamauga, among others. Mustered out of service March 18, 1865, Solon married Czarina Hyde. They would have eight children. After the war he aided Clara Barton in her efforts to identify the dead of Andersonville. He lived in Ohio, Indiana, and Missouri, where he started up and lost businesses as a homesteader, a dry goodsman, a real estate developer, and a pharmacist. He retired to California where he died in February 1920. He is buried alongside his beloved Czarina in a small Civil War section in Inglewood Cemetery, Inglewood, California. Solon Hyde's racial stereotyping exemplifies attitudes commonly held during and after the Civil War.

CHAPTER I

The Battle of Chickamauga

IT was Saturday, the 19th of September, 1863—a lovely fall morning. The sun's rays were mellowed by the haze of Indian summer, and the air was crisp with early frost and cool for northern Georgia.

About half-past eight, after a hard night's march from the extreme right of Gen. Rosecrans's army, we were halted near the extreme left, and given a short time to rest and prepare our rations. The suddenness of the move and the caution exercised in carrying it out were accepted evidences that we were in the neighborhood of the enemy and preparing to engage in battle, whether on the offensive or defensive we knew not.

Our breakfast disposed of, we were once more ordered into line and, after a brief time, were led into position in line of battle. Our regiment was the Seventeenth Ohio Volunteer Infantry, under the command of Colonel John M. Connell, and Lieutenant-Colonel Durbin Ward (since Gen. Durbin Ward) of the First Brigade, Third Division (Gen. Brannan), of the Fourteenth Army Corps, General George H. Thomas commanding.

Already several artillery shots had been fired by the enemy, one of which fell near where we were halted in line before being placed in final position. It was a grand sight to see regiment after regiment wheeling into line, their bright guns flashing the reflected rays of the morning sun. A remarkable stillness seemed to settle over the men, the voices of the commanding officers sounding clear on the September air. Orderlies were busy in carrying orders, and ever and anon the air was shaken by the heavy boom of cannon or pierced by the peculiar shriek of ball.

Thus we found ourselves entering the battle of Chickamauga, Georgia, some six or eight miles south of Chattanooga, Tennessee. I do no discredit to brave men when I say there were pale cheeks to be seen along that line, for coupled with them were the flashing eye, firm, steady step, and defiant look that betokened determination. Their muskets were grasped in steady hands. It seemed to me, as I looked upon those ranks of men, their muskets held at "order arms," that a jest at that moment would have been most inappropriate.

Immediately in front, with unlimbered guns, was the battery of our brigade preparing to give its initiatory shot. Already the firing along the skirmish line was becoming general, not only in our front, but on, on, on, in the distance to the right, until the sounds lost their individuality in a deep rumbling that told, in the language of conflict, that another page of protest was being written in characters of blood against the false idea of secession,—characters which are indelible and sacred.

For a distance of nearly six miles, could the eye have followed it, the sunshine glistened along a line of bristling bayonets, and wreaths of blue smoke arising above the tree-tops served to locate the line of battle formed by the contending armies. The rattling of batteries taking new positions, and the hurried shifting of brigades and regiments, the flying hither and thither of couriers, the clanking of the iron scabbards of moving cavalrymen, and clouds of smoke and dust, showed the work to have begun in earnest.

I had little time for mental notes as I sat my horse beside an ambulance, for, borne on a stretcher by two comrades, came the first sad fruit of this harvest of death,—a wounded man whom I, as hospital steward, was ordered to carry to a place convenient for a hospital.

Water being the great essential at a field hospital, we loaded the poor fellow into the ambulance and started in search of a good spot, which we found at Cloud's Spring, nearly a mile away, —a beautiful spring that burst out at the foot of the line of hills skirting the Chickamauga valley on the west, in the midst of a thick, shady grove that extended up the hillside to the left, embracing the Cloud residence on the summit. It seemed as if nature was extending her hands to us in the hour of our extremity, in presenting this twofold blessing—ample shade and an abundance of cool, pure water. A hundred yards to the right ran the Chattanooga road, stretching to the left over a spur of the hills, which at this point took the form of a semi-amphitheatre ranged around the spring and grove, its open side looking toward the battlefield. At the point on the hill where the road was lost to sight in a straggling grove stood a wooden church. In the other direction the road led toward the battlefield and for some distance skirted an open field overgrown with rank weeds to the height of a man's head. Near the spring, in whose water minnows were sporting, stood a log spring-house which received a portion of the water from the spring through a wooden trough. All these surroundings I observed as my eyes took in the advantages of the location for the work in hand, while we busied ourselves in preparing the ground and erecting tents for the reception and comfort of the wounded that might be thrown on our hands.

The hospital wagon was sent in search of straw for bedding, of which a good supply was happily found in an old barn near by. Our stores of sanitary goods were unpacked; instruments were examined and put in order, and lint and bandages were put in convenient places and opened out for work.

The noise of battle to our right was terrible. In an hour, perhaps, from the time we put up the first tent and displayed the red hospital flag, there were twenty tents on the ground, all full of wounded men, while the ambulances were bringing others from the field in such numbers as to make it impossible to care for them properly. We made pallets of straw for them under the trees, while those who were slightly wounded had in a measure to take care of themselves or to assist in caring for the less fortunate.

There were many examples of noble heroism exhibited by those who were severely, though not dangerously, wounded,—a spirit of unselfishness remarkable and commendable. I remember one instance of a man who had been shot through the windpipe by a side shot. On being approached by an attendant with bandages, he said: "Never mind me; give me some lint and bandages and I will bind it up myself; you go and see those who are more in need of attention."

Poor fellow, every time he drew breath the air whistled through his mutilated throat like a leaky bellows until he covered it with compresses and bound them on with his handkerchief. Soon afterward I saw him pitching his dog-tent under one of the trees. Such are the cases of heroism that never find a place in history, and yet are more truly heroic than some that are immortalized by polished columns and flattering song.

Our surgeons attended to the wounds as rapidly as the nature of the cases would admit, having divided themselves into squads in order to facilitate the work and prevent clashing. To each squad was assigned a particular duty, as to one the task of attending to minor cases as they came in; to another the cutting out of balls. Others, again, passed on cases for amputation, still others to bandaging and dressing flesh wounds; prescribing and administering stimulants and morphine to those in immediate want of them; or operating upon those cases decided upon as requiring immediate amputation. Yet, notwithstanding this systematic division of labor, it took time to see to all with new cases accumulating rapidly, and many poor fellows were beyond the reach of human aid before they could be cared for, and had passed the veil that intervenes between life and the great hereafter.

Those were bitter, sad hours, with so many needing help, but it could not be otherwise. Some had to be neglected, if inability to attend to all could be called neglect. The wounded were accumulating fast, all the ambulances being busy. The battle was raging fiercely off to our right, and now and then a random cannon-shot would pass over our heads, or a shell burst in air, shaking it like the voice of a shrieking demon. We knew from the sound of the musketry that the ground was being hotly contested, and we were conscious, too, as the din settled more and more to the right, that our boys were being pressed closely and falling back reluctantly. The sound of the musketry fire was not unlike the ominous muttering roar of a sweeping tornado, or the unbroken thunder of the plunging cataract. Accompanying it was the rapid deep booming of the artillery, mingled with the indescribable shrieking whistle of flying shells and the quick sharp report of those that exploded in the air—the most harmless, and yet most calculated to carry terror to the soul. The very earth seemed to tremble beneath the clang and clash of the uproar: even now, though intervening years deaden the sound, the recollection of it is painfully real. The groans of the wounded and dying around us, friend or foe,—for our ambulances brought in Confederate wounded when they chanced to find any; the horridly repulsive nature of some of the wounds; the stiffened corpses whose distorted features showed the extreme agony under which they had died; the wild cries and maledictions of those who had become crazed by their sufferings,—combined to fill up a memory picture that can never be forgotten.

All through the day, without intermission, while our hands were busied with the wounded, our ears were filled with the noise of battle. The sun that gladdened the early morn with such radiance now cast a sickly, doubtful light through the leaden cloud of smoke that hung as a pall over the scene, as if to hide from the eyes of Heaven the horrible carnage covering the plain below. Ever and anon an increased vehemence of the musketry fire, followed by cheers, told of a resisted charge, though whether of friend or foe we could not tell. It was certain, however, from the changing position, that our boys were slowly falling back, so that by night they must have been nearly a mile in the rear of their morning station. What an ensanguined mile it must have been if the dead were at all in proportion to the wounded!

With the shadows of evening came a cessation of fighting, but so accustomed had we become to the din that the stillness seemed unreal and oppressive, even to a sensation of dread. The coolness of the night air caused the cloud of smoke that hung over us through the day to settle into the valley, loading the air with the peculiar scent of burnt powder. As the shades of night deepened the gloom increased. The timber burning in places, set on fire by bursting shells, was reflected upon the smoky clouds and gave out a faint, trembling light at once weird and ghostly. Many bodies of the dead were consumed by these fires, and no doubt many wounded, who were too helpless to crawl away, fell victims to this double torture. The stillness of the night, broken only by the cries and groans of the wounded, and, occasionally, by the report of a shell or musket, was an evidence that both armies were taking needed rest after their hard day's work. The men who all day had been intent on repelling an advancing foe now had time for reflection. The roll-call gave them an idea of their thinned ranks and of the terrible trial through which the survivors had passed unscathed, as name after name was called with no response. They recalled how during the excitement of a charge they had seen this one or that one fall, whether dead or wounded they could not tell; yet the remembrance was so vague that it now seemed like a dream, albeit made real by the absence of the messmate.

Night brought us a season of comparative quiet in the hospital, and we gladly availed ourselves of the opportunity to secure a few hours' rest. The day had been a weary one to us, not only physically, but mentally, as our nerves had been kept to the utmost tension by the sight of so much suffering. A bed of straw beneath one of the trees seemed a luxury. Tired though we were, our sleep was often disturbed by the heart-piercing cries of a wounded man nearing death, as he called out, "Water, water, water! my God, give me water!"

These cries were borne to us across the night from a dense undergrowth perhaps a quarter of a mile away. Yet we dared not venture out to give the cooling drink, as the enemy's pickets were not far away in that direction. The cries grew fainter and fainter, until they reached us as a mere whisper. These struggles of immortal souls nearing their eternal home, loath to leave their shattered tenements, alone on the field of battle, without a friendly hand to wipe the death-damp from the brow, or pillow for the aching head or rest for the shattered limb, were calculated to awaken sympathy in the most callous heart. The wounded in our quarters had settled into a state of remarkable quietness, the cool air perhaps having an anaesthetic effect upon the wounds that disposed the men to sleep and rest.

CHAPTER II

Captured by Forrest's Cavalry

MORNING came at last,—the Sabbath morn, beautiful and bright as ever. But war knows no Sabbath. The rising sun had scarcely cast his first rays across the valley ere random shots were heard along the line, which soon increased until it seemed that the whole line must be engaged. The rebels had been reinforced during the night by troops from Lee's army in Virginia, who went into the fight fresh and vigorous, while our boys were minus the dead and wounded of the day before. The odds were terribly against them and we trembled for the results of the day's fighting.

We were now so far to the left of the field (in fact to the right in rear of the Confederate forces) that we did not receive many of the wounded. This was well, as our accommodations were already full and we had taken possession of the church spoken of above. During the day our hospital flag drew the attention of the rebel sharpshooters, and they began to send in their leaden compliments, while a battery let drive a number of shells, most of which passed over our heads and struck in the hillside beyond. Of course they were harmless at that altitude, but they kept up an infernal screeching and whizzing, and became so provokingly familiar as to nip twigs over our heads. This caused a panicky feeling among some of the surgeons, which increased with each new screech until the feeling became epidemic, resulting in a complete skedaddle of the medical force over the hill beyond the church,—each

6

one, as he ran, grabbing, as by instinct, an instrument case or some imple-
ment of the craft.

As they went zigzagging across the open space that lay between
our camp and the hill at that point, I had to laugh in spite of my own
danger. I had taken refuge behind a tree, from which I had a good view
of them. There was something in the situation midway between the grand
and the ridiculous, but inclining so much more towards the latter than
the former, that I laughed outright. As they came into the open space,
the Confederate sharpshooters let drive at them, and as the balls went
"zip-zip" by them they seemed to crouch until their chins and knees
came close together. When they got into the shelter of the trees they
would stretch up to their full proportions and run like deer. My laugh
attracted the attention of Assistant Surgeon Benedict, of our regiment,
who, seeing me behind the tree, asked if I intended to remain. I told him
I intended to stay with the wounded.

"If you do, so will I," he said, and he took to a tree.

Meanwhile I was conscious of a feeling coming over me of my
tremendous size in comparison with the tree I was behind, which seemed
to decrease in proportion to my increase until it became most uncom-
fortably small. The sharpshooters had evidently got their eyes on us. A
ball nipped a twig near my head. I told the doctor they were becoming
reckless and we had better make for the spring-house. We were an enthusiastic crowd, the doctor and I, and so intensely interested that the
suggestion was taken as a motion put and carried, and we went to zigzagging,—expertly too, I suppose, since we had profited by the long
line of surgeons who had preceded us. It was not nearly so funny to
practise muscular contraction myself as it was to be in a safe place and
watch somebody else contract, and I am free to confess to a feeling of
great relief the moment I was under cover of the spring-house. When a
person comes to analyze the spiteful whistle of a minié ball, and has
time to reflect and calculate upon the amount of daylight it might let
into his carcass, it begets peculiar sensations and a desire akin to wishing he were not there.

We had scarcely time to congratulate ourselves, however, as a shell
went crashing through the top of a tree that stood near by, covering us
with leaves and bark, bursting as it struck the ground just beyond, and
setting fire to the loose straw. It was rapidly spreading toward one of the
tents. Acting on the impulse of the moment I seized a bucket, dipped it
full of water from the spring, and started to save the tent, but had not
gone ten steps beyond the shelter of the house when "whiz!" went a ball
so close to my head that I dropped, the ball striking the bank beyond.
Benedict thought I was certainly struck and called to know if I was killed.
Fearing to show myself erect, I crawled back on my belly like a snake,

thankful for the friendly shelter. I told Benedict I preferred letting the tent burn to exposing myself as a mark for sharpshooters. The tent was destroyed, but fortunately there was but one man in it, a poor fellow who had been brought in a short time before the panic, wounded just above the ankle, the foot dangling by the integuments. He managed to hobble out of the way dragging his dangling foot.

While we were talking about this circumstance and locating the direction from which the shell came, we were startled by a yelling as if a legion of demons had broken loose from the weeds beyond the road. Looking up, we were surprised to see a brigade of Confederates advancing on our quarters at the "double-quick." Without a moment's thought I ran to the amputation table, and, grabbing up the sheet that we had thrown over it, ran out to meet the advancing column, waving this impromptu flag of truce. It was rather a bloody one, but answered in this case. Advancing to the officer in command, who was riding in front, with a revolver in each hand and his bridle reins hanging loosely over the pommel of the saddle, I saluted him without saying a word.

"What has become of all the men who were here?" he asked.

"All who were able have but a short time since retired out of reach of your shells and sharpshooters, sir," I replied.

"Whose headquarters are they?"

"It is a general field hospital, sir."

"We supposed it was some general's headquarters," he replied.

I then asked, "To whom have I the honor of surrendering?"

"To Col. Scott, of the—Tennessee Regiment of Cavalry, commanding the—Brigade of Forrest's Cavalry. (They had dismounted to make the charge.)

Again saluting him, I said, "Colonel, you have captured a field hospital; we have a large number of wounded, many of whom belong to your own army. We are short of hospital supplies. Will you be kind enough, therefore, to request your men not to disturb our bedding, as we need all we have?"

He answered very kindly, "Nothing shall be interfered with, sir," and, turning immediately to a captain standing by, said: "Captain—,detail a guard and give them instructions to allow no one to interfere with anything necessary to the comfort of the men."

He then ordered his men to rest at will and they soon scattered among the tents in search of friends, of whom they found a number. I remarked to one of them:

"Well, you have gobbled us this time."

"Yes," he said, very pleasantly, "but it's time we were getting some advantage; we've had to do all the running heretofore, and it's very discouraging to have to do all the running."

While, as I have said, I acted upon first thought in regard to advancing to meet the charge, and it proved salutary in the end, after it was all over and I had time to reflect on it, I was amazed at my presumption. I am glad to say that not an article necessary for the comfort or welfare of the men was molested in any way during the Confederate occupancy of the ground, which must have extended through several hours, during which time "Yank" and "Reb" mingled together in conversation as pleasantly as though there were no question of difference between them. Each seemed studiously to avoid giving expression to anything that could be considered offensive. In all my subsequent experience as a prisoner among the Confederates I always found the rank and file (with a few exceptions) to be genuine men and generous foes.

While I was busy in attending the wants of the wounded I had not noticed a commotion among the men of the Colonel's command, until I heard him give the order in hurried tones: "Fall in, men! fall in! get into line double quick!"

Stepping out in front of the tent to ascertain the cause, I beheld on top of the hill a line of bluecoats advancing to our relief. It made our pulses beat quick, notwithstanding the fact that our social visit with the enemy bad been of rather a pleasant nature. The new comers proved to be a reserve under Gen. Granger, I think.

The Confederate Colonel, meanwhile, had fallen back into the weeds with his force, without, apparently, having been discovered by the advancing column. I noticed five of his men so busily engaged in conversation with some of their wounded friends, for whom we had made beds under a tree, that they had not heard the order to fall in. Stepping up to them I asked if they would not assist to move their friends into the shade. At once they laid down their guns to assist. By the time we had the men well cared for, our men were on us. The surprise of the Confederates, when they discovered their dilemma, was serio-comic. They did not dare to run, but quietly, with undisguised disgust, submitted to the inevitable. As they were being marched to the rear one of them said to me: "This comes from helping you to move those men instead of attending to our own business, as we should have done."

As our reserve charged through our quarters and were passing on, I approached an officer who appeared to be in command of that portion of the line, and said:

"For God's sake, don't take your men in that direction, unless you want to slaughter them, because it will throw you in the rear of the main body of the Rebel army who are driving our men, and Forrest's cavalry has just fallen back into the weeds, ready to close in behind you and cut you off, placing you at their mercy."

Self-importance was one of the curses of our army officers in many instances, and such intelligence, coming from one not under commission, was bound to be ignored. The Federal column charged on and soon passed out of sight. Forrest's men closed leisurely behind them and soon disappeared in pursuit. How the springing of the trap resulted I never knew, but the roar of musketry in that direction soon after gave indication of hard fighting. Some of the Confederates with whom I talked afterwards claimed that the corps was badly cut to pieces. Be that as it may, the noise indicated hot work, and I could readily believe the enemy's report of the result. Our skedaddled surgeons had sufficiently recovered from their panic to return under cover of the reserve and resume work. In stress for room we took possession of the Cloud house, on the hill, for hospital use; but here, again, our flag drew the attention of the Rebel battery, and a number of shots were fired at the house, one of which passed through it, killing a staff officer who was lying wounded on the floor. The Confederates claimed afterwards that they mistook the flag, which was red, for a battery flag, which would have been yellow,— rather a lame excuse.

The news from the front now became discouraging. A portion of our army was reported to have retired from the field, but we could hear tremendous fighting in the distance and knew from the sound that it was not the irregular firing that would have characterized a retreat. Late in the afternoon one of our regimental ambulance drivers came in with the intelligence that our lieutenant-colonel (Durbin Ward) was borne from the field, shot through the lungs. He told also of the death of Captain Ricketts, one of our noblest officers and purest men. It was quite evident that our army was defeated and we were certain that we would soon be in the hands of the enemy again. We seriously debated whether to take advantage of the opportunity and save ourselves from being taken prisoners, leaving the wounded to their sufferings, or to remain at our post regardless of results. We decided to remain.

In this connection I had quite a talk with our chaplain, James H. Gardner, who, at the breaking out of the war, was principal of a school at Shelbyville, Tennessee, and a preacher of the Methodist Episcopal Church North. Refusal to unite his interests with those of the South to the extent of taking up arms in her defense was sufficient to make him a marked man. Freedom of thought, of speech, and of action, were tolerated in the South in those days only as they might be subservient to Southern interests, to all of which he was antagonistic. He fled for his life, and was hunted as a fugitive. After months of anxious hiding and dodging he reached our lines soon after the battle of Murfreesboro (Stone River), after which he was commissioned chaplain and assigned to our regiment, reaching us at Triune, Tennessee. Being from the same part of Ohio as myself, and acquainted with each other by reputation, an intimacy soon struck up between us which warmed into close friendship. The discouraging news from the front made him nervous and apprehensive. He now said to me:

"I don't know what to do. Here we are; our army is driven from the field, and these wounded men claim our attention and need all our care. We are liable to be made prisoners at any moment; some of Forrest's Tennesseeans will recognize me, and my life will not be worth a farthing in their hands. I believe they would hang me like a dog should they find me wearing the garb of a Union soldier. Tell me what to do: would I be doing wrong to leave these men, even under such circumstances? I'll do just as you say."

Our horses were standing near by, hitched under the same tree. I said to him,—

"So far as these men are concerned, I do not know that you can do them any good by remaining; certainly you could not if the *dénouement* should be such as you fear. If you go immediately you may be able to make your escape. There is your horse. My advice to you is to mount without a moment's delay and make for Chattanooga."

He mounted his horse and loped away. I did not see him again until, after the close of the war, I recognized him at the station in Zanesville, Ohio. He did not recognize me at first. The privations of prison life had left me a wreck beyond recognition, but all the warmth of his generous nature was thrown into the hearty handshake and greeting when I made myself known to him. In the few minutes we had together we rehearsed personal history rapidly. I also had an introduction to his bride, who was with him. I indulge in these little incidents because I love to cherish the memory of my campaign friends.

So discouraging were the reports that now came from the front that it was with intense satisfaction that we saw the sun disappear and night close in around us, as with darkness came an end of fighting. Again the smoke settled down into the valley and the wounded became quiet.

Chapter III

Southern Men and Southern Views

THIS night there was not that marked stillness which characterized that of the previous day. Throughout the darkness we could hear the noise of the troops moving beyond the ridge,—confirmatory evidence of our troops abandoning the field. Several of our nurses took advantage of the night and made good their escape; our regimental hospital cook, John Harmon, got off in this way. Soon after sunrise next morning (Monday), two horsemen emerged from the underbrush in our front and rode leisurely across the open space to our quarters, as leisurely dismounted, tied their horses, and came to our mess, saying they thought they would come and breakfast with us. They proved to be Generals Forrest and Cheatham, of Confederate fame. This confirmed our fears that we were prisoners. General Cheatham commanded a division of infantry in Gen. Bragg's army and was a leader of no mean note. General Forrest was a commander of cavalry of great fame but rather irregular in his manner of warfare. The bearing of the two men, as they sat with us around our mess-table, was a true index to the character of each.

General Cheatham enjoyed several cups of coffee with a gusto that evinced unfeigned satisfaction, and spoke of the pleasure he took in a cup of choice Rio. General Forrest, with all the superciliousness of an offended mogul, simulated contempt for such luxuries.

"Not," he said, "but that I am fond of coffee, and the like, but because we have been deprived of them by the iron heel of a tyrannizing government and a damnable, inhuman blockade, that cuts us off from intercourse with the outside world, and thus deprives us of them. I *scorn*" (his tone had to be heard to be appreciated) "to indulge in them until I can do it in an established Confederacy, whose independence has been won by the strong right arm of Southern chivalry, and when we can flaunt our flag in the face of our oppressors, a free and independent South."

General Cheatham laughed a dry kind of laugh and passed his cup for more coffee, denoting the very sensible conviction that the present is all that we can justly claim of life, and that a bird in the hand is worth countless multitudes in the bush.

During the progress of the meal the conversation very naturally turned on the day's fight and its results. General Cheatham said:

"Gentlemen, I must say that I had to admire the bravery and fortitude with which your men fought, and the doggedness with which they repelled our charges, fighting in many cases until they were literally shot down in their tracks. They fought well, gentlemen; they fought well; no men could have done better; all the glory we can claim is that we hold the field, and against such a foe it is a glory. But we hold it only by force of numbers, and our glory is dearly bought; our loss is fearful,— equal to, if not greater than, yours. Yes, we hold the field at a fearful sacrifice. We had the men, and General Bragg issued an order to all his division commanders to press your lines in double column, and press you so closely that you could not make your artillery effective, and to keep our front column full we did so, but 'twas at a fearful cost of life,— fearful, fearful, fearful! Why, the men seemed to melt away; in many places the dead were piled, or looked as though they had been mowed down in swaths."

It seemed to touch him as he dwelt upon the carnage, and recalled the battle scenes with an emotion that forced us to acknowledge him a brave man, honest in his conviction of the justness of the cause for which he fought.

General Forrest was full of braggadocio; they had given the Yankees a terrible whipping and had routed them, demoralized, from the field. They had captured an immense stand of arms; our army was in full and disorganized retreat, and so utterly demoralized it would take months to reorganize it, if it could be reorganized at all. He intended to have his command in Chattanooga that night, then advance on Knoxville, and would push the Yankee army to the Ohio River by Saturday night. He must hurry up and get his boys on the wing, in order to complete the victory,—and as he rode away he left on our minds the impression of a man without heart or soul.

The truth is, at the battle of Chickamauga the Confederates were as badly whipped as were the Northern forces, and if it had not been for the unfortunate misconstruing of an order, by which Wood's division was taken from the centre, creating a gap and cutting our army in two, the battle would certainly have resulted differently. I heard General Cheatham and several of the Confederate commanders say that up to that time the battle was in doubt, and that when the movement was made it was so inexplicable to them that they feared to take advantage of it, lest it should turn out to be a cunningly laid trap; but as soon as they became convinced it was a blunder, they had no more fears of the result, as it turned the whole tide in their favor. Had it not been for the stubborn stand made by the heroic band under that noble hero, General George H. Thomas, it certainly would have resulted in the utter routing of the Union army. Well is he called the "Rock of Chickamauga."

As quite a valuable amount of hospital stores had been captured at our hospital, a detail was made to take charge of them, and the prisoners were put under the supervision of Major Clare of General Bragg's staff. I think he was from Montgomery, Alabama. We found him to be a gentleman and he entered freely into conversation with the prisoners. He would say, when talking with us on any of the issues of the war:

"Now, gentlemen, I want you to give your opinions on these things as freely as you would if you were around your own camp-fires. Don't let your views be biased by the fact that you are prisoners."

Associated with him was a young ensign from the British navy, a Mr. Burns, who had been granted leave of absence from Her Majesty's service that he might offer his sword to the Confederate cause, aching, I suppose, to have his name emblazoned alongside Lafayette's in American history. He had succeeded in running the blockade at Charleston a few months before, and for his zeal was appointed to General Bragg's staff with a commission as captain. He was chuckful of conceit and had a lordly contempt for anything not English. The major said of him, "He is a good kind of fellow, spends his gold lavishly, and is a tip-top good mess-fellow on that account." He was an enthusiastic advocate of Southern rights and bitterly denounced the United States government for presuming to resist the efforts of the Southerners to establish a government of their own according to their own peculiar ideas.

The Confederacy at this time was very much buoyed up by the prospect of England's recognition of its belligerent rights, and felt confident that the news of the reverses of our army at Chickamauga would have a tendency to hasten it. In truth, it did look as though that day was about to dawn upon them. In this feeling Ensign Burns heartily shared. In conversation one day with Major Clare and the ensign in regard to the probability of such a thing as England's interference, the major asked me:

"What in your opinion, would be the effect, upon the North, of such interference on the part of England?"

I said it would be the best thing that could happen; it would be a godsend to the North and death to the Confederacy.

"Why?" he asked in astonishment.

"Because upon the question of war with England there would be a solid North and that element that now retards and opposes the prosecution of the war from sympathy for you would be arrayed as an army of invasion that in four weeks would overrun Canada and be made harmless as Southern sympathizers. The result would be that you would be no better off, and England would soon not have a foothold on American soil, as we would take Canada so quickly it would make their heads swim."

The ensign scouted the idea as grossly fanatical and impossible. Clare said that that was a phase of the case that had never entered his mind before, and it looked plausible, though he thought it would have the effect of forcing the North to recognize the independence of the South.

The men who were left under Clare to guard us were a portion of John Morgan's command. One night, as I stepped out of the tent, I noticed the guard reading a letter by the light of the fire. Seeing me, he handed it to me and asked if its contents were correct. I recognized the letter as one that I had received from Ohio a little while before, giving me a description of the raid and capture of Morgan, in which the writer said: "Morgan is now safely lodged in the Ohio Penitentiary, his head shaved, and wearing stripes, which is a great deal better than he deserves." I told him that Morgan was undoubtedly in the penitentiary, but as to shaving his head and dressing him in stripes, the garb of the common prisoner, I presumed that that was not correct, though the writer might have inferred so from the fact of his being an inmate of that institution.

"Well," he said, "I am one of Morgan's men, and it would not do to tell the boys that Morgan was treated in that way."

"Now," I said, "I would like to know how you came into possession of that letter, which, being my property, I know you have no right to."

"Well," he said, "one of the boys gave it to me a while ago."

"Then," I rejoined, "one of the boys has evidently been where he had no right to be," and, going into the tent, I found that they had stolen my valise. It contained my clothing, papers, and letters. I tried to have them return a number of photographs, but failed.

I took advantage of an especially dark night to get to the boxes containing our regimental hospital drugs, as they had not been disturbed since we unloaded them. I knew just where to put my hands on over twenty ounces of quinine, a drug that at that time, in the South, commanded the fabulous sum of $250 an ounce. I very soon diminished the value of their capture that much. I then got one of the nurses, and we gathered up all the guns we could find and put them *hors de combat* by giving them a twist in the fork of a tree. One of the regimental mail-carriers left his mail-sack with us on the first day of the fight. It contained a number of letters for the North; these we destroyed by burning them one at a time in our tent so as not to attract attention.

It was sometimes quite amusing, as well as instructive, to hear Southerners of the upper class conversing about the causes of the war, as well as the object of the leaders in forcing secession on the South. One gentleman especially, from Charleston, South Carolina, who spent several days at our quarters, held views so entirely different from any I had before heard, and expressed them so candidly and unreservedly, making them appear so reasonable withal, that they seemed to me to contain the solution of the whole Southern problem. He was evidently a man of high mental culture and a Huguenot by descent, as I heard him tell a gentleman with whom he was conversing. His dress was that of a civilian from the higher walks of life, and by his deportment he conveyed the impression of being a man who had never sniffed plebeian air. In answer to a question asked by one of the surgeons, he expressed himself as follows:

"You-all at the North have been taught to look upon this war as a contest inaugurated in the interest of slavery,—on the side of the South for its perpetuation; on the side of the North for its suppression and overthrow: but, gentlemen, that is only a phase growing out of the war itself, and is secondary. The war is *not* a question of to-day or yesterday, or of Lincoln's election as President, though that was opportune as an excuse. For more than forty years the South has been preparing for it gradually. True, the negro was the mighty lever in the hands of our statesmen and orators, in moving the mudsills of the South to espouse the Southern cause, for which they have nothing in common with us. They were made to believe that you-all were encroaching on the rights of the South, on *their* rights, by fighting to free our slaves. Why, there never was a more absurd argument bearing its own lie on its face, if they had only stopped to consider. It was an imposition on ignorance, but such is the power of infatuation. Go to nine-tenths of our men and ask them what they are fighting for, and they will tell you for their rights. Ask them what those rights are, and they will tell you slavery, although they never owned a slave in their lives, and in many cases are even below the slave in intelligence and culture; for the negro, from the relation he sustains to his master, is necessarily brought more or less within the circle of refinement and culture, and thus, if he is an intelligent negro, becomes more or less cultured, while the poor whites, from their social inferiority, no matter what their character, cannot avail themselves of such advantages. Hence their children are reared in ignorance, in many cases worse than the negroes. Yet they are firmly of the belief that you-all are trampling on their rights. Nonsense! our leaders won't tell you so; our wealthy slaveholders—the ones most interested—won't tell you so, if they are candid. They will tell you that what we want is an aristocracy. That's what we are fighting for. That's what our training and mode of life demands. That's what we will have, and nothing short of that will satisfy the ambition of Southern chivalry. We may not reach it in this struggle, but we will train our young men to work for it in the years to come, to reach it at any sacrifice and get control of prominent places in the government, as we had under Buchanan, and shape affairs to this end."

It seemed to me that if these doctrines could be preached to those despised mudsills who composed the bulk of the Southern army and were giving their lives to the cause, it would have been more potent in disarming the South than marshalled hosts and bristling bayonets. Though the ignorance of the average mudsill was what Nasby would call "trooly sublime," it did not seem to me to merit such base ingratitude; and, after that gentleman's exposition of the *casus belli*, "Southern rights" looked to me like a refuge of lies, hideous and deformed.

Chapter IV

Going into Durance

A S we were held on the battlefield, or rather at the hospital, ten or twelve days, until arrangements could be made to exchange the wounded, we had an opportunity of going over a part of the ground over which our boys had fought so stubbornly and bravely. If there had been nothing there but the broken bushes, scarred trees, and trodden grass to indicate the severity of the engagement, these in themselves would have been sufficient. The trunks of the trees were lacerated and scarred from the ground to the top; here and there huge limbs had been cut off by cannon-shot, and in places the ground torn into furrows indicated the site of a battery. All these, with the scattered fragments of exploded shells and numerous solid balls, were sufficient evidence. But we had far more significant and painful tokens, in the sad, sickening sight of our dead scattered over the field where they had fallen, in many cases naked, generally partially stripped of their clothing, and all with their pockets turned inside out. The army cormorant had paid his respects to each. Decomposition had already set in, so that none were recognizable, but were repulsive in their putrescence. Mark the contrast, and show me the humanity: the Confederate dead had all been carefully hunted up and given decent burial; but not so the corpses of the "Lincoln hirelings." Their carcasses might lie there and rot, and their bones blanch in the noonday sun. No Confederate spade should dig the trench, no hand be raised to give them Christian burial. Shame, shame, boasted chivalry! That same army had forgotten how many times, per-

18

haps, these same boys, now rotting on the battle-ground of Chickamauga, had assisted in raising the mound over Confederate dead left scattered on other battlefields in Yankee hands; but now—the only time in the history of Bragg's army when they had a chance to show like respect to our dead—they had not the magnanimity to do so, and not until our men had again performed a like ceremony for them at Lookout Mountain and Mission Ridge, and had regained the field of Chickamauga, did those blanched bones find a grave, and then it was by the hands of their victorious friends.

Near where our regiment went into line on the first morning of the fight, stood a log house of the old-fashioned two-part style, connected by a porch or open space. It was occupied by an old lady and her two daughters. Here a number of wounded had found shelter, bunking down on the floor as they could make room. During the cannonading a solid shot from one of our batteries, after passing through a log smokehouse in the yard, came crashing through the door into the room where the men were lying, striking the floor under the drawn-up knees of one of the men and passing out through the side of the house just high enough to miss the men lying next the wall,—certainly a very remarkable escape, as it could not have struck at any other part and missed a man, and not then if he had not drawn up his knees to rest his hands. The experience of the old lady and her girls must have been of rather an exciting character, as the battle raged around them. I will give her description of it as she gave it to me herself a few days after, when we went to remove the wounded men from her house. She said:

"On the first mawnin', when you-all came marching up the road thar, and stopped over in the lot, I told the gearels we or'ter go away from hyar; but we did not know whar to go to, so we thought we mought about as well stay whar we ware, as maybe thar wouldn't be no fout no way, but, my souls! wasn't thar? Why, purty soon the guns begin firen', and the men begin to holer'n. The gearels they crawled under the bed a screamen', and I just had to sit still and hold my head in my apron, it just plumb deafened me, the noise did. The first thing we knowed, our yard was full of soljers a shootin' as fast like as they could. I reckon we ware three of the scardest wimmen you ever sot your eyes on, if you had seen us. We just broke right outer the house and struck for the timber as hard as we could run, but we couldn't run no way, 'pears like, without we run right into the fout. It just 'peared like they ware foughtin everywhar, and we just turned round and cut plumb straight for home and crawled under the house; we just expected to be killed every minit. We crawled right under among the men,—thar ware lots of 'em under thar; and thar we stayed laying just as flat on the ground as we could, with our faces covered up in our aprons, until they had done gone past, and then we crawled out'n. My souls! such a sight as thar was I never dreamed of before. I just plumb didn't know the place no mo'. The fences was all broke down, and dead and wounded men ware layin' around hyar just thick,—'peared like thar was five dead men layin' out'n the yard, and fo mo' out thar on the road, and a whole lot out beyond the crib, and down thar in the lot. Poor fellows, some of them lay thar just like they was restin', thar eyes open wide and smilin' like, and they stone dead. It was just the awfulest time I ever seen, it made me heart-sick, so I just had to sit right down and cry, and the wounded—some of them had crawled into the house and was layin' on the flo'. 'Twas just the awfulest time I ever seed, and I won't forget it as long as I live."

I noticed a number of graves in the garden, one with a headstone marking the grave of an officer; as there were but three Yankee dead that I could see, I judged they must have been mostly Confederate dead the old lady saw, especially as they had all been decently buried save the three exceptions. As an example of the force of a cannonshot, not far from the house stood a tall tree perhaps sixteen inches through at the butt. This had been cut off about twenty feet from the ground by a shell, the top giving every appearance of having jumped clear of the stump, striking the ground in an upright position.

Arrangements having been made for the exchange of the wounded, a train of our ambulances came to carry them to our lines. I had given considerable attention to a captain—I think his name was Carr—belonging to an Illinois regiment, who had been hit in the leg and foot by a fragment of shell, making a very ugly wound, the flesh being torn from the leg, and the missile passing through the foot at the instep, crushing the bone. He was so grateful for the attention I had given him that when he came to be moved he proffered me his watch as a recompense. I told him I was glad if I had been of any benefit to him, but, as we were likely to be sent to Richmond, most likely the watch would be taken from me as contraband of war (subsequent events proved my predictions to be correct); but if, when he got through the lines, he would write to my folks and tell them I was a prisoner and well, he would confer a favor on me and relieve my friends of much anxiety. He promised to do so, and I found he had been true his promise, for when I returned from prison, they showed me the letter. But the grateful fellow had given me such an exalted name I could hardly recognize myself as being the one referred to. Instances of this kind are the flowers that spring up to beautify the pathway of life.

Major Clare very kindly gave us permission to write letters to our friends and send them through the lines by the ambulance train. We put them in charge of the surgeon who was to accompany the train,—an Armenian who had been sent by his people to be educated in the United

States. Having chosen the medical profession, and finished his course about the time the war broke out, he concluded that the field would be the place to get a practical knowledge of surgery, so he offered his services and received his commission as assistant surgeon in the regular army. I have often thought how mysteriously and with what wisdom the Almighty rules affairs pertaining to the spread of his spiritual kingdom. Now, if that poor Armenian, instead of being sent through the lines, had been suffered to feel and see the hideous deformity of the Christian spirit that ruled in Dixie, and had lived through it all, and returned to Armenia to tell his story, the missionaries of the Cross might never have gained a foot-hold in his country. It looked to me as unjust in our government not to have made arrangements for all the noncombatants to be exchanged, instead of suffering us to go into the "prison pens of the South."

Having got all of the wounded loaded into the ambulances, we bade adieu to Cloud's Spring, the scene of so much suffering, and took up our line of march, the wounded for Chattanooga, we for Chickamauga, a station from which point we were to take cars for Richmond, Virginia. On our way to the station we passed through the pioneer corps of the Confederate army. As we were trudging along afoot, one of the guards who was on horseback told me to get up behind him and ride, a courtesy of which I gladly availed myself, and we jogged on together. He was not feeling well, and as I had some brandy in my canteen I told him to drink some of it. In return for this he gave me a silver ten-cent piece, which served me a very good turn when sick myself in prison.

While we were waiting at the depot for a train, a very fine-looking artillery officer came riding along the line, inquiring if there were any Ohio soldiers there; he wanted to learn something of a brother who was in the Federal army. On inquiry we learned that that brother was Granville Moody, the "Fighting Parson." Brother against brother! At the railroad we were reinforced by the surgeons and by help from Crawfish Springs Hospital, giving us a combined force of sixty-two surgeons and assistant surgeons, besides eight or ten hospital stewards. From the station we could distinguish the dim outline of Lookout Mountain looming up in the twilight against the sky, the fires of the Rebel camps being plainly visible on its summit and sides, while camp-fires which we presumed to be those of our friends could be seen in the valley below around Chattanooga, the objective point of the campaign,—and it in the possession of our army, notwithstanding our reverses at Chickamauga.

Soon after dark we were ordered aboard the train, which was composed principally of ordinary freight cars. As there was not room in these for all, the surgeons and commissioned officers were put into a passenger coach. By using a little cheek I insinuated myself among them, and secured first-class accommodations for war times. We found the car dimly lighted by a single tallow-dip candle in the front end, around which the few passengers—all Confederate soldiers, or, at least, all men—had collected like moths, so that they did not know really that we were Yankees, if, indeed, they noticed us at all as we came in from the rear platform.

Their conversation was carried on in animated style without interruption, sometimes considerably to our edification, though not entirely to our justification. Especially was this the case in the conversation of two of them who had gotten into quite a warm discussion upon the relative merits and demerits of Yankees as a class, in which we were forced to take some pretty hard rubs and "see oursel's as ithers see us." We had to acknowledge one as our champion, from the fact that he had espoused our cause and was trying to prove that there were just as good, honest men in the whole Lincoln army as there were among the Confederates, and that, as a class, they would stand comparison. The opposition contended there was not an honest man in the whole Lincoln army, but that they were a set of thieves and blacklegs, from "old Lincoln," the commander-in-chief, down to the lowest private in the ranks, and this assertion he attempted to prove by a long story of how he, a green youth from North Carolina, who "had never travelled much," had been neatly swindled by a pair of bunco men in Philadelphia and relieved of some three hundred and fifty dollars. When he drew the conclusion, from his adventure,— "No, sir! you need not talk to me of gentlemen among them, for *I* know them by experience, and from that very day I have been a rank secessionist," the roar that went up from our party would have to be heard to be appreciated. We had never before had even the pleasure of knowing the *locality* of the "original secessionist," but now that we had him before us, we could definitely point him out and say, "*Behold the man.*" This incident was a striking illustration of the smallness of the point on which the destiny of a nation may be balanced.

It had now become quite dark, our engine steamed up, the whistle blew, and we were soon rattling along "beyond the lines," prisoners of war in Dixie. It was well we could not unveil the future and see the misery and horror that were in store for us. As it was, we confidently expected that a few weeks at farthest would see us again safely quartered with our regiment, but we based too much on our being noncombatants, as the sequel shows.

CHAPTER V

"Away Down South in Dixie!"

OUR advent among the natives seemed to meet general approval and to give a corresponding degree of satisfaction. That portion of the Confederacy seemed to be on its "high heels," and we were welcomed as a kind of first-fruits of Bragg's bagging. It seemed as though it was a fulfillment of a promise he had made them a long time before and had never been able to keep until now. Even the young ladies from the classic walls of Marietta's French seminary, who came dancing down the slope that led from the school to the railroad, seemed solicitous in regard to Gen. Bragg's health, and sung out: "How is Mr. Bragg?" Then, brandishing small stilettos at us they would cry, "Oh you detestable Yanks! You Lincoln hirelings! So Mr. Bragg has got you at last, has he? Good for Mr. Bragg!"

We really began to think ourselves, considering the number of times we had known Mr. Bragg to abandon the field without bagging any game, that our delegation was pretty good for Mr. Bragg. In due time we reached Atlanta, and were congratulating ourselves that we had safely run the Bragg gauntlet, when, as we filed out of the depot on our way to the stockade, an old lady, hearing the confusion, but not clearly discerning the multitude, adjusted her glasses astride her nose, and then, taking in the situation at a glance, shrieked out, as she shook her fists at us:

"Yi, yi! he, he! and you seed Mr. Bragg, did you? How's Mr. Bragg?"

"Damn Bragg!" said one of the men, whose patience had become exhausted by the monotony of the thing. "Damn Bragg and the whole Confederacy with him; who in hell cares for Bragg?"

"Hi, yi, yi!" chimed in the old lady, and we marched on to the "bull-pen."

There was nothing very imposing or awe-inspiring about its external appearance. We were made to pay an entrance fee at the gate, of canteens, pocket-knives, blankets, tin cups, etc. As the fellow stripped me of my canteen I told him he had better confiscate that, as it contained a superior article of Yankee brandy. "Don't use such stuff," he said with contempt. But I noticed that he watched very closely where the canteen fell when he threw it on the pile, and seemed careful to have it fall "right side up with care,"—a tender solicitude that belied his contempt for the article. While they were bringing us into line preparatory to stripping us, a voice called my name from beyond the gate, saying: "You'd better throw your knife over here if you don't want to lose it; the 'Johnnies' are short on pocketknives, and they will take it, sure." Luckily I had two and turned over the poorest one. This was our first "picking." On getting inside I found the voice came from Bill Comstock, of Company K, of my regiment.

This was our first experience in a rebel prison stockade. We found quite a number of wounded who had been sent back from the front instead of being exchanged. Whatever became of them I never knew, but they must have had a serious time if they remained prisoners long. The pen was pretty well filled, so much so that we found some difficulty in finding room under shelter to spread our beds. As I had been deprived of my blanket and rubber at the gate, in common with all uncommissioned soldiers, I would have found bedmaking a mere farce had not Dr. Benedict, our assistant surgeon, kindly shared his blanket with me, and we made out very well. There we saw our first picture of Southern capacity for diabolism. It gave us an idea of what they were capable of doing in inhumanity, and substantiated the stories we had heard so often from the lips of East Tennesseeans when they came as refugees to our camps in the early days of the war,—stories which we then thought were tinged with an over-intensity prompted by feelings of malice. We could not then understand how they could be possible, though subsequent experience proved to us that they were terrible truths. One such case was that of an old man who had been outspoken in his denunciation of the secession movement in its infancy, and had refused to give it any support or countenance. He had been imprisoned early in the war, but succeeded in making his escape. By means of bloodhounds he was hunted down and retaken, and to prevent a recurrence of escape was put in irons and chained to his room, in which condition he had been confined a number of months when we saw him. His unkempt locks, as white as snow, his tottering limbs and sunken eyes, showed but too plainly that the days of his incarceration were nearly over; that be would soon be beyond the reach of the venom of his enemies.

After a few days' rest we were again put aboard the cars, and "On to Richmond" was the cry. If we had not been prisoners and our future uncertain, this trip through Georgia would have been more pleasant than otherwise. We were occupying cattle-cars and had aboard a Roman Catholic chaplain, an Irishman, whose hatred to anything "secesh" was as intense as the Devil's hatred for holy water; his blood fairly boiled at the insults offered by the natives. We must have been the first delegation to pass over this road, and our train seemed to have been heralded; we found a crowd awaiting us at every station, anxious to get a sight of the Yanks. Of course, each gathering would have its remarks to make and innuendoes to fling at us, and these would raise the chaplain's ire to a perfect frenzy. He would shake his fists at the crowd through the open sides of the car in a most defiant manner, a proceeding which would only provoke more chaff. Then he would gnash his teeth, froth at the mouth, stamp his feet, and jump up and down in his rage, while his eyes fairly spoke annihilation. A wild beast at bay could not have shown more venom in its actions.

The train was generally beset at all prominent points by "pie-venders," as we styled them, though they generally had cakes, rye coffee, chestnuts, etc. These—generally boys and women with an eye to business—kept civil tongues, as the prisoners were their best customers. The negroes, gathered on the outskirts of the crowd, seemed to eye us with feelings of awe and admiration. At one place where we stopped, a tight board fence seven or eight feet in height extended alongside of the track, and from behind this we could hear the subdued voices of a number of persons in earnest conversation. Pretty soon one woolly head, and then another, slowly appeared above the fence, until their eyes became visible, when down they went like dipper ducks dodging bullets. Then we heard them say:

"Why, dey looks just like any odder white folks; don't got no horns at all."

Becoming more and more assured, they finally ventured the question. "Is you-uns Yankees?"

When they found that we were, their minds seemed relieved of a heavy burden, and we found by inquiry that these poor creatures had been made to believe that we were just such a race of people as Darwin had been hunting for, having tails and horns. Indeed, all the people apparently expected to see a semi-barbarous crew, from whose clutches they had better keep at a safe distance. If we could only have improvised a pair of horns and a tail for our Irish chaplain and let him spring out among them, there would have resulted a scattering similar to that caused by a hawk sweeping down on a covey of partridges, especially if he had been in one of his fits of frenzy.

Arriving at Millen late in the evening, and having to change cars, we were quartered for the night in a warehouse close to the railroad. We had to buy our food from the citizens, as the Confederacy had not issued any to us as yet, since our leaving Atlanta. Next morning, however, they issued us cooked rations.

At Augusta we spent several hours before crossing into South Carolina. We were rather favorably impressed with the city; its broad streets, shaded by a row of trees on either side, gave it an appearance at once captivating and elegant. A Sabbath-like silence seemed to pervade the place; its streets were nearly deserted, and no clamorous crowds gathered around us to satisfy their curiosity. We enjoyed our several hours' rest on the outskirts of the town unmolested. It may have been owing to the hour of the day, as we were there about noon.

I was informed by a citizen, with whom I afterward became acquainted, that the business of the town, before the war, was carried on mostly by Northern men, and that merchants of Augusta preferred Northern help to their own people on account of the greater energy with which they engaged in their work. I expressed my surprise at this, but he frankly admitted that the youth of the South who by education were qualified to carry on business were, by their mode of life and habits, unfitted for the work, were not sought after for such places, and seldom sought them themselves.

After we crossed on to the "sacred soil" of South Carolina, we were taken three or four miles out and side-tracked, to give us an opportunity to prepare our rations for dinner, which we did on a bluff overlooking the railroad. Being told that we would likely remain here until toward night, we amused ourselves as best we could, not being under very strict guard. A beautiful clear stream offered an inviting place to bathe, of which we availed ourselves; nearly three weeks as prisoners, and a part of that time aboard cars and sleeping in warehouses and shanties, had rendered ablutions not only acceptable, but necessary. We also had time to rinse our socks and shirts and dry them in the sunshine.

About sundown we boarded the train. Dr. Benedict and I, having secured an armful apiece of cedar boughs, spread them on the floor and with his blanket laid over them made an excellent bed, which secured us a good night's rest. Sunrise next morning found us at Columbia. We could not see much of the city and were not permitted to get off the cars, only stopping for a few moments for a clear track.

Our passage through the turbulent State of South Carolina was not marked with any special interest. The swamps and rivers, low sandy lands, pine woods and live oaks, their boughs draped with long pendant moss, while they brought their share of novelty to our Northern minds, did not imbue us with any special feeling of reverence, that we should fall down and worship her "sacred soil" and remove our shoes from our feet because of its sacredness. Certainly the country had its charms, but they did not realize our ideas of Paradise by any means. We did admire the dainty beauty of some of her daughters, but there was a peculiar forty-five-degree angling of the nose perceptible in those we saw when on exhibition as "Yanks," a peculiar flipping of the dress skirt, and defiant poise of the head, that we could not some way harmonize with our idea of angelic beings.

The cars moved on, and soon carried us among the pines of North Carolina, a name always associated with tar and tar-making in our schoolboy days. As we passed through we wondered why our old geographies had not added persimmons to the chief products of the State. We found the scenery more diversified than in South Carolina, making our ride much less monotonous. The train took a very roundabout way, without stopping, by way of Charlotte, Greensboro, Raleigh and Weldon to Petersburg, Virginia, at which point we arrived in the night. Leaving the train, we filed up one of the principal streets and camped near the river north of town. Considering its proximity to the seat of war the city presented an unusually quiet appearance. As we marched through it that night not a light was visible in any of the houses, and not a person, aside from our own party, could be seen on the streets. The doleful clank, clank, clank of our feet on the stone pavement sounded back from the dark, blank walls of the buildings with an emptiness that might fitly have represented a midnight visit to the exhumed streets of Pompeii, or some other dead city of the past.

We were not given much time for rest; long before day we were groping our way through a dense fog to the train. We supposed this night move was a piece of military precaution, as Richmond was only about two hours' run distant, and our route would necessarily pass through their lines of defense, and too much Yankee observation behind the scenes was not advisable. The train ran slowly, and in the dim, foggy light of early morning we recognized that we were once more in the region of military operations. Extensive earthworks and lines of defense were to be seen at all commanding points, and the desolating footprints of war were unmistakable. Few troops, however, were visible along the line of the road, being too early for camps to be astir.

About two hours' run brought us to Manchester, a manufacturing village on the south bank of the James River, opposite Richmond; before us ran the swift waters of the James, and beyond, wrapped in the mists and quiet of early morning, lay Richmond, the great bone of contention, the seat of Southern empire and its stronghold. As we crossed the bridge we had a view of Belle Island, a low, sandy island in the river at the head of the rapids, nature's barrier against tide water. It had already become noted as a place of torment for prisoners, yet when we had read these reports in the papers, we were disposed to receive them with a measure of allowance, as the overdrawn pictures of Northern fanaticism. But as it appeared that morning, half hidden by the river mists that settled over it, our eyes beheld enough to convince us that its reputation was well merited. The sight filled us with dread; even at that early hour the hum of voices from the prisoners could be plainly heard. What an appeal for mercy it must have been, lying there in plain view of Richmond, of her Capitol halls, from the windows of which it must have been plainly visible; in sight of many of her public buildings, her private residences, her Christian churches and everyday life,—a perpetual reminder of Confederate inhumanity and barbarism. Ah, no! I do not wonder the South wants bygones to be forgotten, and would forget the dastardly acts she performed in the name of Liberty and "Southern Rights." Neither do I wonder that Cain sought to hide from the face of the Almighty and deny that he was his brother's keeper. The curse of Cain will hang over the South until the last mover in secession is laid away for his final rest; and as long as any survive, the prison pens of the South should be kept fresh in their memory. It is just that they should be: yea, more! it would be but just that the South should be taxed to pension those whose lives have been rendered years of suffering by the treatment received as prisoners in their hands.

CHAPTER VI

Libby and Pemberton Prisons

WE reached Richmond on the 11th of October, the train stopping at the crossing of Cary Street, down which we were marched to the right. On the left-hand side, some distance down, we passed a large brick building with barred windows, from which squalid, tattered forms peered at us. Heavens! we thought, is such the fate to which we are so quietly marching? One of the guards informed us this was "Castle Thunder," the Bastile of Richmond, the dread of Confederate soldier as well as of Yankee prisoner, for here they confined military offenders from their own army as well as "Yanks" who incurred their special displeasure. We had seen enough to send our hearts and hopes down to zero. As we were marching along, each one apparently wrapped in his own thoughts, we passed an old Irishwoman standing on the sidewalk. Her rough exterior held a heart full of sympathy, and her knowledge of the misery to which we were marching seemed to touch a tender chord in her nature. Crossing herself devoutly, and reverently raising her eyes heavenward, she said, "May God take pity on ye's, poor fellows!" She evidently knew the relentless character of the men who would have us in their charge.

At last we were halted in front of a huge three-story building on the south side of the street, fronting on Cary Street on the north and the river landing on the south. Over the front door on the northwest corner of the building was a wooden awning to which was attached a sign,

"LIBBY & SON, SHIP CHANDLERS."

Here we were, then, under the walls of that historic place known as "Libby Prison," within whose doors were crowded for systematic torture those who were so unfortunate as to fall into Rebel hands. We had not much time to study its external proportions. The commissioned officers were ordered to step out of the ranks and filed off into one of the rooms. We smaller fry were then ordered into another room on the lower floor. The officer in charge, throwing open the door, gave the command: "Step in lively there, God damn you!"—an infernal command from an infernal commander.

We stepped in and were swallowed up, finding ourselves in a long lower room with three or four prior occupants. These told us that if we had not already been robbed of our valuables we would better secrete them, as we would be searched. Some of the boys succeeded in concealing their watches and gold pens.

Very soon an officer came in with a guard and ordered us to fall into line. Then, commencing at the head of the line, they began a systematic search, confiscating anything they could find of the least possible value. Fortunately I had but seven dollars in money, but this was greedily confiscated. Greenbacks were beginning to look up in the Confederacy even then. Our squad seemed to be of the "Job's turkey" order, completely poverty-stricken, so that financially we were not much of a strike for the searcher, who was the Captain Turner so frequently mentioned in connection with Richmond prison life.

It seemed to be the aim of the Rebel authorities to put men in charge of the prisons who were notorious on account of their brutal natures,—bullies, and, I doubt not, cowards at the front, for no truly brave man would vent his spleen on an unarmed prisoner who had no means of defending himself, and whose surroundings were such that prudence would forbid resistance. This is the most charitable aspect I can put upon the matter; for if such persons were not chosen intentionally, but were taken from the army without regard to their peculiar fitness in this respect, it would seem to prove that, as a whole, the Rebel army was a set of blackguards and barbarians, and I cannot make that assertion. Justice to the true Southern soldier compels me to say that we generally found them true as steel to soldierly principles, and generous to a fallen foe. Hence we must attach the responsibility where it belongs,—to the skirts of Jefferson Davis and his coadjutors, the manipulators of the Confederacy in the Capitol of Richmond.

We spent only one day and a night in Libby and were then sent into Pemberton Building, on the opposite side of the street, its west line and Libby's east line being on the same parallel north and south. An alley extended along the east end of Libby and the west side of Pemberton, Libby Prison presenting its side to Cary Street, and Pemberton's Building an end. The lot across the alley was vacant. The east half of the building, known as Smith's Building, was also full of prisoners. It fronted on Cary Street and ran easterly to a cross street.

I am thus particular in describing the buildings, because many persons suppose that the Richmond prisons were all one, called "Libby Prison" whereas Libby was only one of a number, all under the same management, the officers having their headquarters in the west end of Libby, on the first floor. The cook-house was in the same building, and it may be to this fact that the Richmond prison system is known as "Libby." The Libby Building was used almost exclusively as an officers' prison and hospital. The Pemberton Building was a four-story brick warehouse, with a basement, the fourth floor being a garret, and the roof a lean-to to Smith's Building, making the room perhaps ten feet on one side and just high enough on the lower side to admit of a person sitting on the floor comfortably. There were two windows at each end of the room, the only means of light and ventilation. The room contained perhaps one-third less floor room than the rest of the rooms in the building. The remaining rooms were well lighted and ventilated by windows in the west side and at both ends.

Here 750 of us "Yanks" were quartered, giving 200 to each of the three main rooms and 150 to the garret. The squad to which I belonged occupied the garret. This was not allotting to each man any more room than is supposed to justly belong to each member of the human family as his final resting-place. When we came to lie down at night the whole floor was pretty well covered, making it very difficult to get around without stepping on a neighbor. The rooms below were more aristocratic, having gas to light them, so that they could see to get around among the sleeping crowd.

But our quarters, like garret quarters generally, were minus such modern improvements, and, the room standing north and south, it became night with us very soon after sundown. When night proper closed in, we were in palpable darkness, blackness itself, the roof being so low. The tin roof, too, rendering it air-tight, the atmosphere was at times stifling. Then, in addition to the much-breathed air of our own room, we received through the stairway an additional amount from the rooms below, so that our atmosphere was poison itself. A cup of water left standing on the floor over night became stagnant and unfit for use,—really putrid, so that it stank. At times it seemed almost impossible to breathe, it was so close. Frequently, when lying down, I have had to get up before I could inflate my lungs, my chest feeling as though a hand of iron had grasped me in its clutches. A number of times I awoke to find myself sitting up and struggling for breath, my head seeming really to burst and my eyes to spring from their sockets. Our position was about the centre of the room, close to the stairway, so that what little fresh air came in at the windows was robbed of its oxygen before it reached us. It was always worse at night than in the daytime, when persons walking around helped to keep the air in motion. During the day, too, we could go down on the lower floors.

Our evenings were generally spent in vocalizing patriotic and other songs and hymns. We had several good singers and managed to spend the evenings very well. When anything was started that all could join in, we fairly made the tin roof jingle. It was not an unusual thing to have our melodies broken by cries of "Get off my leg!" or "Take that, damn you!" accompanied by an ominous thud or grunt (that most of us understood because we had been there), caused by some luckless fellow who, in attempting to reach the stairway in the dark, had trespassed on some neighbor's foot, receiving in return a kick that would cause him to lose his bearing and topple on to someone else with like results, until he was as likely to reach the stairs on his head as any other way. Such events happened so frequently that we called going to the stairway after night, "running the gauntlet," and when it became necessary for any one to make the trip, those along the line would receive warning by his calling, "Look out ahead, I'm going to run the gauntlet!"—so that those who were awake would draw up their feet and make as clear a way as possible.

Each morning we were called into line four deep and counted. This duty was performed in our building (and I suppose in all the rest) by a young man named Ross, who was said to be a deserter from a New York regiment. I cannot vouch for the correctness of the report, but for the credit of the Federal army it was as well that he should be where he was, as he could certainly have been no special credit to any community.

After roll-call, or, more properly, after count, we received our rations, which in Richmond usually consisted of a pint of boiled sweet potatoes, half a pound of bread, and a small piece of cooked beef or pork. Sometimes a pint of pea soup was substituted for potatoes. This constituted a ration for twenty-four hours. The cooking was done in a very slovenly manner, but we were not disposed to find fault with that, as it was generally understood by the prison authorities that we had stomachs like ostriches, that could tolerate anything, from a junk bottle to an india-rubber boot. Of course, where there was such a large family to provide for, they could not devote much time to such superfluities as washing and preparing the raw material. Consequently, when we found pine leaves, straw, and such other stuff as they had been stored in, among the potatoes, or when our pea soup was covered with bugs, we pulled them out or skimmed them off without a word of complaint or disapproval, unless, as was sometimes the case, the foreign matter was in such quantity as to take too large a percentage of the allotted measure. Then we did feel disposed to grumble, for even when it was all food we had nothing to spare. After we had become more accustomed to prison fare, however, we became less careful in skimming off the bugs, esteeming them as necessary to filling up the chinks. So we took it, as one of the boys suggested, "blind." "Try it," said he, "and see how nice they crack between your teeth."

I had often, in boyhood days, wondered at the persistency of a dog gnawing at a bone with such meagre results, and never was fully able to appreciate his sagacity in so doing until, as prisoners, we were compelled to look deeper than the outside to find any substance in some of our rations, the bones having been fairly picked before they reached us; hence we carefully crushed the joints and extracted all the substance from the medullary portion by chewing it. In this way we could get a good deal of satisfaction out of bones which by the uninitiated would have been thrown away as useless.

Chapter VII

The Sugar Riot

AFTER we had been in Pemberton some weeks, and had studied the views from all the windows; had talked about exchange until the theme had become stale and threadbare; watched the ebb and flow of the tide in James River until it had become monotonous; had speculated upon the mission of a little tugboat that used to run down the canal every day, with a cannon elevated on a post at its prow, which we dubbed "the Confederate Navy" and "the flag-of-truce boat,"—time began to hang heavy on our hands. True, we sometimes had a test of championship among some of the boys, yet not enough to vary the monotony a great deal. Finally those on the lower floor began to wonder what the basement of the building contained. Investigation being one of the marked traits of the average Yankee, the boys on the lower floor, being fair representatives of the race, did not theorize long on the subject.

When first brought into the building from the street, we had entered a small office room from which the stairway ran to the upper floors; but we had noticed a door leading from the office also into what we knew must be a basement. Now, what that basement contained, if anything, was the problem for solution. Two hours' work with an old case knife sufficed to cut out a hole large enough to allow an explorer to pass through into the darkness below. All this required extreme caution, in order not to arouse the guards, who occupied the rooms in front, lest a spirit of counter-investigation be aroused on their part. Yet had any of the guards made their appearance on the floor, they would not have noticed anything unusual going on. They might even have gone to the locality of the hole, but their suspicions would not have been excited by seeing two men sitting cross-legged on their blankets, busily at work on bone trinkets, nor would they have been likely to attach any significance to a number of raps with a knife on the floor, as the fellow was only tightening his knife-handle. No alarm having been given, the agreed signal from below announced that the explorer had come to the front to report.

"What do you find?"

"Hist! Not too loud; I hear the guard talking. I find nothing but large hogsheads."

"Full or empty?"

"Can't tell, it's too dark to see anything."

"What do you think?—have you any idea?"

"It smells like sugar; but help me up—all right!—give us your hand—wait until it gets dark out of doors and we will open one."

So far so good and very good, as the fellow's trousers showed where he had rubbed against some of the drainings. The hole was then closed to await the darkness of night.

Near where we lay on the upper floor was a bricked-up doorway, and it required no great amount of reasoning to deduce the probability that a region beyond must have necessitated a door, and, if so, what did that region contain? An old case knife was soon at work picking out the mortar from between the bricks, one of which was soon loosened, then another, until one was pushed out on the other side. Through the hole a voice reached us from beyond.

"Hello there!"

"Hello yourself."

"You're knocking dirt on my bed."

"Hell, you say!"

"Who are you?"

"Starved Yank. Who are you?"

"Ditto."

"What command?"

"Gunboat 'Rattler,' U.S. Marines."

"Where are you from?"

"Army of the Cumberland."

"What news over there,—anything about exchange?"

"Exchange be damned; it's played out—can't agree on the nigger."

"Damn the nigger and the Commissioners too. Any news from the front?"

"Big fight in the West."

"What part?"

"Near Chattanooga."

"Who whipped?"

"Glorious victory for our side. Drove them from their position on the top of the mountain. Captured nearly all their artillery and turned their guns on them, routing them completely."

"Who was in command?"

"Old Joe Hooker and Grant."

"How did you find it out?—where did you get the news?"

"One of the boys got a box from home, and one of the papers wrapped around the things contained a report of it."

"Can't you get us the paper?"

"Will try."

In due time the well-thumbed paper was passed through the hole and we were eagerly devouring the news. Oh, how we swelled and feasted, gloated and emphasized, as "That's my regiment!" and "That's *my* regiment!" fell from this one and that, as regiment after regiment was called off as having been engaged. It was as good as a feast of fat things to us, and the impression that would have been conveyed to the mind of an uninterested party would certainly have been that we were from an army of phlebotomists, as every fellow dubbed his regiment the "bloody so and so," and eulogized it with "Bully for the bloody boys!"

While it brought such good news it was not unmixed with gall, for among the list of killed and wounded we found many names of comrades that we held in high esteem as soldiers and friends. Among them was Major Butterfield of my own regiment, who died from the effect of a wound received. Yet this victory was indeed glorious news; we felt as if our boys were retrieving their loss at Chickamauga most gloriously. Then Forrest's prophecy came into our minds, and we wondered what he now thought of flaunting the "Stars and Bars" in Uncle Sam's face and drinking tea and coffee in an independent Confederacy. We had heard the old negro news-carrier crying, "A great fight in the West," some time before, but did not know any more about it until we received the news from that paper.

This old darkey news-carrier was quite a character in Richmond. We found that his crying a great battle always meant good news for us, though he never gave any particulars and seemed entirely oblivious to our presence as he went shuffling along the street, with his papers strung over a stick hung in front of him. We noticed that the guards, as a rule, cared little for papers, seldom buying any, and seeming to care little about what was going on outside of Richmond. Some few of the officers, however, would buy occasionally.

But to return to the basement. Further investigation in that direction, and the bursting of one of the hogsheads, proved our explorer to have been correct: they were full of sugar, and the boys immediately began making drafts upon it at a reckless rate, drawing it up through the hole in blankets, haversacks, oyster-can buckets,—anything that would hold more than a handful. Everybody had sugar, and so abundantly that we could eat it dry on our bread, or fix up a mixture of bread and sugar and water as fancy dictated.

The success of our investigation was reported through the hole in the wall to Smith's building, and an exploring expedition was soon gotten up on that side of the house, and the floor tapped. Next morning a voice came through the hole:

"Ship ahoy!"

"Aye, aye, sir!"

"We've visited the hold."

"Did you find anything?"

"Aye, that we did,—salt; barrels of salt, sacks of salt, salt, salt, salt, nothing but salt! Wouldn't you like to exchange some for sugar?"

"Certainly!"

So the hole in the wall became the channel for an interchange of commodities, exporting sugar and importing salt. Quite a trade was carried on in this way for several days, but the spirit of monopoly began to manifest itself in our building, and those who claimed the territory on which the shaft had been sunk declared that a duty should be paid on all sugar imported by the upper floors, while the upper floors declared for free trade and smugglers' rights, resolving that sugar they would have if they had to fight for it. Thus the house became divided, the minority seeking to dictate to the majority. A rebellion was inaugurated, the tocsin of war was sounded, and a call made for volunteers to go down and raise the blockade. Leaders were chosen and the hosts were marshalled. The plan was for some of the boys to go down into the basement and pass the sugar up, while others would be there to receive it, and still others, stripped for battle, would see fair play. No objection was made to their going down, but as soon as a haversack was passed up full of sugar the straps were cut by the minority, letting the sugar back. The first string cut was like the first shot fired at Fort Sumter. The blood of peace receded and the blood of war came to the front.

It is a well-proven fact that "when Satan rules, the Devil's to pay" and this was no exception. The relief corps came up to the support of their friends, and the fight began—a regular sugar riot. I was asleep when it began, but the noise soon awoke me. It sounded like bedlam on a frolic; the building fairly shook with the racket. The guards sounded the alarm, and the long roll was beaten. The news of an outbreak of prisoners spread through the town. The relief was called and charged into the building with fixed bayonets. The "Free Traders" came tumbling upstairs in a hurry, and only a few moments sufficed to put all on our floor in the profound slumber of innocence, apparently unconscious that anything out of the usual course had transpired, so that when the officers came to the head of the stairs all was so quiet and dark, they concluded the riot must have had its muscle from the lighted floors, and all the occupants of those floors were made to form in line and remain standing until daylight, a sufficient guard being kept on each floor to enforce the order. When Ross came to call the roll next morning he said he knew we were not engaged in the fuss—we were all so quiet. Thanks to our darkness for once. But that was an end to our prosperity and speculation in sugar: selfishness was our ruin. Thereafter we had to eat our bread and water, with the remorseful thought of "what might have been" if we could have lived together in peace and enjoyed the mutual benefit arising from our discovery.

The Richmond papers contained an account of the affair next day, in which it was stated that three hogsheads of sugar had been taken and wasted in the *mêlée*. The stock of nearly a hundred hogsheads was owned by speculators, and it was all taken away. Our jailers claimed that they knew we were getting the sugar all the time, but as it belonged to a set of sharks, who were holding it to take advantage of the necessities of the people by waiting for higher prices, they were perfectly willing we should have it if we could have behaved ourselves. But we were disposed to look on such talk as "whitewash." Prison authorities were not generally so well disposed toward us as all that, inasmuch as we had several times been made poorer by their cupidity. We were more disposed to think if they had had any suspicions of the sugar being there, they would have taken it themselves and blamed the stealing on us. In fact, I think the true feeling of the colony was expressed by one of the boys named Foster, a member of the Eighty-second Indiana Regiment, who was standing in line next to me when the officer made the statement. Whispering to me, he said:

"Don't you suppose he knows that we know he is lying about that? The dirty pup!—cuss him!—I'd like to cram a few fistsful down his crop."

The absence of sugar and the presence of a number of black eyes and banged noses were noticeable effects of the fracas, but peace and harmony were restored by the removal of the cause. Imports and exports were checked by the blockade: we had checkmated ourselves.

CHAPTER VIII

Transferred to Danville

SOON after the riot I was taken from Pemberton to one of the hospitals to assist in taking care of the sick prisoners. The building used as a hospital was a large tobacco-house several blocks from the prison and on the next street north. Here I was put in charge of a ward (as each separate room was called) containing perhaps forty beds, all occupied by those who had had to succumb to exposure and hard usage.

Although I had been a prisoner now for a number of weeks, the scene at the hospital was a revelation of horror, giving me my first insight into the sufferings of our men on Belle Island, most of the sick in the ward being from there. Up to that time it was the most heart-touching sight I had ever seen. Though I had passed over several fields of carnage immediately after fighting had ceased, the sight of the dead and dying did not seem to appeal to the senses as did the sight of those dirt-begrimed, half-starved, disease-stricken, powerless men that were put in my care in that tobacco-house. Poor fellows! they were not declared sick enough to need hospital nursing until they were beyond the reach of remedies. The result of exposure was beyond my conception of possibilities, but I was only on the threshold then. Subsequent experience taught me that there is nothing so bad but it might be worse.

The position of the island, the absence of any accommodation for the men, together with the chilly autumn rains, were a triple alliance against which the strongest constitutions could not long stand. Pneumonia, chronic diarrhea, and diphtheria finished up the work with fearful promptitude. The physician in charge of the ward was a resident of Richmond and did all he could for the sufferers, but medical skill and appliances were of little use. To leave men exposed in the buildings and on the island until they were beyond the reach of human skill, and then bring them to the hospital, was simply a cruel, blind subterfuge. A little attention given to their comfort at their quarters would have been much more potent in saving life than all the hospital practice they could employ later, if saving life had truly been the object.

Hard as the case already seemed, I soon found that it was rendered worse by a set of cormorants hanging around the hospital, ostensibly connected with it for prudential reasons, whose eyes seemed to take an inventory of the worldly effects of each patient that entered, and whose real business was to speculate in the clothing, blankets, and shoes of those who died. These we were ordered to turn over to the gang as soon as death claimed the real owner. At the head of this ring was a person claiming to belong to the Seventeenth Indiana Volunteers, and a prisoner, which might have been true, though from some cause he was a privileged character, coming and going as be pleased without a guard. To defeat this speculation in a measure, when one died who had a good blanket, pair of shoes, or any article of clothing, I would exchange them with some of the sick having poorer ones and turn over the tatters. I found that the same party was favoring the boys (so he made believe) by buying bread and butter for them in the city. As this seemed to be his whole business, and his residence was not in the building that I could see, I thought I would investigate and see if his bread-buying was, as he claimed, simply to accommodate the prisoners. I asked one of the guards at what price he would get me bread and butter, and if he could get them. He told me he could get me all I wanted and would be glad to do so, and at figures that showed that the prisoners' friend had been charging the boys three or four times what the stuff cost him,—in fact I was told he had made over a thousand dollars in his shameful speculation. I checked that by telling the men how to get their bread. But the result was that after a week's trial I was sent back to prison—evidently proving to be the wrong man for the place. Doubtless the Indiana man was the cause, as he seemed to be in the confidence of those in charge of the hospital.

On my way back to prison we halted a short time in front of Libby. Dr. Herrick, my regimental surgeon, who was an inmate of Libby, happened to see me from one of the upper windows. He asked where I had been, etc., and said they expected to be exchanged in a few days, negotiations having been about completed for the exchange of medical officers. Of course they were feeling in good spirits over the prospect. I told him I had been to the hospital, and charged him, if they were exchanged, for God's sake to try to have some arrangement made to have our sick exchanged and cared for, as they were dying off like sheep. The officer who had charge of us ran up to one of the guards, jerked the gun out of his hand, and cocked it, saying to me, "You —, hold your tongue or I'll shoot you." The doctor threw me out a pair of drawers and socks, which were truly a valuable accession to my wardrobe, as the weather was getting quite cool and I was thinly clad.

On returning to prison we were put into the east end. We were now in what was called Smith's Building. We found that the men were becoming disheartened and giving way to despondency. Our imprisonment was growing discouragingly long, and cold weather was fast coming on, which few, if any, were prepared, with proper clothing or by physical condition, to meet.

To add to our discomfort the news from City Point, the place of exchange, was very discouraging. General Grant was opposed to exchanging the well-fed Confederate prisoners for men disabled by sickness and exposure and advised that it be stopped. In fact there was a deadlock between the commissioners of exchange which was not likely to result in action very soon. It was a sheer piece of nonsense that so many lives should have been left to the whims and foibles of a couple of commissioners. The Northern people could have had no idea of how we were treated, or they would simply have demanded that our exchange be made regardless of formality or the expressed wish of General Grant. It was one of the most provokingly foolish pieces of formality developed during the whole war, and one that resulted in the death of over forty thousand men by slow torture, and the crippling for life of many more. We were abandoned to our fate simply as "a military necessity."

If we could have had reading-matter to occupy our minds, it would have assisted very much in keeping us from despondency. As it was, our only pastimes were in playing cards, checkers, chess, and like games, and in manufacturing trinkets out of bones, in which some of the men became very expert, making some things that displayed much skill and ingenuity considering the rudeness of the implements they had to work with. These consisted merely of old knives, pieces of knifeblades, and bits of glass. For drills they used pins and needles, running them with a bow. Of course, under these conditions, the work consumed time and it also kept the mind employed, which was an important factor in prison life. A deck of cards was a sight to see after we had used them for several months,—the corners worn off until they were of an oval shape, and so greasy that it was hard to distinguish one from the other. A deck was seldom idle during the day; we passed them around and kept them on duty, ministering in their way to lighten the tedium of the long hours.

Generally, once a day,—about noon, when we had the strongest light,—we spent an hour or two in the necessary pastime of removing vermin from our clothes and bodies. Woe to the poor fellow who had not strength to perform this work, if he had no friend to do it for him. It was really astonishing where the torments came from; for, no matter how carefully we might perform the work to-day, to-morrow there seemed to be just as many.

We had but a scant supply of water at most, our building being supplied by a one-inch iron pipe, with a faucet on each of the three floors. Some days it was impossible to get enough to drink, and to get any for bathing purposes and washing our clothes was out of the question. We hardly dared to use it for our hands and faces. No soap was issued to us, so that even if the water supply had been sufficient it would have been a difficult matter to have kept ourselves in a presentable condition. Occasionally men were assigned to carry water from the river to scrub the floors. This was the only sanitary move I ever saw made, and it soon played out. We were a dirt-begrimed set, looking more like negroes than white men.

It was a monotonous life, this weary waiting for exchanges, and yet we had had a comparatively short experience. The only sound that reached us from without was the steady "tramp, tramp, tramp," of the guards on the brick pavements below, some of whom, wearing wooden-soled shoes, varied the sound to a "clog, clog, clog." During the night it was the duty of each sentry to cry out the number of his post and the hour, beginning at Post No. I, ending with "All's well"; in this way the officers knew they were all awake and at their posts.

Some of the guards were very much disposed to trade with those of the boys who had managed to secrete their money. Those who lacked cash would trade their blankets, shoes, and coats for things to eat. From the back windows we had a view of a poulterer's yard, and could see him each day putting his flock through the stuffing process, fattening them for market. The boys would call to him that they were fat enough; that if he would send them up they would pick them for him.

When we were put into Smith's Building it varied the monotony a little, affording us an opportunity of studying Richmond from another side of the house. On Sunday afternoons, when the weather was fair, the streets presented a more animated appearance, seeming to be a favorite promenade for the negroes and devil-may-care women of the city, who would promenade for hours back and forth with the guards. A great many of the negroes had finely dressed white children in charge, and among all of them was a spirit of holiday jollity that put the idea of war and its horrors entirely out of sight, so accustomed may the mind become to stern facts as to accept them with an indifference that seems astounding from a civic standpoint. Sometimes, as we were spectators of the busy promenade, we had to accept a little of the spirit of bravado from the pent-up wrath of the promenaders, mixed occasionally with a laughable episode. We seldom got sight of a horse and buggy while in Richmond, and saw very few men not in soldiers' garb. We supposed that the horses had been pressed into the cavalry service, and the able-bodied men into the home guard.

About this time the city was thrown into a state of excitement by the escape of Colonel Straight and a number of officers from Libby. They had tunnelled under the alley spoken of at the east end of the building into a vacant lot or court, from which they scattered. The outbreak seemed to awaken a fear that the collecting of so many prisoners within the city was not a safe policy, as there might be an outbreak which, if properly carried out, with the concerted action of Union men resident in the city, would give the place into Yankee hands. While such an event might have been possible if there could have been preconcerted action among the prisoners, it was scarcely possible, owing to the isolated situation of the various buildings used as prison quarters, and the close guard maintained over each, to bring around such an event, unless, indeed, abettors could be found among the Confederate soldiers themselves. The fear once begotten, however, resulted in the establishing of a depot for prisoners at Danville, southwest of Richmond and near the North Carolina line, and vague rumors soon began to reach us that we were to be moved there as a place of greater safety. These rumors were not calculated to strengthen our faith in exchanges, and had a very depressing effect upon many of the boys, who seemed to lose hope and gave way to depression of spirits that soon brought them under the power of disease. It seemed like a long time to us, as we counted up nearly three months of our own experience as prisoners; and we looked on several who had been prisoners six or seven months as veritable heroes. Our short experience, however, with the scant, unwholesome fare, the exposure and anxiety natural to our condition, was beginning to make its effects seen on the boys, many of whom had to be taken to the hospital for treatment.

In this way time dragged along until about the 15th of December. Early in the morning we were ordered to vacate our building, each one receiving a small loaf of corn bread as he passed into the street. We were marched up Cary Street until we came to the bridge, over which we crossed to Manchester. Again the James River rolled between us and Richmond, and we interpreted the move to mean Danville and postponement of exchange. As in most military moves we were ahead of transportation and had to wait several hours before the train was ready to receive us.

The air seemed very chilly, coming, as we had, from the crowded building and many of the boys being destitute of hats and shoes, but its freshness and purity seemed to infuse new life into us. We amused ourselves and got our blood into circulation by playing leap frog. Our blood was so sluggish that it took considerable stirring around to keep us warm.

About an hour after sunrise the train steamed up on the Danville railroad, and we were ordered to board it, settling all doubt as to our destination. A change brought its novelties if nothing else, and there was a tonic property attaching to it that did us good. We were in just such a spirit and bodily condition that "anything for a change" was desirable and was received with thankfulness, though the end was yet in darkness. Our last glimpse of Richmond, like our first, was in the quiet of early morning, but we had had an experience in the city from which we learned how a quiet exterior might cover a heart full of misery and woe. We drew a breath of relief as her last spire disappeared from our view, for we knew that, though it pointed silently heavenward, its foundation was laid in a place akin to hell.

The Richmond and Danville railroad passed through a section of country that did not impress us very favorably. Much of the land seemed to have been worn out and abandoned and was growing up to young pines for some distance out from Richmond. There were no towns of any size along the whole route, and only three or four stations, so that the road looked like one of the most unnecessary ones in the world from a local point of view. But from the military standpoint it was the most important road in the whole Confederacy, facilitating the throwing of troops from the East to the West, and *vice versa,* as was done several times to the great discomfort of our armies. We made a halt about the middle of the day at a station in the woods, where we were allowed to get water. A number of the boys secreted themselves in the brush and failed to respond to the "All aboard" of those in command. Whether they succeeded in making good their escape I never knew. At another point, in running a long down grade, someone cut the train, so that at the next up grade the engine took part of the train some distance before the discovery was made. This provoked considerable profanity on the part of the guards, and put the "Yanks" into pretty good humor. We made such slow time that we did not reach Danville until late in the night.

As we were expected by that train, a delegation of soldiers, and not a few citizens, were awaiting our arrival to act as escort. We were not, however, "tendered the freedom of the city" by the mayor, but were immediately ordered into line by the soldiers, who, with fixed bayonets, marched us to the quarters that had been prepared for our accommodation, a negro martial band leading the way to the lively strains of "Dixie." They belabored the drums with a vigor surprising for darkeys, and stepped off with the pride peculiar to the race. We presume the "Johnnies" thought that this African band would be a humiliating joke on us, but we rather enjoyed it, as being the grandest reception we had received on the whole tour, or, as a big Irishman expressed it:

"Begorra, ain't that fine now; and ain't it gintlemanly in the divils to be afther thrating us to such music and military honor?"

It was quite a distance from the depot to our assigned quarters, and with the music and our noise combined I feel sure that many peaceful dreams were given a hideous aspect along our line of march, and many a refreshing slumber broken. We could hear windows raised, and see nightcapped heads protruding from some of them, in anxious inquiry as to the cause of the tumult; but the end came at last, and we were lodged in a four-story brick tobacco-house, our hearts gladdened by the assurance that rations would be forthcoming in an hour or two. Many of the boys had eaten up the loaf issued at Richmond before we boarded the cars in the morning. The rough ride had given us sharp appetites, and the fair promise of something to eat so soon buoyed us up, but we soon found that they computed time in a different manner to that which we had been taught in our youth, for the two hours consumed the balance of the night, the whole of next day, and until near midnight the next night. I had been prudent enough to husband my supply in anticipation of such an event, and did not suffer so much, but those who had been so indiscreet with their little loaves suffered the keen pangs of hunger. Our first ration consisted of a good-sized piece of very dark, heavy bread (apparently baked in large sheets about two inches thick) and boiled corned beef. The bread tasted very well, but I never could imagine from what kind of flour it was made.

CHAPTER IX

Mode of Life and Rations at Danville

WHEN morning came we found we were quartered in one of four large tobacco factories, built one on the north (Prison No. 1), two on the west (Nos. 2 and 3), and our building (No. 4) on the south sides of an open square containing about one city block, the Dan River running in a northeasterly direction near to and in rear of Nos. 1 and 2. The building on the north side and our building were of brick, the others of frame construction; each had four stories including a garret. Back of No. 3, on the river bank, or nearly so, was another large building, at that time used as a woollen factory, run by the Confederate government, in the manufacturing of Confederate gray and army blankets. To the southwest of No. 4, on a rising piece of ground, stood another large building, used as barracks by the guard. The four buildings fronting on the square were used as prisons and were full. I believe there were still other prisons in various parts of the city, but those on the square were all that I ever saw.

Here we underwent another search by a crippled man who walked with a cane. When he came in the first morning with a guard and ordered us into line, we did so quickly, supposing it was for the purpose of counting rations. But he soon undeceived us by beginning at the head of the line to search us. I happened to be third man in the line; he took from me a silver penholder and two gold pens that had escaped Turner at Richmond, and hesitated whether to take some postage stamps, but finally said I might keep them. He then took my name in a small book with a description of the articles, saying:

"These things will be returned to you when you leave this place. We only take them that you may have nothing with which to corrupt the guards."

I told him they must have a very poor opinion of the fidelity of their guards to suppose they could be so easily bought; that it was needless to offer an apology, as I understood it all, as he was not the first person by whom I had had the honor of being searched as a prisoner; that I had had the pleasure of being fleeced at Atlanta, skinned by Turner at Richmond, and was prepared to stand a small gutting at his hands; that we had been told the same thing at Richmond, but they had forgotten it,—at least they held on to the booty. He turned fairly livid with rage, but as he was only supported by one guard he wisely choked down his wrath. One of the guards told us that the things were sold at auction a few days afterward.

I do not suppose he secured anything of value on the lower floor. The boys on the next floor had been taking observations through a large auger-hole that had been bored for a pulley-rope, and, justly surmising that their turn would come next, had made what preparation they could to meet the emergency, and had succeeded so well that by the time the cripple got upstairs they were the most destitute set of men imaginable. We had learned the art of concealment at Richmond; paper money was pressed into the caps of our army buttons, and the covers returned, so as to show no signs of ever having been disturbed. One of the boys hollowed out a place in a stone large enough to hold his watch, and, covering the place with clay, suffered the stone to lie on the floor. Once, while they were being searched for knives, the officer in charge struck the stone with his foot with such force as to send it rolling across the floor, but it remained true to the secret entrusted to it and escaped without creating suspicion. Another saved his watch by cutting his ration of bread, putting his watch in the centre, and carefully fastening the bread together with wooden pins.

We had the privilege of a small yard, perhaps twenty by forty feet, enclosed by a high, tight, board fence. The well in this enclosure, about thirty feet deep, afforded an abundant supply of excellent water, a very decided improvement on the Richmond hydrant water.

Investigation disclosed a basement to our building wherein were stored a quantity of tobacco stems and a number of sheets of tin. The latter were quickly converted into stewpans by turning up the edges and turning the corners in against the sides, timely and important discovery and inventions which later were turned to good account. The tobacco stems were an ambrosial feast to the old smokers; they were eagerly sought after and as highly prized as their rations. Some of the prisoners had managed to keep their pipes through the past vicissitudes of prison life, and these were in great demand. They were always in use and were seldom allowed to get cold during the day, as they were generally spoken for several smokes ahead; in fact, in the middle of the night, a starry glow could frequently be seen that marked the pipe on its mission of comfort among the boys.

We sometimes had wood issued to us, and now to look back and see the value we attached to it is really amusing. They issued about one-third of a cord at a time, which, when divided among seven hundred men, gave but a small stick to each,—about the size of a small stick of stove wood, which had to suffice for a week or more. To give an idea of its value and the manner in which we had to divide it in order to give each man his ration, I will give the process in detail. It was issued to us in the ordinary cord sticks, which were divided as equally as possible among the floors in quantity corresponding to the number of men on the floor. Each floor then divided its quantity among the squads on the floor as equitably as possible; then, that there might be no possible room for grumbling, after it was divided into piles corresponding to the number of squads on the floor, one man turned his back. The sergeant then pointed to a pile and called out, "Whose is this?" the other naming the squads as they came to his mind until all were gone. From this choice there was no appeal. Each squad then made a division of its wood to the individual members. In order to do this the sticks had to be split up into kindlings, and, seeing that we had no tools of any kind, the "Johnnies" having taken even our knives, the difficulty the task may be imagined. On our floor we had a railroad spike and a piece of iron about six inches long by one inch wide, one side of which had been hammered down to an edge. These, with a small chunk of wood for a beetle, were our only implements with which to convert those rough sticks into fragments sufficiently small to make a fair issue to the men. Suffice it to say, it was a hard day's work to divide up three or four such sticks into proper size to give each man his share, and sometimes, when the wood was especially hard and knotty, two days would be consumed in dividing the ration among a squad. After each one had received his ration, it was still further split into slivers like straws, and carefully bound into bundles, which on our floor we usually hung to the rafter over our sleeping-place. A ration thus worked up would make a bundle about the size of an ordinary forearm, which we hoarded as carefully as if it had been gold.

Now, it may be asked, Why all this work for so little? Well, we could trade our shoes, blouses, trinkets made from bones, etc., with the guards, getting rice in exchange, and when we drew a ration of meat containing a bone we pounded the bone up into fragments, and, boiling the pith with the rice, made a very acceptable soup, far superior to any issued to us from the cookhouse. We accomplished the cooking by digging a small trench in the yard, over which we placed the pans made from the tin spoken of; in the trench we placed our fire, keeping up a fervent heat by constantly blowing it, but putting only a splint or two in at a time, so as not to use too much fuel. We had to do our cooking on all fours, in order to get our faces down so as to blow under the pans. It is astonishing how quickly we could cook a dish of rice in this way, and the very small amount of wood necessary to accomplish it, a small handful being sufficient. Our bread-crusts we scorched and made into coffee, boiling it in fruit cans, and making the one fire do for all. After all was done the fire was put out, and every small bit of unconsumed wood was carefully gathered up. It requires a prison experience to understand properly the importance attaching to these circumstances. Viewed in the light of the uninitiated, or even now in retrospect, they look like small matters well calculated to provoke a smile. To us, at that time, they were of momentous, nay, of vital importance.

The rations issued to us after the first few days were of the poorest kind and revoltingly cooked. It was a very common thing to find rat-dung cooked in the rice; our pea soup, made from a kind of black pea cultivated abundantly through the South, and fully ripe when gathered, was always covered with pea bugs, which floated on top; cabbage soup was sometimes substituted for pea soup, and this was worse, if possible, than the other, as only the outside leaves, covered with worms, were used in making it. The peas, or cabbage, as the case might be, were boiled with the meat,—either corned beef or bacon,—which was put into the mess kettle without being properly prepared and cleaned, and frequently our meat rations consisted of ham and shoulder bones from which the juicy parts of the meat had been cut before they were issued to us, as though they had been refuse from the town or from our own guards. The water in which everything was cooked was taken from the Dan River and was very muddy, so that the soup always contained more or less grit; hence, you can readily see the importance attaching to our crude method of working over our rations and treating them with pure water from the well, and why the tin stewpans were of such value.

Then, too, the time consumed in the preparation of meals kept our minds engaged, giving us a mental rest from the morbid state into which we were liable to be brought by constantly brooding over our condition. A careful study of the cases which had to be sent to the hospital convinced me that many diseases had their origin in mental rather than physical conditions,—conditions which finally brought the unfortunate one beyond the reach of aid.

CHAPTER X

Cold, Smallpox, and Scurvy

THE weather was growing cold and we were illy prepared to meet it, clad as we were and insufficiently fed. Many of the boys had traded their blouses for rice, leaving but a tattered shirt and pants to keep them warm. Our future had indeed a gloomy outlook, and disease began to make inroads into our ranks. The despair of near exchange had a very depressing influence on the sick, seemingly depriving them of all mental power to resist disease. Our sanitary condition was bad in the extreme, and no provisions were made to heat our quarters. A few days after our arrival a Mr. D——— came into No. 4 and called for a hospital steward. I was pointed out to him. He inquired if there were any in the building needing hospital attention and left some medicine with me to give to those suffering from diarrhea, instructing the sick to be at the entrance room in the morning at surgeon's call. Toward the latter part of December the sick were accumulating so that it became necessary to open a new hospital, and through the influence of Mr. D———I was given charge of a ward. Here, though as closely under guard, we were much better provided for than in prison, having a bunk and straw bed to sleep on and good warm fires. I found the sick were provided for as well as circumstances would permit; each patient had a bunk to himself, and our food was more abundant and prepared with some degree of cleanliness and care. The buildings were under the immediate care of Drs. Boyd and Hunter. The former was a genial, old-fashioned fellow, free from ostentation, and running over with fun. I think he was not a regimental surgeon. Dr. Hunter, who wore the uniform of the army and was by birth a Marylander and a member of a Maryland regiment, was more distant in his manners and not given to communication.

Dr. Boyd called my attention one day to an old white-headed darkey leading an old, white, raw-boned horse near the building, and said:

"An incident occurred a few days since, in which that old couple were actors, that may seem a little novel to a Northern man. That old horse was sold under the hammer, and that old darkey bought him in for ten dollars, which ordinarily he had a right to do; but it happens that the old fellow has no home, and, under the law, is a vagrant. The city, being chargeable with the care of vagrants, provides them with homes by putting them up at auction and selling them to the person who will keep them for what work they can do. Well, the old fellow was put up, but no one wanted him, so he became city property. Now, you see, he owns the horse, and the city owns him, and so the city will put him to carting dirt or any other work he may be capable of doing, and will have to see they are both properly cared for. Yes, there are some funny things growing out of slavery, as you will see if you remain in the South long."

During the holidays the weather turned very cold. The New Year's Day of 1864 is remembered all over the country on account of its severity, and Danville was no exception. The sick were rapidly increasing on our hands, every day bringing its quota. Their recitals of their sufferings in the prison buildings during the cold snap were heartrending. With the mercury at four degrees below zero, and the men in the condition I have described, without fires, it requires no vivid imagination to paint their miseries. For two days and nights they had to keep up an almost constant walking to keep from freezing to death, hardly daring to take the sleep necessary, lest they never should awaken. It must have been extreme torture and I was truly thankful for that Providence which had saved me from this trial.

The building used for a hospital to which they first took us was a large brick tobacco warehouse, so centrally located in the town that the people began to complain of its proximity to their dwellings, especially as smallpox bad broken out in the prisons, and they feared its spread in the city.

Justice to the South here demands a few words in regard to statements I have frequently seen made by prisoners; namely, that the surgeons of the Confederate army vaccinated the prisoners with impure virus and with virus taken from smallpox patients. Of course, I can only speak for Danville, but the assertion is absurd, locate it where you will. The fact is, the men were not vaccinated at all until the disease had made its appearance, and all had been exposed to it. Then, too, scurvy was making rapid inroads among the men, so that it was really dangerous to open a sore on the person such as was likely to result from a vaccine pustule. In fact, so poisoned were our systems that I would rather have taken the chances on smallpox than to open a suppurating sore, almost certain to follow vaccination in a system full of scurvy, and everything about having a tendency to foster gangrene. All the virus I saw bore the U.S. mark and was mostly from Philadelphia. The disease was in a very modified form; I suppose the men were sufficiently dieted for it; certainly, at least, there was no adipose tissue to interfere. The mortality was very light from this cause compared with the mortality from pneumonia and chronic diarrhea accompanied by a low state of the system. In fact, it ran its course with many of the boys without causing much discomfort aside from a few pustules, while pneumonia or chronic diarrhea, once fastened, seldom let go its grip save in death. There seemed to be no rallying force to build on and assist treatment. About all we could do with such cases was to ease them off from the shores of time. The surgeons did all in their power, but their means were limited.

In the latter part of January the sick were removed from my ward and we returned to No. 4. How eagerly the boys pressed around us to know if we had any news of exchange; but we were not the messengers of hope. We were surprised to see what a difference the five weeks we had been out made in the looks of the men. During the cold snap they had built fires indoors from the ration wood, taking bricks from the walls to make a safe foundation. Then they would crouch around the fires and draw their blankets around them so as to hold the heat in. Of course, this filled the house with smoke and gave the boys a dried-halibut look. The tales they told us of their sufferings during the cold spell were tales of horror, confirming the reports brought us by the sick. Rumors now began to reach us of a contemplated move little calculated to make us desire the change, especially after reading an editorial on the subject in one of the Richmond papers. I cut out the extract, intending to keep it as a proof of the spirit that ruled in the treatment of prisoners, but lost it with many other extracts of similar character in attempting to make my escape. It was as nearly as possible in these words:

"A move is in contemplation among officials and has been recommended, having for its object the removal of the Yankee prisoners now confined in Richmond and Danville to the cornfields of central Georgia. We think this would be a wise move, as it will take them nearer the base from which their supplies are brought, doing away with transporting it to them, and placing them also where the climate may tell upon them as heavily as our army is doing in front."

CHAPTER XI

More Hospital Duty

A FTER several weeks I was again drafted for hospital duty. Our boys were coming down so fast it became necessary to increase the hospital room to meet the demand. The authorities took possession of three buildings which had been specially erected as a general hospital for the use of their army in Virginia. They were located in the eastern part of the city, and probably outside the corporation limits. They were airy and comfortable, and were located on a very pretty knoll overlooking Dan River and giving a fine view of its meanderings among the hills for several miles. Each building was fifty by two hundred feet, boxed with rough lumber, and two stories high. A hall above and below divided them into four wards, each containing sixty bunks, and each bunk supplied with a straw bed, straw pillows, and sufficient covering of quilts to make the men comfortable. The walls and ceiling were nicely whitewashed and festooned with evergreens, as if loving hands of the gentler sex had been plying their handiwork in the mission of mercy. It was done for the sons of the South, but we Northerners appreciated and enjoyed the effect. Without exception they were the best arranged and most commodious hospital buildings I saw in the South. An abundance of water bubbling up in a spring near by probably had much to do with its location. Everything was new, and affairs were under the surveillance of a number of Confederate supernumeraries, generally of the kid-glove class, sent here to be out of danger, who, to keep up the shadow of a necessity, attended to their several offices quite attentively. A laundry department kept us supplied with changes of bed linen and shirts to a limited extent. For those of us who could walk, our meals were prepared at the cookhouse and were served in a comfortable dining-room in the rear of the building. Those who were bedfast were served at their bunks, and the food was unusually well prepared. Taking all in all, we had reason to be thankful for this mollifier of our otherwise wretched condition.

Our mode of procedure when we received a patient from either of the prisons was to strip him naked and stand him in a tub of warm water, if he had strength to stand; if not, we supported him in an upright position until he could be thoroughly scrubbed and cleaned with soap. We then gave him a clean shirt and drawers and put him to bed. This generally occurred about two o'clock in the afternoon, and in most cases they would soon fall asleep and we would hear no more from them till next morning. The bath, straw bed, and warm covering were luxuries they never got in the prison quarters, where the hard floor had been their bed, in most cases with no covering at all. Poor fellows! the beds we gave them were a rest to their weary limbs that wooed them to slumber.

I was put in charge of Ward No. 3, the upper room on the east side of the most easterly building and nearest the spring. This building was under the supervision of Dr. Dance, a Confederate surgeon of whom I formed a very high opinion for his gentlemanly treatment of myself and the sick of my ward.

Scurvy was now becoming alarmingly prevalent, and formed, when combined with chronic diarrhea (as it generally was) or with pneumonia, a combination at once hard to control with the medicines we had at our hands. Drs. Hunter and Dance, with Dr. Fontleroy as director, did all they could for the boys, but the mortality was heavy. The poor fellows needed food more than medicine; vegetable food would have done more good as a curative than all the medicines that could have been given them. It may possibly have been the promptings of a desire to give the patients the benefit of an antiscorbutic diet that led the authorities to have a wagon-load of the outside leaves of cabbages, worm-laden and dirt-discolored, thrown into one of the small rooms spoken of in No. 4 prison, with the announcement, "Help yourselves, Yanks; they are for you; pitch in!" It was an ingenious mingling of the animal and vegetable pretty evenly divided, but the boys made fair soup from it,—understand me, I mean *prison soup*, though it was a compound an average Northern hog would turn from in disgust. It was simply a philosophical acceptation of a principle laid down by an old gentleman named "Hobson," whom, no doubt, we have all had quoted to us,—"That or nothing."

There was living near the hospital a lady, whose name I fear has slipped my memory, though I think it was Rodgers, the widow of a Confederate lieutenant killed in front of Richmond. She seemed to fill the position of matron or to have held that position during the occupancy of the buildings by their men. At any rate, she deserves kindly mention on account of the many kindnesses extended to our *very* sick boys, many of whom received delicacies which only a woman's hand knows how to administer,—the smoothing of a pillow, a word of cheer or sympathy, or the moistening of fevered lips with lime-juice from a silver cup which she usually carried. We were visited frequently also by Rev. Dr. Carmichael, of the Episcopal Church, who distributed Testaments among the boys and gave spiritual advice to any who desired it, in a kindly way that won him a place in the affections of the men. I love to refer to such characters, for they deserve to be kindly remembered. From what I saw I think they did the best they could for our sick in Danville.

I once unintentionally touched Dr. Fontleroy's dignity by making a suggestion regarding a patient who was very low with typhoid fever, in that wakeful, wild state it sometimes assumes, with the skin dry and hot. While the doctor was examining him, I said:

"You will get a good effect from a heavy Dover's powder administered to him to-night."

"Don't you know, sir," he said, "you might about as well kill him as to give him any opiate in the condition he is in? No, sir, a Dover's powder given him now would kill him."

Well, I made up my mind he would die if he did not get one, so I went to the office and got a ten-grain powder, combining some camphor with it, and administered it to him about eight o'clock. He soon quieted down and fell asleep, his skin became moist, and next day, when the doctor made his round, the patient was rational.

"Now," said he, as he came to examine the man, "what do you think of your Dover's powder? I never saw a greater change in my life in one night."

But I held my peace and did not mention my treatment.

The movement of prisoners to Andersonville had begun, and Dr. Dance came in one morning and said he had orders to send every man in his wards who could walk, back to the prisons, to be sent south. He continued:

"They intend using this building for a smallpox hospital. Now, if you will take charge of a ward of smallpox I think I can manage so that you can remain."

After duly weighing the matter I concluded that my chances of taking the disease were about as good in the prison as in the hospital, so I told him I would take charge and remain, preferring even the chances of smallpox to the privations of Andersonville. I could not down the ghost raised by the editorials in regard to Andersonville. They struck me at the time as being the coolest survey of a probable mortuary result that I had ever read or heard. It was murder not only premeditated, but publicly recommended. And the locating of the stockade at Andersonville was a grand supplement to such a spirit, and worthy the genius of its advocates and projectors. It is useless to tell me that the locality of Andersonville was not well studied. Yet, notwithstanding all the adduced testimony in the case, men will stand up in the halls of Congress and declare that the inhuman treatment of prisoners was unknown to them and to the Confederate authorities at Richmond. Such assertions are preposterous and bear falsehood on their very face, with the stench of Belle Island wafted to their nostrils by every breeze blowing from the south, the island itself in view of the windows of the Capitol, and their morning papers bearing editorials of this character to their very desks. To deny all knowledge of these things is to put the stamp of ignorance and incapacity upon their pseudo-government and Chief Executive. Yet I do not wonder that they attempt to deny all knowledge of it. Its recollection ought to be sufficient to cover them with shame so great they never could raise cheek sufficient to ask to be doorkeepers, even, in the Capitol at Washington.

Chapter XII

Attempts to Escape

BUT I find I am getting ahead of my diary and must return to my experience after my first return to prison in January. Soon after my return some of the boys conceived the idea of making an escape by tunnelling out. Among them were several members of the Eighteenth U.S. Infantry, D. S. Wilder, Tooker, and others whose names have been forgotten.

The place decided on for the experiment was beneath the floor of our office room on the west side of the building. Having made all necessary observation from an upper window, it was decided that it would be necessary to go down six feet in order to pass under a drain before striking a lateral direction under the street into a vacant lot beyond. These preliminaries being agreed upon, work was commenced by sinking the shaft. The tunnel proper was about three feet high by two feet wide. As I had secured a number of candles while out, my share was to furnish the light, the others doing the work. And hard work it must have been, too, with only case knives to loosen the hard clay and the diggers' hands to throw the dirt back, which was done by passing it between their legs while in a kneeling position.

After the soil was brought to the surface it had to be carefully packed away under the floor. The air was so close that the men could only work a few minutes at a time and then come out for air. In this way several weeks were consumed and the utmost secrecy was exercised. All work had to be done by daylight, as a guard was stationed on the lower floor every night. At night the diggers would report progress, and we would lay plans for our course after we got out, for we did not have a thought of failure. In this way work progressed until we reckoned that one more day would complete it. Our hearts beat high with hope: we could almost fancy ourselves free men in God's country.

Next day the men went to work to complete the tunnel so far that nothing would remain to be done but to break through to the surface. But "the best laid plans of mice and men gang aft agley." On that eventful day a Confederate officer and squad of men filed into the building, marched up to the place where the boys got under the floor, and called:

"Come out of there, you damned Yankees, you."

They then took them out and made them dig down and fill up the tunnel. Quite a number of citizens came down to see the hole the Yankee gophers had dug. The plan had been revealed by a prisoner, a sergeant from Michigan, who expected by his perfidy to gain Confederate favor. Indignation filled the breasts of all who were initiated into the secret of the tunnel, for, notwithstanding the fact that weeks had been consumed in its preparation, but few in the building had any suspicion of its existence, and their ruling was that he who would betray his friends under such circumstances ought to die by the hands of the men he had betrayed, and I doubt not such would have been his fate if the officers had not given him a place in one of the other buildings. For this attempt at making an escape we were not permitted to use the lower floor, from sundown to sunrise, except in squads of six at a time, for the purpose of answering nature's calls. The last man of the six had to return before another six were permitted to pass. This was a punishment whose severity none can know but those who felt its weight. Men who were suffering from chronic diarrhea and scarcely able to stand or walk, had to take their places in line, wait their turn, come back, and fall into line again. I have frequently stood in line from dark until ten o'clock before my chance would come. I do not know that a more inhuman punishment could have been devised outside of starvation; it was simply torture. Major Moffit, who had command at Danville, ably seconded by Lieut. Mews of the Eighteenth Virginia Infantry, were the brutal originators of this order. After a time they modified the punishment by providing slightly better accommodations.

I believe there were only three successful efforts made to escape from our building. The first was soon after our arrival at Danville. A cross-eyed, apparently half-witted fellow took an axe that was in the yard, broke the gate-fastening one evening, and ran; the guard emptied his gun at him, but missed him in the dark, and we heard no more of him. For this act they took from us the axe.

The next case was that of two men who slept on the lower floor near a window. They allowed us to have the windows open at that time. These fellows, watching their chance when the guard's back was toward them, jumped out and ran; he fired, but the darkness favored them, and we never heard from them again, which is the only evidence we had of their success. For this act our windows were boarded up from the outside. The third attempt was made by a couple of men from the roof of the shed on the west side. One succeeded in swinging off all right, but the other received the contents of the guard's gun, the ball entering the armpit posteriorly and passing up through the shoulder, shattering the accromian process. (The guard was standing under him when he fired.) The poor fellow was taken into the building, and it was several days before they would permit examination by a surgeon.

I was told this by the young man himself, who was put into my ward in No. 4 hospital after I was taken out the second time, about the 1st of May, 1864. Dr. Fontleroy and I differed again, he claiming it was only a flesh wound and would soon heal. I held that from its direction it could scarcely fail to shatter the process, and that if I were correct, a day or two would prove it by the working out of spiculae of bone. If, on the other hand, he were correct, the absence of the spiculae would sufficiently attest his views. That night I had occasion to take several splinters from the wound and showed them to the doctor next morning. This young man was still at the hospital when I left on the 3d of July, his system so full of scurvy that the wound could not heal, and I had my serious doubts if he would ever recover. For this attempt at escape all the upper windows were boarded up even to the garret.

On one occasion I was standing at the fence in the yard, in company with a Mr. Spears, who was having some conversation with one of the guards through the fence. Suddenly the guard brought down his gun and fired at Spears, but the latter happened to move just as the man aimed. He got pretty well spattered with splinters, and was so effectually scared that, to use his own expression, he "shook for an hour." The ball passed through the west back window, struck the floor near the old tobacco-press, and bounded out through the front door. It was remarkable that no one was struck, as quite a number of prisoners were on the lower floor at the time.

On another occasion several of us were enjoying the view from the garret front window, when, in trying to direct their attention to a certain point on the opposite side of Dan River, I chanced to extend my arm beyond the window. Hearing a guard call, "Take in your arm thar," I cast my eye downward and beheld him taking deliberate aim at my arm. I obeyed the order with promptness, no doubt to his disappointment, as a large percentage of the Danville guards were men who did not value the life of a Yankee very highly, and seemed on the alert for a pretext to shed blood. As an instance of their disregard of life, I may mention the following incident: Nearly opposite our building, on the west side, stood a small house occupied by some negro washerwomen, one of whom, while hanging out a washing, was deliberately shot at by a guard of No. 3, the ball breaking her arm. Several of our boys who were looking out of the windows at the time were witnesses of the whole affair, and saw nothing in the actions of the woman to provoke the act. It just seemed to be the leaven of the Devil working in them that had to have vent some way in the shedding of blood. The guard reloaded his gun and continued patrolling his beat as if nothing had happened, and no attention was given to the matter by the officers. They held negroes and Yanks about on a par. They used every pretext to render us uncomfortable, nor did they require an overt act on our part, for their fertile brains could manufacture one.

At one time the authorities claimed to have discovered that an outbreak was being organized in our building, and sent in an armed body to take from us all knives or anything that could be used as a weapon of defense. As such things had been pretty well picked up before, about all the knives we had were manufactured from hoop iron found at the time the tin and tobacco stems were discovered. As they began their search on the lower floor, those of the next floor gathered all their knives and put them in one corner under a blanket. They then put several blankets on top and placed a man there to play sick. When the "Johnnies" came to the corner where he lay tossing and struggling in apparent delirium, two of the boys holding him down, they wanted to know what ailed him. "*Just coming down with smallpox*, poor fellow; he is delirious and the symptoms are—." But they made for the stairway with an alacrity that seemed to say, "No smallpox in mine, thank you!" So we saved our knives. I don't know whether these little deceptions will be brought up against us in the court of Heaven, but I certainly think we were justified in whipping the Devil around any stump we could catch him behind.

The daily counting in our building was attended to by an Englishman named Noles, a kind-hearted man, though a great stutterer, a Confederate by force of circumstances, and always dressed in black velvet. He came into the building one morning and took five of us up to headquarters. He said to me, as we were passing up the street, "I g-guess yo-yo-you go-going this t-t-time sh-sh-shure p-p-pop!" At headquarters we were shown a number of gold pens and pencils and told to select ours from them; of course they were not there. We were then taken back to prison. I never could understand the force of that move, or what object they had in it, as they asked us no questions.

Next morning there was an order, for the sick to report at the entrance door. The doctor sent word that he wanted to see me. He told me that Dr. Hunter had told him to bring me out to be on hand next morning, and he would take me to the hospital again. I was there on time next day and was again put in charge of my old ward. I then found that the orders were to send the men of Prison No. 4 to Andersonville as soon as transportation could be procured for them. This was in the latter part of April, 1864.

After the escape of General Morgan from Columbus, he made a visit to Danville for the purpose of recruiting from among the prisoners. He sent word to the hospital that if there were any prisoners there who would like to talk with him he would be pleased to call and have a talk with them. As he did not put in an appearance, the presumption is that no one cared enough about him to want to have a talk with him. We were not investing very heavily in Confederate stock at that time, though some did take the oath of allegiance as a possible means of prolonging life and getting out of prison.

CHAPTER **XIII**

"Beast" Butler and Southern Rights

HAVING occasion to go into the office one morning while at No. 3, one of the attachés who had been reading a paper, turning to me, broke out in violent defamation of General Butler. It was an account of Butler's appointment as Commissioner of Exchange that had touched him up so; in fact his appointment to that position was a bitter pill for the South to swallow, as they had declared him an outlaw. After the fellow had said his say, I asked:

"What has the 'Beast' been up to now? Has he been speculating in spoons again?"

"No," said he, "but look what an insult your government has offered to us in asking us to treat with that outlaw; it don't look as though they cared much about getting you-all exchanged, as they ought to know no Southern man would recognize him in any official character or demean himself by having intercourse with him. Why, he has openly insulted every lady in the South by his beastly order at New Orleans, and now for your government to ask any Southern gentleman to demean himself by any show of equality with him is more than the South will stand."

"To what special order do you refer at New Orleans?" I asked.

He then read to me Butler's celebrated order No. 28, in regard to the women of that city,—a story which is too well known to all to need repetition here.

"*There!* what do you think of *that*, and having that dirty dog appointed as Commissioner of Exchange?" he asked, as he threw down

the paper and struck the table a blow that made things rattle as he exclaimed: "Damned if I'd live under the United States government again
for anything. How would you like it?"

"Well," I said, "it has the merit of plainness, anyway, and I fail to
see anything wrong or out of place in it that would characterize it as an
insult. Certainly it was proper, if the ladies of New Orleans did not know
enough to behave themselves with becoming propriety, for Butler to teach
them; and, in order that they might not ignorantly err, it looks to me like
a gentlemanly act in him to define the offence beforehand and to announce the penalty attaching thereto, as it put the ladies on their guard
and no doubt shielded them from real insult by the soldiers. Just reverse
the order of things, and suppose the city was in the North and under
Southern rule, would you not consider it proper to make all citizens pay
due respect to your flag and soldiers?"

"Certainly," he said, "but don't you see how he has insulted some
of the finest ladies of the city, and through them every woman in the
South?"

"Ah," I rejoined, "just there is where you err in judging Butler and
make your position questionable, for I have more respect for the good
sense of the better class than to believe that they would so far forget
themselves as to conduct themselves in that way. But, admitting that
they did, it was not for Butler to draw any discriminating lines. If the
better class put themselves upon the same footing with 'women of the
town,' they, and not Butler, were to blame if they were brought under
the same judgment and condemnation. There should be no caste or condition of society that could shield them from the penalty of transgress-
ing the laws; all are supposed to be governed by them alike,—rich and
poor, high and low, male and female."

"Yes," he said, "your view of the case is reasonable."

"Then," I said, "the citizens of New Orleans are under obligation
to Butler for the great hygienic improvement he has made in the city."

"Very true," he said.

"Then you will have to admit, after all, that the 'Beast' is not entirely savage."

"Well, he is no gentleman, any way," he returned.

I told him I could not say as to that, but that it would be no detri-
ment to the United States if we had a few more Butlers. As to his acting
as Commissioner of Exchange, or the policy of appointing him to the
position, I was not prepared to say. Certainly, if my government thought
he was the man, I could not say otherwise; and so far as the result to the
Confederacy was concerned, we did not recognize such a thing as yet,
and there were some doubts yet if there ever would be.

"For whom did you vote for President," I was asked one day.

"My first vote was cast for John Bell, sir."

"You *did*? Well, that's strange. I voted for him, too, and here we are, one in the Northern army and one in the Southern."

"Not at all strange," I said politically. "I was in sympathy with the South, having been taught to look upon her rights as a sacred institution under the Constitution; but when she showed the cloven foot in firing on Fort Sumter, my sympathy was gone; in that act she disrobed herself, and did more toward opening the eyes of the North than all the fiery speeches that had been made, or ordinances of secession that had been passed. It proves your injured rights to be but a pretext, a sham."

CHAPTER **XIV**

The Spring Campaign of 1864

THE war cloud now began to assume a threatening aspect, and hung lowering over the Eastern army. The stereotyped "All quiet on the Potomac" bid fair to give place to the bustle incident to an energetic campaign. General Grant, having been put in command there, was putting things into shape for an offensive movement, and was pushing matters with such vigor that all able-bodied Southerners were ordered to join their commands at once in order to check his advance.

The authorities at Danville were directed to get the buildings we were occupying in readiness for their own men from in front of Richmond; and all our Confederate attachés had peremptory orders to join their regiments immediately. It caused considerable consternation among them. They had no desire to shoulder a musket and go into active duty again. One of them said to me:

"When the war first broke out it appeared as though we couldn't get to the front fast enough; we wanted to go right into you-all, tooth and toe-nail; but now, doggoned if we don't want to get home just as bad and a good deal more. But while it was an easy matter to get into the army, getting out is quite another matter. If I had it to do over again, they might do their own fighting; they'd never get me to shoulder a musket and leave my home."

All of our boys who could walk were sent in a few days to Andersonville. We were moved to the smallpox camp, perhaps a mile west of town, some time in May. Every day, almost, we would hear of heavy fighting around Richmond. Dr. Hunter asked me one day why our government allowed Grant to slaughter his men so unnecessarily, when they were accomplishing no good. Another day he spoke of Lee taking a great number of prisoners, and of our boys being forced to charge until the Confederate artillery literally ploughed through ranks of dead piled in heaps.

"Your men," he said, "charged up like drunken men. What do you think of that kind of work; don't you think it's madness?"

I laughed and told him I would like to hear the other side of the story, as I would be better prepared to judge of the rashness of the act; but from his standpoint it certainly did have a foolish and extraordinary look, and I could offer no explanation.

We found our new quarters very pleasantly located on a commanding knoll thinly covered with trees, beneath which the boys could rest and enjoy sunshine and pure air. A marked improvement was soon manifest in most of the cases. Dr. Hunter, who had entire charge here, had us gather greens for them, and when the berries ripened they were also supplied, a treat highly appreciated by all and most beneficial to those suffering from scurvy and chronic diarrhea. On one occasion he sent Mr. Schroeder, the hospital steward of a Missouri regiment, and myself under guard to the matrons to get some delicacy for one of the men, and instructed us to call at the guardhouse and ask for an extra guard to go with us after berries. We delivered the message in what we thought pretty good style, but the officer of the day broke out in a tirade of abuse against us that was very ungentlemanly and altogether un-called for, adding, "If Dr. Hunter wants you-all to go berrying, tell him to go with you himself, or to furnish his own guard. I have sent all the men I am going to detail there to-day."

A lieutenant, sitting by, said he didn't "go much on that Dr. Hunter, any way."

We delivered the message and told the doctor what we had overheard the lieutenant say. His indignation was intense and beyond expression.

"I'll teach that damned Virginian what Maryland is made of," he said, and, mounting his horse, started to hunt him up. Next day, when he came out, he said:

"Well I made that fellow take that back, or, at least, deny saying anything of the kind. I told him I could prove it. I believe he said it to you, but, damn him, he did not dare give me any such order himself; he can cuss an unarmed prisoner, but he mustn't try any such impudence on me to my face."

The doctor was a very staunch rebel, but a generous one. It made him very angry, however, to find a Southern man a prisoner in the hospital, as he did about the middle of June; he said he could very readily forgive a Northern man entertaining opinions differing from his, but he had no charity for Southern traitors. The man was brought in suffering from pneumonia of such a severe type that he had to be dropped from a group that was being sent to Andersonville. On the doctor's asking his name and regiment he found that he was from North Carolina.

"What!" he said, taking a step or two backward, "from North Carolina?"

"Yes."

"Born there?"

"Yes."

"Living there when the war broke out?"

"Yes."

"And in the Yankee army, too?"

"Yes, sir."

"Well, damn you! you may die, you ought to,"—and he turned away. Then in a few moments he came to me and said, "Do all you can for that man; poor fellow, he will not last long, any way."

Three days later the prisoner died. The morning after, when the doctor came out, I said:

"Well, your wish in regard to Dale is fulfilled; he is dead."

"I did not wish to have him die," he said. "But it did make me mad for a moment when he said he was a North Carolinian, fighting in the Yankee army,—fighting against his own people and rights. I didn't understand it, I cannot understand it. It's not right."

CHAPTER XV

Our Escape from Danville

W E had over us at this hospital two Confederates; one a Mr. Walters, from Charleston; and the other a brother of Gov. Holden of North Carolina; he had been disabled for field duty by a wound in the elbow which gave him a stiff joint. We found both of them very pleasant gentlemen, seldom interfering with the running of the wards more than to see that all were on hand. As the 4th of July was drawing near I told Mr. Holden in a joking way that I had never been accustomed to being deprived of my liberty on that day, and they must be keenly on the alert or I would have my usual holiday.

"All right," he said, "I'll see to you and keep you within bounds."

Several of us had, however, been laying plans to "skip out" on the night of the 3d,—Schroeder, Sergeant Carlisle, of a Michigan regiment, a big Irishman whom we called Mat, and myself. Carlisle said he would attend to the manner of our escape, as he was pretty well acquainted with several guards of approachable disposition. He was our cook and knew that a man's prejudices could be overcome by appeals to his stomach. By the aid of one of our boys named Thurston, who assisted Mr. Walters in keeping the records and making reports, I gained access to a map of Virginia, from which I furtively drew a map of our part of the State. We tried to get Thurston to join us, but he preferred abiding his time and standing chances of exchange to running the risk of an escape. He bound himself to secrecy, however, in regard to the move. Mr. Walters seemed to suspect something, possibly from what I had said to Mr. Holden, and would come into my ward every night about ten o'clock.

Meanwhile Carlisle had secured his man and arranged to have him on the beat next the cookhouse on the eve of the 3d, to pass us out immediately after calling eleven o'clock, the price for this accommodation being a blanket apiece. He had also prepared rations to last us several days. The evening of the 3d came at last; everything was in readiness, and we were awaiting the hour. A few moments before eleven Mr. Walters came into the ward and inquired if I was in; then, seeing me on my bunk apparently fast asleep, he passed out through the southwest door.

Then Schroeder and I went into the cookroom, blankets in hand, where we found Carlisle and Mat. As soon as "All well!" was sounded by the guards we slipped out, dropping our blankets at the guard's feet as we passed. The building stood four or five steps from the edge of a deep ravine on the east, down the side of which we slid with as little noise as possible, following the course of the ravine to Dan River.

I must confess to strange feelings when we stood outside the guard lines; my nerves were keyed to their utmost tension, and my whole being tingled with emotion and the possibilities of the venture. For nearly ten months we had been constantly under the range of guns ready to bore us on the least provocation, and now, under darkness of the night and still in close proximity to those same guns, we stood free, and yet not free, and possibly in greater jeopardy than as prisoners. Yet even this foretaste of freedom made us leap with joy and thanksgiving. Our studied plan was to cross the Dan River as quickly as possible and get it between us and the town, after which we would push our way in the direction of Lynchburg. On reaching the river an insurmountable difficulty arose, because of the inability of Schroeder and Mat to swim. This was very annoying under the circumstances, a feature not on the programme, and one for which we had made no provision. The river was wide, deep, and swift in current. Farther advance in that direction was simply impossible, and it behoved us to be moving, as we had partially to retrace our steps and to make a detour in order to avoid the hospital. Our only chance was to follow up the south side of the river, which at this point makes a bend in the direction of North Carolina.

We heard the guards crying "Midnight and all well!"—from which we judged that our escape had not yet been discovered. As we passed near the ferry, we unfortunately, as we thought, aroused a dog whose bark was taken up and answered by all the canine race for miles around, making us quake with fear, though in the end the chorus was an advantage, as it enabled us to locate habitations ahead, and so shape our course as to avoid them.

Passing in a southerly direction until we struck the railroad running from Danville to Greenboro', we followed it for several miles and then struck off in the direction of the river. The surface of the country was very much broken, and, not being in very good condition to travel, we found it necessary to make frequent rests. Still, by the time the gray of dawn began to streak the east, we were some distance from the hospital, and again near the river, and, we judged, a ferry, as we thought we could distinguish the sound of a chain and the stamping of horses as they passed on and off the flat-boat.

As daylight advanced we found a hiding-place in a fallen tree-top on a timbered hillside, which gave us a good command of the road without danger of exposing ourselves. After eating a lunch we disposed ourselves to sleep, one remaining awake to keep watch.

We lay low all day, scarcely daring to speak above a whisper for fear there might be listening ears. Our apprehensions were aroused by the appearance of two unarmed men who halted and stood some time in earnest conversation in a ravine below and not over a hundred yards from us. Our Irishman was asleep, and making what we thought a tremendous noise snoring; but we did not dare to wake him lest he should make some exclamation that would lead to our discovery. The men carried on their conversation in such low tones that, while we could hear the voices, we could not distinguish what they said. After what seemed to us a protracted interview they separated, going in different directions. Their meeting thus, in this secluded hollow, and parting, as we thought, with some degree of caution, filled us with suspense, as we feared they might have heard of our escape and had some clew to our being in the woods. Thus we interpreted their separation to mean a more thorough search. We saw nothing more of them, however, and as the afternoon wore away we began to feel safe again. Toward evening, however, a negro boy came into the woods calling cattle. He actually mounted the stem of the tree under which we lay, and stood so close that I could plainly see the white of his eyes, and at one time I thought he was looking right at me. If Mat, who was still sleeping, had given a lusty snore, our discovery would have been certain. We felt suspicious of the boy, for there had not been a cow in sight or hearing all day, and we inclined to the belief that he was sent to draw us from our hiding-place. Night, however, closed around and we breathed easier.

So passed the 4th of July, 1864, quietly, and yet full of excitement; breathing the air of freedom, and yet not free; full of the joy that hope brings, and still conscious that any moment might see our cup dashed in fragments at our feet. As the gloom of night deepened around us we ate another meal and congratulated ourselves on our success so far. We told Mat he would have to try and sleep without snoring so lustily. "And don't I try to do that same wid all me might?" was his rejoinder.

About ten o'clock we ventured out, going in single file, myself in the lead. We had arranged to travel thus for greater safety, as by keeping a sufficient distance apart we would not be tempted to carry on conversation. At the same time, should the leader fall into a trap, those behind might have time to make their escape. Still we kept sufficiently near to keep the next ahead in view, and the leader's movements were to be followed in every motion as near as practicable. In this way we reached the road near where we left it when taking to the woods at daybreak. Halting before I stepped out to see if all was clear, I heard some one, nearly opposite in the bush, speak in an undertone to his horse. I immediately struck off at a right angle, looking along the line to see if my movement was discovered by the one behind me. I saw them moving by the flank; but this brought Mat, who was in the rear, to the edge of a bank which, in the darkness, he did not observe until he found himself rolling down with the noise of a young avalanche, counteracting all our prudence and filling us with apprehension, as we could hear him thinking aloud in strong Hibernian accents. As no alarm was given, although the noise must have been heard by the party whom we were trying to dodge, this led us to believe that the mission of the two men to the ravine in the morning was for some sinister purpose,—probably horse-stealing,—and that they were probably as anxious to escape detection as we were. At any rate, they did not follow us; so, continuing the flank movement several hundred yards, we again ventured forward toward the road, where we halted for consultation.

Our night traveling, though full of excitement, was very fatiguing, as we did not dare to follow public roads; and travel through the timber, so near the river, made our way dark, rough, and broken; sometimes we would get into a place so dark that we could not get out until we struck a match. We got some very severe falls and tumbles over logs and into ditches, besides many entanglements in briars and thickets. Carlisle and Mat became discouraged. Our provisions, prepared before we left Danville, soon became mouldy and unfit to eat, so we had to make our stopping-places with reference to getting blackberries and huckleberries. Occasionally we found green apples, but we subsisted mostly on blackberries. Twice we found some small potatoes, which we had to eat raw, as we never dared to make a fire. We suffered for water during the day, as we had no canteens to carry it in and did not dare to venture out in daylight to hunt for it.

Chapter **XVI**

Friendly "Contrabands"

IN this way we traveled five nights; on the sixth evening, as we came from our cover after eating heartily of huckleberries, we came to a fence at the edge of some timber, and sat there waiting for the moon to rise. After fully discussing the situation and the probabilities of succeeding in our venture, I told them I thought that now we had better separate and go each man for himself, as it would be necessary to have more substantial food than we had been having for three days past, and our hopes of getting it were from the people, which we could do singly with less danger of being suspected than if we were in a squad.

Mr. Schroeder, who was nearsighted, said with some Teutonic emphasis:

"Mein Gott, Hyte! I vill not at all consent to dat; I vill go mit you, for by myself I could not one ting do; you must not tink of such a ting."

He was a splendid fellow, had been a druggist in St. Charles, Missouri, and he and I had been together ever since our capture, and I was very loath to part with him. So I told Carlisle if he would take Mat I would take Schroeder and we would try in pairs.

The traveling by night through the heavy dews generally kept our clothes very damp, and lying in them through the day was very trying and had given Mat a severe asthma that almost disabled him; besides, he weighed over two hundred pounds. He said he had concluded that he could not stand any more exposure, and would have to give himself up or trust himself to the mercies of the first house he could find. Carlisle had developed an attack of rheumatism, which stiffened one knee so that he could scarcely walk. He said that if Mat would agree to it they would go over to the plantation quarters and give themselves up. We tried to dissuade them from so doing, and proposed that we should lay over another day, rest up, and skirmish around for something to eat. But they said they had fully made up their minds to the move and would carry it out. From our position on the fence we could see the dim outline of a house. They said they would go in that direction, and if after walking that far they did not feel differently, they would go in there. As the moon rose we bade them good-by and started. I told Schroeder we would go in the direction of the house and conceal ourselves and watch whether they came that way. We had scarcely found a safe hiding-place near the gate when we heard them coming. Passing close by us they walked deliberately up to the front door and knocked, but we could not hear the story they told.

As we were very thirsty we passed around the house near the negro quarters, where we could hear the darkies in full enjoyment of the evening's pastime, giving vent to their mirth in songs and laughter. We almost envied them their happiness. Striking a path leading into the river bottom, we soon came to a large spring, beside which lay a gourd inviting us to quench our thirst. From the character of the ground we supposed we must be near the river, and thought such a plantation would be likely to have a "little red canoe" tied up somewhere along the bank. We started to hunt it up. To reach the river we had to pass through a large cornfield. The soil was sandy and had been recently worked, rendering the walking extremely tiring. We failed to find a boat, and, to add to our troubles, a gun was fired at the mansion, which we interpreted to be an understood signal to arouse the country to be on the watch for travelers. This, with the extreme nerve tension caused by Mat's and Carlisle's parting, seemed to take away my strength. To confirm our belief, we could hear voices in the direction of the river.

We seemed overcome with exhaustion, and I told Schroeder I could not go any farther. Collecting some willow boughs from the spring branch, we made a bed, and drew the tops of the corn together to make a shelter from the dew. So nearly had we exhausted our physical natures, weakened as we were by our past confinement and our recent fasting, that we soon fell asleep,—deep, restful sleep that held us locked in its embrace until day began to dawn. In its increasing light we could see, not far off, a steep timbered bluff, and equally near, in another direction, the outline of the house. Already we could hear some stir in that direction and deemed a quick move to the bluff our safest course. As a retreat we found it all we could desire, and more than we anticipated, for blackberries grew in abundance. The thick underbrush and absence of any paths assured us we would be safe from observation; our previous night's rest rendered day sleep unnecessary, and we had ample time to collect our berries and lay plans for future action.

The negroes were working all day in the cornfield below us, and a part of the time they were so near that we could hear their conversation. There were about twenty of both sexes, and we were highly entertained by their actions. There seemed to be a division among them, one body accusing the other of having stolen a part of their rations; then a war of words resulted until their vocabulary of abuse was exhausted, and there would be a lull for a time. We heard them discussing the action of our chums in giving themselves up, and their expressions being favorable toward them gave us some hope. We could see that our presence had not been revealed by them.

The overseer came out on horseback two or three times, each time carrying a large umbrella over him and accompanied by a big dog. The path lay right at the foot of the bluff, and so near that I could have tossed a stone on top of his umbrella had circumstances allowed such a demonstration. The dog seemed to suspect our presence, for as he followed his master he would stop every little while and sniff up our way, and then walk on with his nose in air as though he "smelt the blood of a Yankee man." We were glad when he left; as we did not dare to move for fear he would see us and push his investigations or draw his master's attention to his actions. We felt thankful to the intervening umbrella.

I told Schroeder he must make up his mind to go over the river that night, and I worked all day preparing saplings from which to construct a raft. We had heard enough from the negroes to believe they would befriend us if we could reach them without being seen by the whites. I made up my mind to get down near the road, watch when they left in the evening, and hail them; yet, lest on close inspection I found an appeal impracticable, I completed my arrangements for the raft, even to selecting suitable rails from a fence near by. Raft-building I found very slow work, having only a small knife with which to cut my withes and peel my bark.

Toward evening I gathered my hat full of berries for our supper, over which we discussed the negro question in all its points, and concluded to trust them if we could hail one without letting too many into the secret. As the sun sank in the west they began leaving their work singly and in pairs. Getting a good position near the path, fortune seemed to favor us. As the next to the last one passed us, something became detached about his horse's harness, which caused him to dismount. I gave a low whistle, which made him look up. Seeming to apprehend the case at once he motioned me back. When the next one came up he told him to lead his horse along, as he wanted to go up on the hill a moment. Coming up to where I was lying, he said:

"Get back, man; don't be seen; get back! I knows who you is; get back!"

"Well," I said, "who am I?"

"You's a Yankee."

"Well, suppose I am a Yankee?"

"I'll help you, but get higher up; get back, and don't be seen."

In answer to my signing for something to eat, he said:

"We don't get very much, but I'll get you something; we only gets things to eat as they is issued to us each day," which accounted for the quarreling over the missing rations.

"Now," said he, "I must go, or they'll 'spicion me. Lay low till it gets dark, then go up to de fence and follow it up till you come to de corner, den lay low till you's called for. Don't be feared; I'll help you over de ribber."

We went near the place designated and concealed ourselves to await further developments, not wishing to venture too close for fear of treachery. Several negroes passed during the evening, but as they seemed unconscious of any expected presence we continued to "lay low" according to instructions, until near midnight, we judged, when a whistle was given from a clump of bushes not far off, which we answered by a similar whistle, at which a young colored man came up, asking:

"Is you-uns l's gwine to put ober de ribber to-night?"

We said we were.

"Keep me in sight den," said he, "and don't be feared."

He kept some distance ahead, walking very fast and passing by the spring, where we again quenched our thirst, not having drunk since we left it the evening before.

"Now, keep very quiet," he said, as he led us, at the foot of the bluff on which the house stood, down the edge of the cornfield, to a place not two rods from where we had searched the night before for a boat. Stopping, he gave a low whistle and received an answer from the weeds near by, from which our man, "Joe," made his appearance, presenting us with some bread and meat, which we put out of sight with an avidity that filled our sable friends with surprise and astonishment, one of them saying: "Golly, you-uns is powerful hungry, ain't you? 'Pears like you can't stop to chaw, but swallow it down whole-like,"—which critical observation was about correct. We were ravenous, and Joe's fat bacon and hoecake were stowed away with surprising rapidity, I suppose.

Our supper ended, from sheer lack of more to eat, Joe said that we had better get over the river, and led the way to a small bayou from which they brought a small canoe or dug-out, cautioning us to sit very steady or we might cause an upset. The current was rapid and about fifteen feet deep. We found that the navigation of the craft was considerable of a task and required great skill to prevent upsetting. I thought then that if I had put my friend aboard the raft the chances are he would have found a safe mooring at the bottom of the river.

It took a full half hour to make a landing some distance below, and then we started on. We asked about the boys; and the darkeys said they had been sent to Greensboro that morning. The gun-firing was to scare the colored folks from raiding some ripe cherries. Joe said that if his father had been there he would have piloted us over the mountains, but he was then out on a similar expedition. Safely over, one of them went several miles with us to put us on the right track and "carry us around an old rebil."

We were considerably elated at our success in getting over the river, but we found we had crossed near the confluence of another stream flowing from a northeasterly direction, which would throw us more in the direction of Danville than we wished. Its current was also, if possible, more rapid than Dan River, and I concluded it was best not to try to cross that night, at least.

CHAPTER XVII

"Jugged" Once More

IT rained hard all next day, but we bunked beside a fallen tree from which we gathered sufficient bark to make a good shelter, and slept comfortably on a bed of leaves. In the evening we made another examination of the stream, but thought best not to venture to cross, so we quitted its banks to avoid the bluffs and traveled along a well-beaten road, stopping at daylight on a wood-covered hill, where we rested several hours before venturing out in search of berries, of which we found plenty, both huckleberries and blackberries.

After satisfying the demands of appetite so far as berries could do so, as we could hear no sound to indicate proximity to a plantation, we thought we might venture to travel by daylight by keeping on the summit of the ridge and maintaining a good lookout, which the character of the ground favored. A little distance away ran the river, which by light of day did not seem so formidable. We concluded to try crossing, even if we went no farther. We found that by stripping off our clothing we could ford the stream, although the water was chin deep. Success in this venture put enthusiasm into us, and we concluded to go to the top of the next ridge, to see what lay beyond; on reaching which we beheld—apparently a few miles distant—the rugged tops of the Blue Ridge. It was a glorious sight to us, and we were wild with delight as we took in the beautiful landscape spread out before us, with the mountains, most beautiful of all, for a background.

From the very start they had been our hope; we felt that if we could reach them we would be free indeed. But it was a question whether we had better venture farther or lay by until darkness favored us, as we could see that the country through which we would have to pass had only narrow belts and clumps of timber, interspersed with fields with fields of golden grain, which was even then being harvested, and we knew that our chances of being discovered would be very much against us. Yet our minds seemed unable to comprehend anything but the mountains. For weary nights we had been toiling to reach them, and now a few hours' march would bring us to them. We suffered our better judgment to be overruled by our eagerness and continued on. Soon after noon we entered a thick undergrowth at the head of a deep ravine, which we afterwards heard was known as "Leatherwood Hole." Near by a number of negroes were harvesting oats, under the supervision of an overseer on horseback. Crawling up behind some pine bushes to reconnoitre, I found myself unpleasantly near him, having only the bushes between us. I did not discover him until I peeped from behind my screen. But the men were just preparing to start in on another round and had their backs toward me,—all save one old darkey, who, stepping back into the bushes, came right on to me so unexpectedly that I thought he was going to yell out, and motioned him to keep silent. After asking him a few questions I inquired if he could get me something to eat. He appeared so frank, though he was about the homeliest negro I ever saw, that I thought we could trust him.

"Go down into the Hole," he said; "the overseer'll be back in a few moments and will see you. I'll come back this evening and see you."

We concealed ourselves, and lay down to get a little sleep. Toward evening the darkey came around and asked what he should get us to eat, suggesting chicken as a part of the proposed bill of fare. I was watching him very closely while he was making his proposition, and noticed that there was a confused expression of the eyes that lacked the nerve of truth, and I said to Schroeder as soon as he left that I did not like the fellow's actions; that we must get out of there immediately, or at least shift our position so as to avoid surprise. We got up to start, when suddenly there sounded a "Halt! halt!" and a man with a gun cocked and ready to fire stepped out before us. At the same time another came up from an opposite direction, the negroes came in on all sides, and we were again prisoners.

"Yankees, by God! Hands up," said the elder of the whites, who proved to be the overseer, the other being his son.

"Mein Gott! dis is too badt," said Schroeder, wringing his hands in anguish. "Hafe ve again to go back to dose prisons. How can ve standt it to do so?" It seemed to weaken him for a moment and he sank to the ground, then, jumping up, he cried, "If only ve could have maked it to the mountains; if only ve had not stopped in this tamd hole. Vhat vill ve now do! Vhat vill become of us! Dis is too badt, too badt, by Gott! I cannot standt dese tings!" Then, looking up and seeing me unmoved, he said: "By Gott! Hyte, how can you be so cool?"

Poor man, while I may have shown a calm exterior, he could not see what was passing through my mind. It was a terrible blow; nearly ten months as prisoners in Virginia under the most favorable aspect of prison life had been terrible, and telling on us physically; but now we knew that Andersonville would be our destination; and, after all the hardships we had encountered in our effort to escape, to be thus balked just as we thought our freedom sure,—and to be balked, too, by the perfidy of a negro,—was about all we could stand.

Our captor's name was Ferguson. He said he was not expecting to find Yankees in the "Hole," but supposed we were deserters from the Confederate army, and he was very sorry he came onto us or tried to capture us. I told him he need not bother his mind on that point; if he would give us something to eat and let us go, or even let us go as we were, we would take care of ourselves. He said he could not do that now, his men were all enrolled and sworn to keep military watch, and word would leak out that he had been helping prisoners to escape, and he would be severely punished for such an offence. On learning my name he said that he had a cousin in Ohio married to a person of the same name. Several times on the way to the house he expressed regret at having captured us, but loyalty to the South demanded his turning us over to the provost marshal at Henry Court House. Arriving at his house, his wife brought us a supper of milk and corn bread, of which we ate heartily. We retained our appetites if we had lost our freedom. Our hunger appeased, and some of the bread remaining, Mrs. Ferguson told us to put it in our haversacks, as it might be some time before we would get anything more to eat.

We had nearly five miles to go to reach Henry Court House, and did not get there until about ten o'clock. I heard Ferguson tell the marshal that the darkey thought we were Confederate deserters. He told us that if we had reached the mountains we would have been safe, as they were full of deserters, who were armed and could not be driven out, and that we were only seven miles from the mountains when we were captured. "Leatherwood Hole," he said, "is an unlucky place to hide in. Only last week I took in two deserters in there." This piece of intelligence did not add to our comfort or good will, though he seemed to intend it as a panacea to our disappointment. We found that in the eleven days we had been out, owing to the perplexing drawbacks presented by the river and the roundabout way we had been compelled to go, we were only forty miles from Danville, though we had traveled more than double that distance.

After taking our names and asking a few questions, the marshal took us to Henry County jail, where we stopped a moment until he could find the keyhole in the dark. The door open, another moment's halt was made until he could strike a match and light a piece of candle three or four inches long. By this ghostly light we found our way up a flight of stairs, through a hall, to a room perhaps sixteen feet square, to enter which we had to stoop, the door being only about four feet high. The floor of the room, sides, and ceiling were hewn logs to which were bolted wagon-tire irons perhaps five inches apart. The inside door was made of the same material, but the iron and wooden doors were separate,— one opening into the room; the other, the iron one, swinging into the hall. To the centre of this one was attached an iron bar that fastened like a hasp over a staple in the centre of the hall, where it was secured by a padlock on the door. We took all this in at a glance by the dim light of the turnkey's candle, as he pushed us in with the assurance that if we attempted an outbreak he would put us in irons.

The room already had an occupant in the person of a negro. The door grated on its hinges, the heavy bolts clicked into their sockets, and we were in the blackest of darkness. By making a circuit of the room on our hands and knees, we found a place free from bars where there was room to lie down. It was not a question of finding the soft side of a board, but of finding a board free from iron bars. Placing our haversacks under our heads, we lay down to try to forget our surroundings in sleep. But as soon as quiet reigned we found ourselves in the most animated community possible. The room was alive with rats. They ran over us, whisking their tails in our faces, and pulling at our haversacks. The corn bread attracted them, and we found that we would have to make some other disposition of our pillows, so we put them on the stove that stood in the centre of the room.

CHAPTER **XVIII**

In Henry County Jail

WE passed a terrible night. The room was so filthy that we could hardly move without raising a stifling dust, and the rats were impudent and troublesome, giving us no rest. If, momentarily off our guard, we dozed, they would attack us in force. I had often read of the courage of rats rendered ravenous by hunger, but this was the only time I had ever had a practical illustration of it. Some time in the night I heard the negro go to the stove and fuss with the haversacks in search of something to eat, but I thought likely the poor fellow fared pretty badly, perhaps worse than we would, so I said nothing to cause him to think he had been discovered.

As night waned the rats drew off their forces and gave us comparative quiet, so that Schroeder fell asleep. The night's mystery was where so many rats could find hiding-places and ready ingress into such a seeming ironclad. Daylight, however, revealed a pipe-hole under the stove, into which a post had been set at an angle of forty-five degrees. Up this post and through this hole they found ready communication from below. There was also a crack between the floor, and the log lining of the cell, giving them a harbor between the walls. When daylight was fully come we found we were in a building whose outer wall was of brick a foot or more thick. Our burglar-proof room inside of this brick wall was lined with eight-inch hewed logs, closely joined and iron-clad as described. Two eighteen-inch-square windows (or rather holes, as they had no glass), heavily barred,—one on the east, looking into the court

81

house yard and toward the town; the other on the west, looking toward the mountains,—revealed the location of the jail to be in the outer part of the town on the edge of the woods. No buildings were visible from it. Our observation, of course, related only to this one room. There were a number of staples and rings in the floor, which the negro said were used in confining a former occupant who was insane, and who must have been a very Hercules, as we could see where he had twisted off several of the lining bars from the floor. When it became sufficiently light to see I asked Schroeder if we had not better eat a bite, and went to the stove for the haversacks.

"Well," I said, "you've taken the bread out, have you?"

"No," said he, "I've not touched them since you put them there last night."

"Well," I said, "what has become of the bread, then? Did you take it, you black rascal? Have you been at those sacks?"

"No, sah, I hasn't."

"You haven't?" (stepping towards him).

"No, massa; 'fore God I hasn't, massa; I hasn't."

"Well, what has become of the bread that was in them last night if you didn't take it?"

"I don't know, massa; indeed I don't; 'spec, do, de rats done got it; dey is mighty bad in hyer, dey is!"—a fact I did not gainsay, and I accepted his version without further controversy. He had been confined there some days as a runaway and was awaiting the coming of his master.

As I have said, from our west window we had a very good, though limited, view of the mountains; but they seemed to mock us as we looked first at them and then at our cell with its ironclad walls and double locks, its filth and stifling air, the small window openings being the only means of ventilation save when they left the inner door open.

During the day a number of boys came around to get a glimpse of the "Yanks." It was amusing to see them circle around and watch the window with open mouths. Finally, one little fellow asked if we had any "bone rings" to sell. I told him I had one I would sell him.

"Well, what will you take for it?"

"Can you get me some onions?"

"Yes, sir."

"Well, bring me a dozen good ones, and I'll give you the ring."

"Will you," he asked; "all right,"—and away he went as fast as he could, with half a dozen boys at his heels. We had not long to wait until he returned with a bunch of nice onions, holding them aloft at arm's length and saying:

"Here they are!"

"Well, how will you get them up?"

"Oh, I'll fix that."

Going down into the depths of his pockets he brought up a string, to the end of which he tied a heavy nail and began the difficult feat of lodging it in the window so that I could reach it. After a number of efforts, in which they all had to try their hand, the task was accomplished. Stepping out so that I could see him, he said:

"Now, you'll send it down, will you, if I send the onions up?"

"Certainly," I said.

Then I heard one of the boys say to him, "I'll just bet he won't when he gets hold of the onions."

"Yes, that man will," said the little fellow, with a childlike confidence that would have compelled a rogue to deal honestly with him. Then, stepping out so that I could see him,—"Pull," he said, "they are all right."

And pull I did with an eagerness which only those in like circumstances could understand, the boys ranging in a row where they could see me take the bunch in. Then, taking the ring from my finger, I passed it down to him.

"All right," he said, holding it up to view, and then examining it critically.

"Well," I asked; "is it nice enough?"

"Oh, yes, sir; nicer than I thought it was,"—and away he went to show the folks at home a ring made by a Yankee prisoner, while we pitched into the onions, consuming them root and branch. I thought I never tasted anything better in my life.

Noticing a number of cavalrymen riding rapidly by the jail and scattering as soon as they struck the open woods toward the mountains, as though in immediate pursuit of some one, I asked the boys what they were after. They said a deserter had escaped from the guard up town, and they were trying to head him off from reaching the mountains. We learned from the negro that an escaped Yankee had been confined in the room we were in about a week before,—he thought he was a sergeant. We looked around to see if we could not find some pencil-marks that would give a clue to the person, but there was no evidence to confirm his story.

A second night with the rats wound up our jail experience, and we were satisfied,—so completely so that in all the years since I have never felt any hankering after a repetition of it, nor can I tell how much that short experience may have influenced me in striving so to shape my ways as to keep clear of jails forever. At any rate, it was my first and last peep inside one.

CHAPTER **XIX**

Across the River Styx

EARLY on the morning of the second day (Monday) before the light of dawn had penetrated the dark room, our door was opened and we were ordered to stand forth. As we had no special toilet preparations to make, no blankets to roll, or knapsack to strap, we were outside before the order could be repeated.

Being taken to a hotel near by, a cold lunch was given us, the scraps of which were put into our haversacks, and we were told we would draw our next rations at Danville. With this happy intelligence the jailer produced a pair of handcuffs. and we were linked together, my right hand to Schroeder's left. This seemed like filling our cup of indignity until it ran over.

In this way we were marched up the main street of the town, manacled together like criminals, with a soldier on either side. And this because, in our devotion to our country, we had tried to take ourselves out of the Confederacy and escape the privations of prison life. I wished we could have paid our respects to Abraham Lincoln that morning as we marched along the street of Henry Court House under the inspiring influence of Rebel bayonets. Certainly, we were becoming rich, if accumulating experiences could be called riches, and still these riches grew on us until we began to feel that the traditional "last straw" could not be far off.

Our handcuffs were such as they used in manacling slaves when they drove them to market, and consisted of a straight bar of three-quarter inch square iron nine or ten inches long. The ends were rounded from a square shoulder long enough to take on a clevis sufficiently large to slip over the wrist, and then had a thread cut to receive a burr to keep the clevis in place. Such was our "jewelry," the indissoluble bond that so united us in sentiment and action,—the latter especially,—that we moved in perfect unison, for the least irregularity in our movements caused a great deal of pain, the irons fitted so closely.

Our guards, three in number, had a horse which they took turns in riding, and we were put to our utmost strength in marching, the heat being great and the road dusty. Once or twice they allowed us to stop and eat some blackberries that grew beside the road, and once, while resting beneath the shade-trees in a dooryard, where we stopped to get water, an aged couple sitting at the door inquired who we were. On learning that we were escaped prisoners being returned to Danville, the old lady sprang to her feet, exclaiming,—

"Poor fellows, how they have to suffer! Won't you let me give them something to eat,— a bowl of milk and bread? They are human beings if they are prisoners; they are not to be blamed for trying to escape."

She brought each of us a bowl of milk and some bread, and said,—

"Eat! It will do you good; you are welcome; I wish I could do more for you. I know you see trouble enough. I feel sorry for you."

"Yes, yes," said the old man, leaning forward on his staff. His long white locks reached nearly to his shoulders and his voice was tremulous with age as he said eagerly:

"Eat all you want; eat all of it."

I rather suspect there was a love of the "Old Flag" burning in the bosoms of that aged couple that refused to bow entirely to the new. The old lady shook hands with us when we left, as we thanked her for her hospitality. She said to the guards as we started on:

"Don't abuse them men; make it as pleasant for them as you can. They have a hard time of it and will have to suffer enough."

Even Schroeder, who was much disposed to think that no good thing could come out of Nazareth, said with more than ordinary appreciativeness, "It is any vay a fine old lady, dat, and dat oldt patriarch, sitting dere leaning on his staff, saying 'Yes, yes, trink it up; eat all you can,' it vas any vay a goot ting; it would have maked a goot picture, vhat!"

Many days after, when he and I were sharing the honors of Andersonville, the memory of that old couple would come, as an oasis in the burning desert of our experience, full of fragrance, to the mind. Their good was living yet in our hearts, and the circumstance was always referred to with reverence and gratitude.

We reached Danville about ten o'clock at night. It took some time to call up the old ferryman, whose hut stood on the opposite side of the stream. I thought of Charon, Cerberus, and the river Styx as we stood there on the river's bank. Not a word was spoken. My thoughts went hither and thither as I reflected on the peculiarity of our position, and tried by speculation to penetrate the future and unravel the net that met us whithersoever we turned. Gloom, impenetrable gloom, covered us as the waters of the sea, and Hope had well nigh died within me. Yes, I felt like a lost soul, the last opportunity gone, standing on the dank borders of the river Styx.

The waters soughing at our feet; the sound of rattling chains, borne to our ears from the impenetrable gloom beyond; the boat, scarcely discernible in the fog, that hung low above the waters, becoming more and more distinct in outline as it neared our shore, revealing the spectre-like form of the old negro, as he "poled" it along, accompanied by a stub-tailed dog, which had taken its position in the prow; our sad, weary forms awaiting their coming, to ferry us across into the world beyond the mist,—completed the similitude. Surely, I thought, a soul never reached the banks of that classic stream in a more used-up condition than we were when we reached Dan River that night, weary, footsore, and mentally and physically used up. I felt as though I had a twenty-pound ball in each groin and similar ones in the hollow of each knee-joint. The muscles of the calves of my legs seemed as though they had been twisted with a marline-spike. Every muscle in my body ached as though I had been pounded and my feet seemed leaden weights.

We heard the guards crying the hour as we passed in sight of the hospital from which we had so recently escaped. It seemed as though it would be impossible to reach the town, so stiff had we become while stopping at the river, but we reached the end at last and were taken to headquarters, where we hoped we would be released from our irons. In this we were disappointed. Finding the burrs a little loose, they took a hatchet and riveted them on, so they could not be removed save by cutting. This was done by Lieutenant Mews of the 18th Virginia Infantry. It seemed to give him intense satisfaction and we supposed he remembered how we had raised Dr. Hunter's ire against him, and this was a kind of petty revenge. In this condition we were taken to Prison No. 1, then empty, and put in a corner on the second floor under the care of a corporal and two guards, whose instructions were to see that we did not leave the corner except as nature required. Handcuffed together, with nothing but the floor to lie on, our shoes serving as pillows,—you can form some idea of our chances for comfort. We had of course to lie so as to favor our manacled wrists, which was hard to do, as the irons fitted so snugly that our wrists had no play in them, the slightest twist occasioning pain more or less severe.

I told the corporal, when I heard his instructions regarding us, that so far as we were concerned he might as well take his men and go to his quarters that night; that we could not get away, even though he left the door open, as I doubted whether, after we had lain half an hour, we could get down stairs if we tried. I know we could not have done so the next morning, as it was all we could do to stand when we got up. The guards were abusive in their manner towards us. One of them said our treatment was better than we deserved; that we ought to be shot; and that if we had stayed north, where we belonged, we would not have got into any such difficulty. I asked him very coolly if he did not think he ought to be at the front.

"By God," he said, jumping up and taking his gun, "I have a notion to shoot you myself."

"Yes," I said, "I should think shooting handcuffed prisoners would suit you better than running the chances of killing some one at the front."

When our rations were brought to us the guards would take the greater portion themselves. In this way they kept us for several days. Dr. Hunter came in several times to see us, but made no effort to get us released from our irons. Though he made no allusion to our escape, he treated us very civilly. Our wrists were swollen and became very painful, the irons partly burying themselves in the flesh, impeding the circulation. I presume they would have suffered us to lose our hands, which we would likely have done in a few more days, had not a squad of prisoners been brought in from in front of Richmond to await transportation to Andersonville. There was quite a howl of indignation when they came in and found us handcuffed and suffering as we were. It was a revelation to some of them, and one not calculated to illumine their outlook, and several expressed a determination to try to escape on the way to Andersonville. Several set to work with an old case knife to try to saw the irons off, but had not made much progress when a man came in with a file and cut them off. I asked permission to keep the pieces. He said he had no instructions further than to file them off, and as they were ruined he presumed there would be no objection to my keeping them; so he left them, but very soon an officer came in and called for them. I told him I would like very much to keep them.

"What for?" he asked. "What benefit will they be to you? What will you do with them?"

"Well," I said, "they will be of no particular benefit, so far as utility is concerned, but of considerable satisfaction to keep as a memento to show to my friends,—the jewelry I had the honor to wear for my country's sake and for an attempt to escape from a Southern prison. For this reason I would prize them highly."

"Well, damn you," he said; *I* want those irons, *you* have no business with them."

"There they are," I said, pointing to where they were lying; "if you want them, pick them up."

He gathered them up and left. It is more than likely that many a poor slave had felt the weight of those handcuffs, but I think, when they fell from our wrists, that their power was broken.

CHAPTER XX

From Danville to Andersonville

NEXT day we were told to hold ourselves in readiness to move, and in the evening we started for Andersonville. Among the guards detailed to accompany us I noticed the one who passed us out the night we made our escape. He was very abusive to the boys, striking them or punching them with his gun if they did not move to suit his ideas. I also noticed the corporal (the one who had had charge of us in the corner) strike a man over the head with his ramrod simply because he happened to step a little out of line at one of our stopping-places.

We frequently had to stop to allow the regular trains to pass. At such times there were generally crowds around; some attracted by curiosity and a desire to vent spleen where there was no danger of retaliation; and others, prompted by speculative instincts, were on hand with pies, cakes, and such other luxuries as generally tempt soldiers. I found that the "Johnnies" were no exception to the rule. They would buy as long as their resources held out or trickery availed anything. The pievenders were usually negroes, generally not over tidy in appearance, but their wares were bought without regard to previous associations. A hearty laugh was indulged in by all hands at the chagrin of one of the guards, who had bought a chicken pie of considerable promise, judging from its appearance, from a big darkey'—" the last of his stock." I noticed that the vender seemed in a hurry to get away as soon as he got his money, but his head was clear. The purchaser sought a place in the shade where he could enjoy the pie at his leisure, but on opening it he found it contained nothing but the head, neck, and toes of a chicken. It was now evident why the darkey had seemed so anxious to get away. He was a living argument against the Southern cry of—"You can't larn a nigger anything." He had grasped the tricks of commerce and could bring profit out of adversity; he was surely learning fast.

The cars used for our transportation were ordinary box cars somewhat the worse for government usage. The guards on duty, two to each car, occupied a position on either side of the door; only one door being kept open. As we had no lights this gave the boys a good opportunity of escaping as soon as it became dark, and quite a number made good use of the opportunity in our car. They cut a hole in the back end or corner of the car, so that when the train slackened on an up grade they could let themselves down at arm's length and drop. Eight or ten made their escape in that way before the leap was discovered. I saw one poor fellow who had jumped from a forward car rolling down a bank. A number of shots were fired at him, but with what effect we did not learn. The train was moving at a pretty high rate of speed, so that he must have received some injury from the concussion, if not from the balls. He made the jump as we were crossing a field, and rolled down the declivity as though he had been thrown with considerable force. He was left to himself, dead or alive. This occurred while we were passing through South Carolina.

Our route was over the same road we had travelled on our trip to Richmond, ten months before. We could not see that the country showed any of the effects of war more than it did on our former passage through it, and we noticed that the farther we got from war's desolating footprints the greater were the insolence and braggadocio of the people. We could not help hoping and wishing that something might yet occur to humiliate them, especially those extreme Southern States that had been so zealous in precipitating the war and urging secession on the rest of the Confederacy. All along our route we could see the negroes carrying on the labors of the plantation, and raising supplies for the soldier in the field, as well as providing for home comfort and consumption. While not enrolled as soldiers, they were nevertheless as important an element to Southern success as were the soldiers in the field; for while the whites furnished the brain and sinews of the war, the negro furnished the rations without which no army can be kept organized. One was as necessary as the other. Trusty negroes would look after the interests of the soldiers' families, so that the men at the front had no anxiety for the welfare of the home circle to worry them. In this respect the South was peculiarly prepared to carry on warfare as long as they could keep their internal organization intact and keep the contending armies in the border States. Any one traveling behind the scenes, as we were, could see how necessary this sable element was to the South. In fact, they were as much enrolled, so far as effect was concerned, in the Southern cause, as were the negroes who were bearing arms for the North.

The South seemed to look upon the arming of the "nigger" by the North as more of an insult to their chivalry than anything else; for while they were willing to give their lives, if necessary, in defence of secession, it was repugnant to them and grossly humiliating to have that rich blood let out by a bullet from a "nigger" soldier. Hence we wished, almost to prayer, that old Mars might set his iron heel in this heart of the Confederacy and make his presence more severely felt, and even while we were thus speculating the same idea was taking tangible shape in the brain of General Sherman, at Atlanta, to be consummated a few months later.

Having safely delivered us at Andersonville, the guard returned to Danville, reporting to the "boys" there that I had tried to escape again by jumping from the train, and had been shot. They even brought forward the person who had committed the laudable deed in attestation of the truthfulness of the report. He said he had shot me through the head, killing me instantly, and he gave the *minutiae* in a most plausible manner. These "boys" being soon after exchanged, one of them, a Mr. Thurston, with whom I had been quite intimate, wrote my friends regarding my death, and sent them several mementoes I had left when I escaped from the hospital. He had no doubt of the correctness of a report coming so direct. I suppose the object of the yarn was to intimidate others from attempting to escape, as I was well known to all our comrades at Danville.

Chapter XXI

Andersonville

WE reached Andersonville about the 25th of July, 1864. This now historic place was simply a railroad station on the road from Macon to Americus, the settlement consisting merely of six or eight houses, mostly military necessities, and an unfinished church; the whole being surrounded by dense pine woods with a heavy growth of under-brush. The stockade was located about half a mile east of the depot, in plain sight, looking down the stream that arose near the town and passed through the stockade after receiving another branch from the north side of the town.

We were marched from the train across the brook spoken of to a double log house situated southwest of the stockade, but nearer than the depot and in full view of the north side of the interior of the stock-ade. The house was partially surrounded by earthworks, quite a force of negroes being then engaged on their completion. We were drawn up in line in front of the house and held there some time in the beating rays of the July sun. Some of the boys were sitting in the ranks when a tall, wiry, nervous-looking man, with prominent teeth and dressed in a white linen suit though without a coat, came out of the house with a roll of papers in his hand. His first salutation was:

"Get in de ranks dere. Got damn you, get in de ranks, or you shan't have a got-damned mouthful to eat to-day. Guardts, vhy in hell don't you standt dem up; get up dare. I say, py Chesus Christ, vhen I vants you to set down I tells you."

This was our introduction to Captain Wirz, the scapegoat of the whole South, and the only rebel of the outfit upon whom the hand of justice fell to the extent of life; and he was a subaltern, one around whom circumstances had thrown the web of fate, in the interminable meshes of which he had become entangled. As the guardian spirit of Andersonville he was responsible to other and higher powers. He was unfortunately possessed of a nature that would have done no discredit to Satan himself; and he was as utterly devoid of feeling and as remorseless as Hell. By these attributes he was peculiarly fitted to fill the position of a tormentor. Why, I ask, was such a man chosen, and by whom chosen, to take charge there? Does not the editorial spoken of in a former chapter fix the actual responsibility? While Wirz was a man who could faithfully execute a piece of work assigned to him, his was not the mind to plan such a scheme and give it shape from chaos. Not at all. Wirz never planned Andersonville. It was an idea conceived in Richmond, deliberately planned and theoretically studied in all its probable details, in the council chambers of Jefferson Davis at the Capitol of the Confederacy. The men there knew whom they were putting in charge at Andersonville, and the qualities of heart and mind that fitted the man for the position, and they were not disappointed. But, I ask any candid man, was it right that Wirz should hang and they go free? It seems to me that Justice herself might have dropped a tear over his grave, as she beheld the end of that simple though too pliant tool in the hands of crafty workmen. Retributive justice had already claimed one life by apoplexy in the person of General Winder, and another one, since, in the person of Ross, by the burning of a hotel in Richmond. Turner, I think, also met a violent death. But they all were merely cat's-paws in the drama.

We were kept standing in the sun so long that several of the boys were prostrated by the heat and became insensible. Finally, after taking our names and assigning us to squads, we were sent to the stockade. The view we got of the inside from the higher ground as we passed to the southwest corner and along the west side across the brook to the north gate was anything but assuring, and we felt as though our march had something of the tragic nature of the charge of the famous Six Hundred.

The stockade was a quadrangular enclosure containing about thirty-two acres, its longest dimension being from north to south. The stream of water spoken of ran through it from west to east, dividing the tract unequally; the southern portion containing about one third and the northerly one the balance. Each side sloped to the stream with good drainage; that on the north being gradual, while that on the south became more abrupt as one neared the water, especially on the east, where there was quite an abrupt bank with a small level plot bordering on the stream, the only really level ground in the stockade. On either side of the stream the ground was very moist for perhaps a hundred feet, the northerly portion being a black mucky swamp, the water apparently oozing from the hill side forming what, at the locating of the prison, was a redwood swamp, difficult to cross. The rest of the ground had been covered with a dense pine forest which was cut off to procure logs for the stockade. The swamp could be crossed by jumping from tuft to tuft, on either side of which the slimy mud was knee-deep. There was a regular crossing of logs at the west side next to the "dead line," but we did not always avail ourselves of this, preferring to run the risk of missing our footing in jumping from sod to sod.

The palisade, or wall, was made of pine logs set on end in the ground as close as they could be set, about fifteen feet remaining above ground. The entrance was by two gates, each sufficiently large to admit a wagon. Both were situated on the west side, one leading into the southerly division, and the other—the main entrance—into the northerly one. These gates were protected by a small square enclosure on the outside. Outside of all this a second line of palisades had been commenced, but was never completed, save a portion on the south and west sides. The greater portion of the trench had been dug, but was suffered to fill up— through lack of energy I suppose. Twenty feet from the wall on the inside all around, except at the gates, was a four-inch line of boards nailed flat on the top of a row of posts projecting three or four feet from the ground. This was the celebrated "dead line," to go between which and the stockade was to enter the court of death. No guard would miss the chance of a shot by ordering us out. They all seemed filled with the Indian's desire to add Yankee scalps to their belts.

On the outside, near the top of the wall, and perhaps two hundred feet apart, accessible by steps from outside, were the sentry-boxes, so built that the top of the wall was about waist-high to the guard. Thus they could see all that was going on within and have a breastwork from which to shoot in case of an outbreak. The waters of the creek, soon after passing the dead line, were made to pass through a crib extending nearly across the enclosure. Here were the sinks, and the water served to keep them clean, the only provision for cleanliness or evidence of care in the whole outfit, and I have often wondered how even this was thought of. Just above the stockade on the west, near the north entrance, stood the cook-house, a board shanty in which were a furnace and kettles for doing the cooking, and an oven for baking our corn bread, which was done by a detail of our own men. All the filth of this passed into the stream, making the water so foul that it was not fit to drink. The stream also received all the filth and wash from the Rebel camps and sinks.

Near the southwest corner outside, and within the second line of palisade, was erected quite a formidable lot of stocks for the punishment of minor offenses. (The method of general punishment was to cut off the rations of the squad offending, or of the whole camp if necessary.) The stocks, which provided for neck, feet, and wrists, were so arranged that the culprit could be invested in all at the same time, and being out in the hot sun without shelter of any kind must have been a first-class purgatory to the unfortunate offender.

Within the earthworks surrounding the house first spoken of were a bomb-proof magazine and several pieces of artillery planted to rake both sides of the stockade. On the west side, near the north end, was a similar earthwork mounting a number of guns bearing on the south side and gates, while on the north and east were rifle-pits and several more field guns. In all, fourteen pieces of artillery stood ominously pointing to some point of the prison, and ready, on the slightest provocation, to belch forth the missiles of death at close range. Near the northwest corner, on the road that led to the cemetery, stood a number of shanties, one of which was occupied by a well-trained pack of bloodhounds, under the supervision of a man whose duty it was to circle the camp every day, to take up the trail of such as might have escaped from the stockade or from those who were outside. He had these dogs trained to the sound of a cow's-horn hunting horn.

Chapter **XXII**

My First Night in the Stockade

S UCH was Andersonville, and our feelings, as we made the march to the north gate, cannot be imagined. As it swung open with a loud creaking noise that could be heard all over the camp, what a view of misery met our eyes! Great God! could it be possible that this motley, haggard crowd that pressed around us had once been soldiers fit for presentation on inspection parade. The gate closed behind us, and we were of them—were shut in. No one but those who have had similar experiences can have any conception of the fearful import of those words "shut in." And no pen, however graphic, can give a description that will convey to the uninitiated mind more than the vaguest idea of the horror and misery that centered in the *"Prison Pen at Andersonville."*

My spirit groaned as I stood looking over the crowd of weary, tattered, emaciated forms, that gathered about us eager for news from without. I use the term "weary" as best suited to convey to the mind the haggard, forlorn, absent look imprinted on the countenances of most of those surrounding us. Grasping us by the hands they would ask, "Any news of exchange?"

Exchange! The forlorn hope, the weakening hawser that bound many of them to life, the daystar for whose arising they had so long hoped, almost against hope, and no wonder. The night had been long and dark, the angel of Death had laid a heavy tribute upon them, and his seal was already set upon many more. It was a sickening sight even to me, accustomed as I had been to prison horrors. Heretofore, however,

96

my observations had been confined to small numbers—less than a thousand; but here were collected over thirty thousand of the most tattered, dirt-begrimed, squalid-looking men the world ever beheld!

But it was not ours to bring words of comfort, and, as the afternoon was fast passing, we had to busy ourselves in hunting up the squad to which we belonged, as we well knew that upon this depended our getting the little that would be issued to us to eat, and among that multitude it was no small matter to find the sergeant of a squad of ninety men. By diligent inquiry we at last found where it met for roll-call once a day, in the morning. This was near the northeast corner of the stockade. The sergeant, however, was located on the south side.

Having ascertained this much, it became necessary for us to find a place to spend the night,— simply a place to lie down. For you must remember that no shelters were prepared by the Confederate government for our comfort at Andersonville. There were no neat whitewashed houses, such as I had seen at Camp Chase, Ohio, in the prison for Southerners, with its nicely laid-out streets,— none of these. The Confederates having completed the stockade, their only further care was in effect to use the vulgar phrase, "Root, hog, or die," which, simmered down, amounted to this:

"If you can't make yourself a shelter out of nothing, lie out in the rain and dew and hot sun."

Thus I could account for the scant clothing on the men. They would cut off the legs of their trousers and the sleeves of their coats, rip them up, and sew them together to form a shelter from the heat of the sun by day—for it beat with an intenseness against those sandhills—and the heavy dews at night. The nights being cool, while the earth retained its heat, a very heavy dew was precipitated, sufficient to dampen a person's clothing through. While this might have no deleterious effect in one night, a continuation of it through weeks had a marked effect in producing the fearful cases of diarrhoea and pneumonia which proved so fatal there.

Many of the boys we noticed had dugouts or subterranean houses, which were treacherous substitutes at best, frequently caving in,—in several instances that came to my knowledge burying the inhabitants alive. As I looked around that evening I noted the many devices made use of in the erection of shelters. I felt that my chances for one were most dubious. Blanket I had none, and no clothing but my shirt, trousers, and blouse, and even if I had had anything to spare, I had no sticks with which to erect a shelter. I felt gloomy enough as I wandered around just as night began to settle around us.

We finally found a place where we could lie, and here Schroeder and I spent our first night in Andersonville. Heavens! What a dreary place as the quiet of night gathered over it, and the motley multitudes settled to rest! The stars seemed to look kindly down upon us from the depths above, and that was all. We had no covering but our clothing and the broad canopy of Heaven; our covering was blue, and so were we. Yet we slept as well as could be expected. I had been suffering from chronic diarrhoea for some time, and the trip from Danville had so nearly worn me out that I was prepared to enjoy rest, even under these adverse circumstances.

I had asked several of the boys to share our bed, and to cheer them up as we disposed ourselves to the best advantage I told them that we need have no fears of falling out of bed, nor of the underpinning giving way, and, as to our bedroom, the ventilation was most excellent. Schroeder, through whose mind ran visions of our recent handcuffing, said:

"It is any how an improvement on our condition in dat tamned corner in Danville, hopplet together like oxes. Ve can any vay turn ofer vithout having to say If you blease, or Py your leaf. Py shingo, dat vas tough! Vhat!"

I must confess I felt but little like commenting. I had seen enough in my passing around to convince me that there were few, if any, redeeming points in our present quarters. What we had to meet was too plainly stamped upon the countenances of the multitude who had thronged around us on our first entrance into the stockade, and I knew that in that crowd I beheld the best conditioned men of the community. If our eyes could have penetrated the frail shelters and seen the abject misery concealed by them, it would have made our blood run cold. In my wanderings I had stooped down and looked into a number, and my eyes had seen enough to convince me we had reached the culmination of Confederate skill in human torture.

Chapter XXIII

Meetings with Old Friends

THE earliest light of dawn found me awake, somewhat stiff, but, refreshed by my night's rest, I was ready to start on a tour of investigation. As Schroeder seemed comfortably resting in the embrace of sleep, I did not disturb him, but started out alone. Already the camp showed considerable life. Picking my way among the little shelters scattered irregularly over the ground; now and then stepping over a sleeping form whose bed, like mine, required no particular care; passing an occasional one engaged in preparing his morning meal from the debris of yesterday's rations, and others lost in the earnest effort to make a cup of coffee from burnt crusts, I came to the swamp, which for a time checked further progress until I had seen several of the old inhabitants cross by stepping from clump to clump. It was a terribly filthy place, many going no farther than this to attend to nature's call.

Once across, I came to a squad engaged in performing their morning's ablutions. The water in the stream being too filthy for use, they were dipping from a hole that had been dug in the sand near by, into which the water filtered. It was a delightful returning, the air at this early hour being cool and fresh. Asking one of them if he would kindly pour some water onto my hands while I washed, "Certainly, certainly!" he said. After I got through I found I had not taken the wiping into consideration, and began wringing the water from my hands.

"Here," said my new friend, "Use my towel,"—handing me a piece of an old blouse. "How does it come," said he, "that I've never seen you before in here. I thought I had seen all the boys."

I told him that as this was my first appearance on the stage at Andersonville, having only arrived the evening before, it was not remarkable.

"What, just came in?" said he; "where have you been all this time?"

I told him at Danville Hospital.

"Well," he exclaimed, extending his hand, "we'll shake hands then."

My mind was busy at work trying to place him, as it is always embarrassing for one to present himself in that friendly way and then have to introduce himself. Finally I ventured:

"Is it you, Rose?"

"What is left of me, certainly. Why, didn't you know me?"

I never had had any special acquaintance with him, but remembered him as being located near the "Hole in the Wall" at Pemberton Building, Richmond, his feet and mine having been neighbors there when we lay down.

Rose was a representative character. I am sorry I cannot name his regiment. He first attracted my attention in Pemberton by being a close student of his pocket Testament and an observer of its teachings,—a genuine Christian under adversity; pure gold, tried in the fire. His light had not grown dim through all the ups and downs of prison life.

Leaving Rose, I passed on up the pitch on the east end of south, and sauntered along, thinking the old squad at Pemberton, and directing my steps toward the only two trees that remained in the stockade,—two very large pines near the southeast corner. My course led me close to a fellow who was busy blowing up his fire under his pan (all old prisoners will understand what this means), and my proximity caused him to look up into my face. Then up he jumped and grasped me by the hand with both of his, exclaiming,—"Hello, steward! How are you?"

"Felix, by the life," I exclaimed; "how are you, old boy?"

"Where did you come from?—when did you get in?—where have you been?"—came so rapidly that I had to let him get through before I began,—" as to getting in, why, I arrived last evening."

"In that squad that came in so late?"

"Yes."

"Where did you sleep?"

"Over on the other side."

"Where's your blanket?"

"Have none."

"Didn't sleep out, did you?"

"Have a faint recollection of so doing."

"Why didn't you come over here?"

"Sure enough," I said laughing.

"That's so, that's so," he said, seeing the point. "But here's my tent, I must make room for you under it. My partner was taken out to the hospital yesterday, and you may take his place, although he gave it to another. We must make room for three."

The thanks with which I accepted Felix's hospitality came from a full heart. Here, very unexpectedly to myself, the question of a shelter was settled in a manner that seemed providential. I had not met Felix since I parted with my squad at Pemberton Building for the hospital, nine months before,—nine dark, eventful months. How many comrades we could name who had patiently endured the bitterness of Rebel hate, while the wick burned low in its socket, and relief came at last through the gates of Death,— "and yet," said he, "*we* are still alive." Then, as I made inquiry for this one and that one of our old squad, some had died, several had been exchanged, and several, besides myself, were in Andersonville.

"By the way," he said, "Dick and John, of your regiment, are just down the street in the first tent on the left as you came up the bluff."

I went down immediately, and, stooping down in front of their quarters, whistled. They had not got up yet, but John was awake, and, seeing me, gave Dick a punch or two in the ribs, saying,—

"Dick, Dick, wake up, here's Hyde, the steward!"

Dick needed no second punching, but bounded out in a hurry to meet me. But John, poor fellow, could only hold out his hand. "You'll have to come in to see me," he said, "I can't get up. I can't walk."

He was a German, John Zigler, one of my hospital mess, as was Dick, whose name was Mains, and we had made many a hard day's march together. I could see by his blackened gums and hue that he was fast yielding to scurvy, and, as I learned he was suffering from diarrhoea in connection with it, I knew he was correct as he said mournfully, "Well, steward, the jigs are about up with me." Then he showed me his swollen, purple-colored feet, on which the skin shone almost like a mirror, and his limbs drawn up so he could not straighten them. "They will never take me out of here alive," he said. "I know that. I don't know what I would do if I did not have Dick to wait on me and take care of me." No medical man had ever seen him, nor medicine been administered to relieve his sufferings.

Dick and John both said I must come and bunk with them. They had plenty of room, death having made vacancies within a few days. I told them Felix had given me room with him, so I guessed I would remain there; but I had a comrade I would like to shelter with them.

"Bring him right along; he's welcome," was their hospitable invitation.

As the sun was about rising I started to hunt up Schroeder, proud of the success that had attended my ramble, and desirous of introducing him to his new home. I had some difficulty in finding my sleeping-place, as the camp was all astir and the crowd changed the appearance of things. I finally spied him, pacing to and fro on a short beat, his hands clasped behind his back, his favorite attitude when perplexed.

"Mein Gott!" he said, "I am any vay glad to see you once more. Vhen I vaked and found you vas gone I did not know. I thought somebody must have carried you off vhile you slept. Vhere, any vay, have you peen dis early?"

I told him how I had run across Felix, who had kindly given me a place in his tent.

"By jingo," he exclaimed, "dat is goot! I am any vay pleased mit dat."

Then I told him I had faired him a place too, and led the way across the swamp. It seemed as though he had never thought that far ahead, and followed me without saying a word, though I had so studied him that I could tell by the twitching of his facial muscles that he did not dare to express himself just then.

When I got back, Felix was "waiting breakfast for me," as he said I would get hungry before I drew my rations. After breakfast he said:

"Come, let us walk around while it is cool and see the city. There is more to be seen here than you have any idea of, and you will have to see it to realize it. We'll go up to Main Street and walk out toward the south gate, leading off by one of the pine trees along a zigzag way euphoniously called Main Street."

While we were slowly walking along, busy in recalling the events of the past nine months, I was suddenly seized by my blouse collar and whirled completely around.

"Can't hear a fellow holler, hey?" was the shout that accompanied a grasp of my hand. I found myself face to face with Williams, a Tennessean, who had been a member of my ward at Danville, and to whom I had given a good blanket when he left for the prison again to be transferred to Andersonville.

"Well, I'm plumb beat this time; why in the world are you in here? I thought you were done exchanged months ago?"

"Haven't been here long? First walk down Main Street," I said.

"Well, it's a mighty hard place. They are killing off a power of the boys; a heap of the Danville boys have done gone since we came here. Have a drink, this is my ranch?"

Dipping down into a barrel, he took up a cup of what he called "beer," but which was nothing more than corn bread and water that had stood until it soured.

"It's not much of a drink," said he; "but it's mighty good for scurvy, and I kind o' like it."

I thought myself it was not much of a drink, but I gulped down a swallow or two out of charity to his good will.

"Come down and see me," continued Williams; "I stay down thar," pointing out his tent.

Felix told him I had come among them entirely destitute, save for what I had on my back.

"Come right down to my tent," reiterated Williams, "I've got an extra cup you can have. I can get along without it. Do you recognize that?" said he, tapping his tent as he stooped to crawl under, "that's the blanket you exchanged with me, and I tell you I've seen the good of it too."

We crawled under the tent and spent some time talking over Danville times and my escape and recapture. Little as these circumstances appear now, they were momentous then, and I love to recall them. Those friendships welded with the hammer of adversity were indissolubly joined, and amid the wreck and ruin of those dark hours they stand forth as bright stars in the depths of ether, each one sending forth its silvery ray to illume the path of memory, and I would not have one of them blotted out until all are swept away together.

"Ah!" said Felix as we passed back to our quarters, "I tell you that's a fine thing,"—pointing to the cup. "I've often felt the need of just such a cup since I've been in here. I tell you it's good and will add to our stock of utensils."

Our water-bucket and soup-pail consisted of boot-tops with wooden bottoms fitted into one end. The signal for roll-call being given, I hastened over to find my squad, and it was no small matter, notwithstanding I thought I had so thoroughly located it in my mind that I would have no difficulty. The sergeant told me my ration would be ready in about two hours, and that I must have something to put it in.

My first ration in Andersonville was a piece of corn bread about as large as the half of an ordinary brick, a small piece of bacon, perhaps three ounces, supposed to be cooked, and half a pint of rice boiled without salt. The bread was simply meal and water mixed and baked without salt. The cooked meat, I noticed, had not been heated hot enough to kill several skippers that flipped out of it.

Felix, like some patriarch of old, was sitting in the door of the tent awaiting my return.

"Well, what did you draw,—something first rate?" he inquired. "A big ration, eh? We'll have to put them together and I will make a 'rolla pot'."

"A what?" I asked.

"A rolla pot," returned he.

"Proceed," I said, "if you know what you are talking about,—I don't."

"That's an Andersonville luxury," replied Felix; "a thing born of circumstances, and I have given it that name for want of a better. You see," he continued, "if you leave that bread until morning it will be sour, so I take out all the soft part and roll it into balls this way,—suiting the action to the words by rolling the bread in the palms of his hands into balls about an inch in diameter. "These," said he, "I put into some water in the stewpan with some of the meat, and boil the whole together, which makes it all the more palatable and cooks it so that it will keep. Besides," be continued, "you'll find most of the meat we draw is so strong that you can't eat it. A little of the rice, added to the soup, makes that endurable and helps to fill up. Then I have the crust left to make coffee."

While he prepared the "rolla pot" I busied myself in splitting out some pine slats about an inch wide and eight inches long, which I wove together after the fashion of basket splints, and made me a substitute for a plate. This was the only plate I had while I remained in the stockade. For a fork I used a sharpened stick, and for a knife a stick made into a wooden spatula which answered all ordinary purposes, as we had no occasion for carving. I found I had been very fortunate in becoming one of Felix's household, in more ways than one. Being one of the "original settlers." he had secured a pine stump, roots and all. This he had stored behind his tent, next to the dead line, where he could watch it, every splinter being valuable. When we got through cooking we gathered up every particle of wood and put out the fire, laying the charred embers carefully away till next time. That you may better get an idea of the value of fuel I will note a little conversation between us to that point.

"What are those fellows doing over there in the swamp?" said I, one day, directing Felix's attention to a dozen or more persons who were wading around in the mire and filth, fuddling around with their arms buried up to their shoulders and feeling carefully as if in search of buried treasures.

"Why," he said, "they are hunting for red-roots to cook with."

"Red-roots!" I echoed,—I suppose in a doubting tone.

"Yes, red-roots. When we first came in here that swamp was covered thick with red-wood bushes as high as your head, or higher, and so thick that a rabbit could not get through them. Now it is as you see,—

every inch has been worked over dozens of times, two feet below the surface, in search of bits of roots to cook with. Tough, isn't it?"

Tough! Good Heavens! Think of those fellows thus working over those four or five acres of filthy swamp in search of the smallest fibres of roots, while just outside the stockade walls on the east and south were thousands of cords of the best of pine wood, and hundreds of cords of tree-tops the butts of which bad been felled in preparing the pen. These tree-tops had been dragged off the prison ground, and now lay outside, going to waste, although the prisoners would gladly have collected them if they could have had permission to do so, under guard. With teams this valuable fuel could have been brought inside and divided so as to give all an opportunity of working over their ration. The only excuse the authorities vouchsafed for not permitting this was that too many of the boys got away, and that they traded and became too intimate with the guards and might plan an outbreak. Weak subterfuges! If they had but said, "It is not the will of the Confederate government that you have that much added to your comfort," they would have struck the nail square on the head, for that is the only reason those poor fellows had to gather roots from the swamp. I made it my business to investigate all that when I was out on parole, and I could attribute the whole thing to nothing but "cussed meanness," well studied and scrupulously applied. There is not a person who was confined there but will testify that the condition of the men might have been bettered a hundredfold without one cent of cost to the Confederate government.

Owing to the bad condition of the water supply the boys had dug a number of wells, some of them forty and fifty feet deep. The sand was of such a character it did not cave in a perpendicular wall. The digging was all done with knives, and the dirt was drawn up in boot-tops. Of course the sand favored the work, but to supply so great a number with good drinking-water was beyond the power of the wells, and there was considerable suffering, with no hopes of anything better as the weather became hotter and the grounds outside became filthier.

Chapter **XXIV**

"Bean Soup! — Hot Bean Soup!"

WELL," said Felix, after we had breakfasted the second morning, "let us continue our walk around the city. We did not get far yesterday."

Passing on the same street as before at the south end, near or quite against the dead line, we came to an extensive enclosure of evergreen boughs and brush. "That," said Felix, "is the Masonic Temple." The square and compass were suspended over the door. Going on to the south gate he pointed to a box nailed on a post. "That," said he, "is the Post Office."

"What? do they allow you to send out letters?"

"Oh yes, just drop them in there unsealed, and they will take them and look over them to see if there is anything contraband; if not they send them through by flag of truce."

"Chalk them one," I said, "that's more than I would have given them credit for,"—and more than they deserved, as I found out when I got outside; for the letters seldom got farther than Wirz's quarters, where they were thrown into a box, and when it got full they would send them heavenward in the form of smoke. Occasionally they would send a lot off—I suppose to keep up an appearance with our government; but the greater portion were burned, and I was really glad the boys inside did not know this, as writing letters seemed to cheer them up and to bring them into communion with home.

Passing down the west side we came to the log crossing. Here I noticed quite a fine spring of pure water close to the dead line.

"There," said Felix, pointing to it, "look at that pure water running there, and see in it one of the strongest evidences of an over-ruling Providence that could be given. Call it a miracle or what you will. Now," he said, "look at the brook covered with grease and slime where it comes into the stockade. When we first came in here that was what we had to drink,—cook house slop, drain from rebel camp, and what not. We could not stand it and went to digging wells to secure drinking-water, but well-digging with our means was slow work, and we could not supply anything like what was necessary. So it continued up to a short time ago, when one day that spring burst out, and has continued to run, as you see it now. Look down either side of the stream and tell me where it could have been better located."

"That's so; it is freer from any possible filtering of filth here than any other place you could put it!"

"Yes. Well, now look again, and tell me if there is a more unlikely spot for a spring to break out. Why did it not break out in the middle or on the edge of the swamp on the north side, or in that naturally springy depression on the south side; or, finally, why did it break out at all?"

Surely God had not forgotten them, and had mercifully interposed in behalf of the boys at Andersonville. I took a cup from the hand of one who had just been drinking, and, stooping down, dipped up a cupful and drank it, feeling that I had partaken of the fruits of a miracle as truly as did Israel's famishing hosts when they drank of the stream that gushed from the smitten rock.

Leaving the spring we passed up near the north gate, where were located a number of our old Pemberton and Danville boys. Here we found "Michigan Steve," whom we used to call "the fighting-cock," on account of the ease with which he could get into a muss and the indifference he always manifested as to whether he came out first or second best, so long as he kept his hand in. Poor fellow! We found him *hors de combat*, his feet and legs drawn up so that he could not walk and almost black with scurvy; his spirit was broken, and he pointed silently to several suppurating sores on his heels and to several toes already sloughing off. He died soon after. "Newt," my old smallpox friend, was looking as fair as any of them, though he was troubled with scurvy. I had to take dinner with him, as he said, for old acquaintance' sake.

"Here you are," said an old man, extending his hand. "Williams" (the Tennesseean) "told me you were in here, and I've watched for you and tried to find you. Do you remember me? I was in your ward at Danville, and when I left you gave me this blanket,"—referring to his tent, and told me I would need it when I came here. I've thought of it so often. It's all the shelter I've had." (It evidently pleased the old man to think that I remembered him.) "Come around and see me often," he said, as I started away, "it's all we've got to do here."

This calling around was of decided benefit to all of us; it helped us to get away from present sufferings; and, as we generally recalled the amusing phases of prison life, we enjoyed many a good hearty laugh, which was as good for us as a tonic. I found that Felix was right when he said "there's lots to see in this place." Almost every time I passed around I found something new,—some phase of suffering, some development of genius or character to surprise one, old friendships to renew. One day I ran onto an old Danville friend named Rohrer. He, like Felix, was a member of that class known as "oldest inhabitants," having been among the first who came to Andersonville in what the boys called the palmy days of the old stockade. From them I learned that when it became necessary to enlarge the stockade,—which was done by adding to the north end,—details were made from among the boys to do the work. These details soon got the name of "speculations,"—a word that may need some explanation, as the terms "Andersonville" and "speculation" would not seem to imply conditions that could be brought together.

Human nature has certain distinctive features inherent to the whole class, and a desire to get hold of the greatest possible amount of the circulating medium of commerce characterizes man everywhere, but this characteristic seemed specially developed in the prison guard at Andersonville. Their palms itched to close on greenbacks (at any rate the authorities gave that as a reason for searching us so often, that we might not corrupt the guards).

So with greenbacks these details could buy beans, flour, rice, bacon, potatoes, salt, soda,—in fact, almost everything in the eatable line. These they managed to get inside the enclosure and sell to the newcomers, or "Fresh Fish," as they termed the new prisoners who were being brought in from the front.

By a special condition of surrender a large force taken in North Carolina had been allowed to retain all their equipage except guns, and, having been recently paid off, were well supplied with money. It was a hard matter for them to stomach the rations issued. They had not been gradually brought down to them, as the old prisoners had, and, rather than eat them so long as their means held out, they would buy biscuit, boiled eggs, bean soup, and such other things as the speculators had to offer at fabulous prices. For instance, for *one dollar* a prisoner might buy any *one* of the following items: three small raw Irish potatoes; a spoonful of salt; a spoonful of soda; three biscuits; or a pint of bean soup. A quarter of a pint of the latter commodity cost forty cents, and soup seemed to be the staple of trade. It required considerable of a purse to maintain such a style of living for any length of time. But when the purse was empty there was the ordinary ration to fall back on.

The main street on the north side, leading from the gate, was dubbed Commercial Row, from its being the place where these things were offered for sale. At almost any hour in the day you could have heard the cry, "Here's your place to buy good bean soup! Hot bean soup! Bean soup, forty cents a dish!" At other places you got the raw material at wholesale. Of course the regular ration could be traded in part payment, and these would be worked over. By this trafficking some of the speculators accumulated sums ranging from a hundred to fifteen hundred dollars, and some few even more.

It was not the retailers who made the money. Their object was to eke out their other rations. It was my opinion that much of the goods was taken from boxes sent by friends in the North and opened at the connivance of, and perhaps by, the officials themselves. I will give an instance to the point. While in Danville one of the boys in Prison No. 4 received a box from home which was open and had evidently suffered evaporation to a fearful extent before it reached him. The authorities claimed that the boxes were opened in Richmond, in order to guard against arms being conveyed to the prisons, and that if anything had been taken out it was taken out there. Among other things left in the box were three boxes of essence of coffee, which the receiver eked out with great care; but alas! an order came in for him to turn over the balance of that essence of coffee, from which we have a right to draw our own conclusions. It showed very conclusively that Major Moffit, or some one under him, had appropriated the missing articles and had found one item at least so good that he wanted more.

It was somewhat amusing to observe the earnest energy with which the soup-venders followed their business. Commercial Row had been partially graded to make a roadway for the wagons that brought in the rations, in consequence of which there was a bank of a foot or two elevation on the upper side. Along on this the dealers were located as close as convenience would admit, each one with some kind of vessel by his side, full of bean soup, while near at hand he had another setting over a fire in a trench, in order that his soup might always come up to the standard of "hot bean soup." Here, always in the same place, as though they held the respective lots by deed or lease, from early noon until late in the evening, they would sit and cry their wares. Some were fortunate enough to possess a blanket to make a shade, but generally they sat in the hot sun. For me they were subjects to study. I used frequently to go along the Row and watch them at their work. No merchant on New York's Broadway ever put more vim and zeal into his business, involving millions, than did these fellows along that bank. Theirs was certainly a laudable zeal. It was a case of life or death. As I have said, they did not make much, but they managed, by very close work, to keep up their original stock, each day's profit going to support life. God knows they were worthy of greater success, but they were content if the day's work left them a good dish in excess. They earned it by the sweat of their brows if ever men did. They were not remarkable for cleanliness, and, dressed in their filthy tatters, some of which required great ingenuity to keep together on their person, would, in the outside world, have been termed objects of disgust. Barefooted and bareheaded, with intermediate spots of nakedness, taken all together, they made the most serio-comic scene ever presented of the most abject poverty and misery struggling for an existence, and it is to be earnestly prayed that the world may never have it duplicated.

CHAPTER XXV

The Execution of the Raiders

THE opportunity presented for obtaining with money an indemnity against starvation by means of the wares offered by the soup-venders rendered a class of men within the stockade so desperate that they did not hesitate to commit murder in order to procure a little money. They were called "raiders." Their actions became so intolerable that no man's life was safe who was suspected of having money, a watch, or any other valuable. A number of murders had been committed; several men had been found dead in their tents, with their skulls smashed by clubs; and others were brained on their way to the spring after night.

Such cases were on the increase. To meet this a police force was secretly organized and gotten into systematic working order. Emboldened by success, the desperadoes became more open in their work, so that the leaders, six in number, were ferreted out and captured. They were all, I believe, foreigners. They were given a fair trial, and after a careful examination of all the witnesses they were adjudged guilty and condemned to die by hanging. A copy of the proceedings (their defence, the testimony of the witnesses, the findings of the jury, and the rulings of the court) were sent out to the prison authorities, who sustained the verdict and sentence and sent in suitable timbers and tools for the erection of a gallows, together with the proper appendages for such a ceremony.

On the 11th of July, 1864, the miscreants were executed simultaneously. The rope of one broke by the force of the drop, and he made a desperate effort to escape, fighting with the energy of desperation rendered terribly intense by the experience he had already had. It was not until he had been cornered in the northeast corner of the stockade that he was again secured and dragged back to the gallows, which had been erected near the south gate. The wretch pleaded for his life; he prayed for mercy; he appealed to the consciences of his executioners; but there was no eye that dared show pity in that crowd of men, who had been rendered desperate by the bloody deeds of the criminals. The executioners forced him up the steps onto the drop, readjusted the cord about his neck, and swung him off alongside his now lifeless companions. It must have been a season of extreme mental agony to him, as he was made to ascend the second time in view of the distorted countenances of his companions in crime and punishment.

Thus ended the most thrilling episode of internal dissension occurring during the history of prison life. All breathed easier after this. The bodies of the executed men were cut down and delivered to the outside authorities, by whom they were interred in the cemetery in a separate trench, their names and manner of death being marked on headboards. The memory of the scene was sufficient to deter any of their followers from committing further crimes. The police force, however, was maintained after that, the members being remunerated by an extra ration each day. They were recognized by their batons (about eighteen inches long) looped to their wrists by leather straps and very good order was maintained by them, everything considered.

Chapter XXVI

Scurvy

THERE was quite a religious element in Andersonville that lived in spite of the quenching tendencies of our surroundings and kept alive the spirit of the good Samaritan. So far as they could they met generally twice a week, near our quarters, for religious worship and consultation. I have heard some very fine exhortations delivered at some of these meetings; possibly the uncouth, rugged sources of the oratory added force and impressiveness to the efforts, but the exercises were really interesting. I often wondered that the guards, from the stations near by, did not sometimes respond with a bullet when they heard invoked the protection of an Arm mightier than man's, in that dark hour, for those neglected by their country because of their starved, diseased condition and the prime condition of those whom they offset in the prisons at the North. The fires of patriotism burned still in their bosoms, and they prayed for the nation and the President, I thought sometimes, with an eloquence that I never heard excelled.

There was a majesty in that little band that challenged the admiration of all who heard, and not a word was uttered or an action committed to thwart their work; nor did it end in that simple though sublime evidence of faith, as shown by their meetings. Many a poor soul was comforted by them, and when he became too weak to care for himself they ministered to him so far as they were able. Though the aid afforded may not have been more than the bringing of a cup of cool water, it was that much given in the spirit of kindness and love. They were a noble set of men, true alike to their country and their God.

Every day I became more and more convinced of the truthfulness of Felix's remark, "There is a great deal to see and learn in Andersonville." I saw some new feature every day. It was a good place to study human nature. We had representatives from all parts of the globe, nearly,—even to the American Indians. Inured, as we generally suppose them to be, to filth and privation, Andersonville was a dose too strong for them, and many passed from its horrors to the "happy hunting-grounds."

I tried to become acquainted with every nook and corner of the pen and to see all that I could of its suffering thousands. I found that my first surmises were correct in regard to the condition of the men being more dreadful than a person would guess by standing at a given point and overlooking the moving multitude. Hundreds died in the pen who never had any medical care whatever, but had to drag out a miserable existence with no attempt being made by the authorities to alleviate their sufferings. Imbedded, I might almost say, in filth; too much reduced to be able to care for themselves; swarming with vermin; their bodies eaten in many instances into repulsive sores, and their scalps eaten raw by lice,—these literally skin-covered skeletons made a sight that was sickening to look upon. Fancy limbs discolored by scurvy, which in some cases had caused the toes to slough off, and even the feet also, in several instances; men dying by inches,—yes, literally dying by inches,— and watching the decay with a sad melancholy that no pen can describe! Indeed the pen that could describe such sufferings would have power "to paint the dying groan."

Especially did this condition apply to the "old prisoners," by which term I mean those who had seen long captivity. I am positive that I am safe in saying that nine out of ten were to a greater or less extent affected. Many of them were beyond walking; in many cases their legs were so drawn up that they were unable to straighten up, and had to crawl on their hands and knees.

I found an old schoolmate, Thomas Barnes, a bugler in the Thirty-first Ohio Infantry, in this condition. Poor fellow! though unable to stand alone, he was trying to keep alive the vital spark by selling tobacco, in this way getting a small pittance to invest in food. I could see each time I visited him, which was nearly every day, that he was fast nearing the last grand camping ground, "the bivouac of the dead." I tried to get him to go to the hospital, but he said it was no use, though he finally consented to go, and died soon after.

It was no uncommon thing to see men wandering in idiocy,—reason, sense, feeling, all dead. This was the saddest of all sights to me. It seemed as though their souls had already taken their departure, leaving the clay tenements to gradual decay. Others again, in apparently as good condition as any of us, and rational in general conversation, could not remember their regiments or the command to which they belonged, while still others could not remember their own names or where they came from.

The great exposure to night air, coupled with insufficient food, had produced night-blindness in a great many, so that as soon as the sun set they were in total darkness until the sun rose again. Such unfortunates had to remain wherever sunset found them, if they had no friends to lead them to their quarters. So far as I could trace such cases, they invariably died in a short time after this condition appeared. I asked one of them if there was pain connected with it, or if there was any sense of weariness to the eye. He said there was not; that the sensation was just as if he had suddenly been taken from daylight to the depths of a cave where no light penetrated; he could feel the darkness as a terrible reality,—a proof, I thought, of the possibility of the "outer darkness" spoken of in Scripture.

Chronic diarrhoea, the sequence of scurvy, was terrible, and in its worst phases disgustingly repulsive. Numbers were so far gone with it, that, their limbs being as described above, they could not get to the sink, and were compelled to dig pits beside their beds. Others, again, having no control over the action of their bowels, were being eaten alive by worms and flies, and dying in their own filth. I have seen cases where it appeared as though the victims had tried to crawl to the sink, had become exhausted, and lain down in the hot sand and died. Coming across the swamp on the east side one day, and reaching the flat already spoken of, I found Rose engaged in washing a man whom he had found in a dying condition. Apparently he had become exhausted in trying to drag himself up the pitch in the path and had fallen back to die. His eyes, nose, mouth, and ears were full of worms, and he was still groaning. I asked Rose if he knew him. "Only as a human being needing help," he said. Where, oh where, rests the responsibility?

These are terrible pictures to review after the lapse of a few years,— revolting pictures. Yet I am recording only what I have seen with my own eyes and passed through in my own experience. But oh, how painfully, how impressively real they were to me then, when I knew that the same fell destroyer was fast mastering me. How like mockery it sounded to me as I lay awake nights and heard the guards calling, "*All is well.*" These sights were all inside the stockade, where there was no medical treatment given, and where all were supposed to be able to care for themselves.

I conversed with several persons, while in the stockade, who claimed to have cured their limbs even after scurvy had made considerable progress. Their manner of procedure was to dig a pit in the moist sand, divest the parts of all clothing, and then get into the pit and pack the sand about them. This operation they had to undergo for a number of days, and each application was continued during several hours. They said the earth appeared to draw the poison out of the system. The swelling of scurvy is of an oedematous character, and it is possible that the pressure of the packed sand might cause a scattering of the poison and aid the kidneys in eliminating it, as being buried to the hips would prevent or at least retard the collection of fluid matter below the pelvic cavity. I had no reason to doubt their statement and simply give it as a nut for physicians to crack.

CHAPTER **XXVII**

Severity of the Guards

I HAD become so accustomed to startling revelations in my walks and talks around the camp, that I had grown into a state of being surprised at nothing. I was startled one day, however, by the unexpected report of a guard's gun near where I was walking on the west side, south of the spring. Running quickly I saw two men reel and fall just above the spring on the north side. On strict inquiry the only solution of the matter that could be given was that in trying to dip up a tin cup of water one of the prisoners had reached under the dead line, and the guard had, in shooting at him, overshot sufficiently to strike into a squad of six or eight men who were standing twenty-five or thirty feet away, wounding two of them. Either that, or it was in harmony with an order that had been issued by Wirz, that the guards should fire into and disperse any undue collection of men near the gates or dead line, and that squad was sufficient to fill the spirit of the order. In either case it was cold-blooded murder.

Nor was this the only case of shooting that had occurred. I had been told of a number more, but this was the only case witnessed by me. No man but a devil incarnate could or would do such a thing, and I always have felt that those who did the shooting ought to be brought to trial though it took years to find them. Such an order was altogether uncalled for, because in the densely crowded condition of the stockade it was an impossibility to prevent collecting in squads. In fact we were an almost solid squad of thirty thousand, make the best disposition we could of ourselves. In truth, room was so scarce that wheelbarrows were sent in, and ground was made by wheeling sand from the north side and dumping it into the swamp. In this way considerable room was made, which was always taken up as soon as leveled off, though it certainly must have been very productive of disease and an unpleasant building spot, so near the filth and stench. Yet this ground was in great demand, causing many fisticuff affairs among contestants for possession. In a community like ours, where it was every man for himself, and rights were necessarily on a narrow basis, muscle was frequently brought into action, though never with any serious damage to the belligerents, as the average fighting weight was very light. I saw two fellows quarrelling over a site on the newly reclaimed territory, each claiming it by right of priority. Words not being sufficient, they finally resorted to blows and were making very fair headway when one of them, not giving heed to the ground, went over, full length, backward into the swamp. His opponent, jumping in astride of him, soon pummelled him under. When the "under dog" arose he was the most comical sight for a human being I ever saw, and, I dare venture, as sweet-scented a one. The spectators enjoyed it hugely and dubbed the fracas "The Battle of the Swamp." The mud-immersed individual received such various names as "The Swamp Angel," "The First Fruits of the Andersonville Resurrection," "Eclipsed Glory," "Buried Animosity," and other such euphonious titles, calculated, as they said, to make a man feel good and look kindly on defeat.

Old Captain Wirz sometimes made his appearance inside the gate, and then arose such a groaning and crying of "Carry him out," "Kill him," etc., as would have to be heard to be realized. I really think he was afraid to venture any farther than just inside, unless surrounded by a strong guard, and I think, also, that he had reason to be afraid.

I have often wondered why they had no Confederate flag floating over us. They had a very nice flagstaff, but during my seven months' sojourn there I never saw the flag once; nor do I remember seeing any regimental flags, though I think the several regiments composing the guards were home guards. There were also two companies of artillery.

Our condition during a rain was very trying, as very few of the shelters would turn water, especially such showers as sometimes fell, when the water seemed to come in solid sheets, wetting everything, even our beds or sleeping-places. The sandy soil soon dried off, so we had no mud. The rains during hot weather were accompanied by the most terrific thunder I ever heard. During one storm the lightning struck four trees standing close to the stockade. Sometimes we stripped off our rags and took a genuine shower-bath. This served, to some extent, to keep down the sandfleas. These were a terrible pest; the sand seemed full of them. Mosquitoes were another source of annoyance, the swamp being a breeding-place for them. Those who had not sufficient clothing to cover their limbs suffered from this source very much, as mosquito-bites on limbs affected by scurvy were very likely to run into terrible sores. We all looked as though we had smallpox, but the helpless and weak were especially tormented by these pests.

Here was a good place to study the endurance of men. I found that the Indians confined there were not enduring as well as the whites. They stayed very close to their quarters, however, and were not given to exercise as much as the whites, which might possibly account for their lack of stamina. So, also, I found that the marines were less hardy than infantrymen, and succumbed much more readily to disease and the privations of scant and inappropriate food. The small, medium-sized, and spare men stood it better than those given to corpulency, and single men better than the married ones, on account of the latter worrying over thoughts of their families. Strangest of all, those who were naturally physically weak were far in advance of those who boasted of their muscle and laughed at trifles when we were first taken.

There was a great tendency to rheumatism and renal diseases. Sand-itch was also prevalent and extremely annoying, especially so when, as sometimes happened, the men's thighs would become so encrusted that they had to lie on their faces to get any comfort at all. The patience of the men under these heavy afflictions was heroic and remarkable. They seldom gave way to outbursts of feeling against the foolish and unwise policy that was keeping them there as prisoners, though we all knew it was the veriest nonsense, no matter what excuse the commissioners of exchange might give in extenuation of their course. If the voice of argument would not convince, the voice of humanity should have been heard, and the Federal Government could well have afforded to grant the Confederacy all they asked, as it would thereby have given a much more enduring evidence of care for its defenders than it did in suffering them to remain subject to months of rebel torture. By so doing it would have heaped coals of fire upon the heads of the enemy. As it was, the chances were for the North to lose prestige. The Confederacy had nothing to lose. It had not even established a character, that it could be stultified. A retrospect of the war reveals many mistakes, chief among which was the policy that abandoned us to our fate as prisoners rather than give in exchange for us "men in good condition to put in the Confederate army." General U. S. Grant, more than any other man, was responsible for our condition, or, rather, retention, as he strongly disapproved of exchange for the reason given above.

Chapter **XXVIII**

A Lucky Call

AS I was becoming weakened by chronic diarrhoea and crippled up by scurvy I was very reluctantly compelled to abandon to a great degree my habit of "looking around the city," and to confine my walks to narrower limits. These tours had afforded a kind of melancholy satisfaction and pleasure, and I hated to be compelled to give them up, not only on account of this pleasure, but for the graver reason that it was an evidence that my vital forces were weakening. While I never for one moment thought I would die a prisoner, this giving way indicated a drifting in that direction. Each day I could note a deeper shade of discoloration of my feet and ankles, and a deeper pitting of the oedematous swelling, accompanied by increased bowel derangement, until, finally, the ominous pit had to be dug beside my bed and I could no longer extend my walk beyond our immediate fireplace.

Felix, who was one of the best-preserved specimens of the "old prisoners" that I had seen, was very attentive and had exhausted his culinary skill in trying to cook our rations so they would agree with me, but to no purpose.

"Well," he said one evening, as we sat in the tent, "if I only had some money to buy some raw beans, I would try selling bean soup over on the Row. I think I could make enough to get us something else to eat."

"How much capital would it require, Felix?" I asked.

"About five dollars," said he; "but it would be all the same if it took five hundred. I could get you about as well as the other."

"Perhaps not," I said, taking a ten-dollar bill out of my pocket and showing it to him. It was one Rohrer had given me some days before, and Felix was not aware of it. I guess that if I had drawn a full-grown elephant out of my pocket he would not have looked more astonished.

"Well!—what?—when?—by gracious!—where the deuce did it come from? I didn't know you had any money," he gasped at last.

"Oh, that's only another miracle of the stockade," I said, "and is certainly ominous of good; go immediately and buy what you want, and prepare for business."

It was very satisfactory to me to see the happy expression that passed over his face as he looked at the bill. He looked his very name—"*Felix*"—"Happy." I watched him as he hurried over the swamp to Commercial Row, and noted success in his very motion as he soon came hurrying back to announce that he bad secured an eligible position, a corner lot on the main path,—"a spanking good place," to use his own words. The tenter had given him the privilege of using his tent front in consideration of a dish of soup a day. Then off he went to secure his beans before it came dark; after which we busied ourselves in splitting wood from the old stumps in order to give him an early start. Morning found him, with his kettle or pan of beans nicely cooked, duly installed as a business man, crying, "Here's your hot bean soup!" with as much vehemence as the best of them, and he was measurably successful. When he came in that evening he reported fifty cents, ahead, saying, with feeling, "Bully, we're all right."

A few evenings afterward Felix sat in the tent, his chin resting on his knees and his hands locked underneath so that he could rock back and forth, —his wonted position when in deep study. Watching him a few moments I said,—

"Well, what is it, Felix? I see you have something on your mind."

"How do you know?" rejoined he. "But I'll tell you. I was thinking, if you had no objection, I'd take that other five dollars and get some meal and salt and soda, and make some light corn bread to sell with my beans."

"Where's your oven," I asked.

"Oh, I'm hunky on the oven," he replied, "I've got a friend over in the northwest corner who has an oven, and he says I may bake with him if I'll furnish the wood."

"All right," I said, "go in,"—and away he went to complete his preparations.

"Light corn bread" was a very palatable bread compared with our ration bread and was made by soaking the soft part of our ration over night. By morning this would be quite sour, and it was then made into a thin batter, soda being added to sweeten and lighten and new meal to thicken it. By the time it was baked the mass would rise and be quite spongy.

So Felix enlarged his business and prospered. His bread sold well. I never asked him if he was making more than our extra ration, though he spoke several times about his banker somewhere on the north side.

While lying in my tent one afternoon I noticed an artist, with his camera, taking some views of the stockade from the guard stands. I wondered who in the great Confederacy would want to keep even a shadow of that reproach to hand down to posterity, and then I thought how the Almighty, in his mysterious Providence, had caused to be preserved some of the records of the nations of the past, to be revealed after hundreds of years, when all knowledge of them had passed away. The day will come, possibly, when that artist's work will be reproduced in attestation of the truth that such a place as Andersonville ever existed.

Some days after this, as I was lying in the tent trying to get some rest, but fast running into the last stages of my disease, I was surprised by the sudden appearance of Felix in front of the tent, nearly out of breath from running.

"Hurry up, hurry up," he said, "they are waiting for you out at the gate. I heard them calling your name, and thought perhaps there was a letter for you, and went over to see; but they have an order to take you out; they want you to put up medicine for our sick in the hospital. I told them I'd bring you. You must go. It will save your life. Hurry, I'll get a man to help you while I go over to the other side and get your part of the money, and when you get outside you can buy vegetables to eat which will cure you."

All the getting ready I had to do was to get up and put on my blouse, which I was using as a pillow. Then, leaning on the shoulder of the comrade who came to assist me, I made my way to the gate as soon as I could. Felix was there, keeping the officer engaged, so that he would not give me up. He slipped into my hand fifteen dollars.

"What!" I said, "have you kept anything yourself?"

"Oh, yes; I've got the stock on hand and five dollars. I'm all right."

With many wishes for my recovery he bade me good-by as I passed out through the gate, and I never saw him again.

As the south gate closed behind us I felt as though I had been called back to life and to the world. Thus again had I been taken, providentially, I must believe, from the very jaws of death. I was taken up to the log house where we were first halted on our introduction to Andersonville, but now it was entirely surrounded by earthworks which changed the appearance very much, the entrance being on the west angle. Here I had to sign a parole that I would not try to make my escape. We were given liberty to go to any place within a mile radius from this house, during daylight, when not on duty at the dispensary. At night we were required to be in our quarters. As I was waiting for them to get the papers ready to take a description, one of them said,—

" You were in charge of a ward in hospital at Danville, were you not?"

"Yes, sir."

"Were you paroled?"

"No, sir."

"Tried to make your escape, didn't you?"

"Yes, sir, I did."

"All right, but we will put you on your honor and give you a trial."

After signing the necessary papers we were told to repair to the dispensary for duty.

My old friend Schroeder, who had preceded me by several weeks, was anxiously awaiting my dismissal from the office. He had been instrumental in getting me out to assist in the work. When I came up to the dispensary he seized me with both hands, "By Gott! I any vay am gladt you have comed. I vas fearful dey vould not findt you mit all dat crowdt in dat damp old pen."

I told him it was by the merest accident that Felix had heard my name called, and had assisted me in getting out.

"Vell, dat vas close; he is any how a first-rate fellow, dat Felix. It vas lucky, py jingo. Dot is so, you look badt, you vould soon de bucket have kickedt over if you had staydt any longer. But come on; come in and rest; you look playdt out. Py jingo, I am proudt of dis."

And I knew he was, generous, kind soul that he was.

Chapter XXIX

The Hospital and Dispensary

THE dispensary was a sixteen-foot square log house without any window, a style peculiar to that section of the country, and had formerly been the negro quarters to the double log house. It stood on the north side of the earthwork, two pieces of artillery being planted just on the east side, bearing on the pen. There were two other druggists besides myself and Schroeder, a Norwegian named Oyen, and a New Yorker named Reed. It was some time before I gained sufficiently in strength to be of any service to them, though I soon noticed a change for the better and began to mend slowly. We got much better fare and had better facilities for cooking; besides, I could get medicine to assist nature in her effort to throw off disease.

The stock of drugs was meagre, consisting, in the main, of "roots and yarbs" packed by the Confederate Medical Dispensary at Macon, Georgia. The United States had so effectually blockaded the Southern ports that it was a difficult matter for them to get drugs that required chemical manipulation, all they had having either run the blockade or been captured from the "Yanks." Consequently we had only a limited quantity of quinine, opium, mercurial preparations, etc., though what we had were generally good and bore the stamp of English manufacture. But the way we sent out those "yarbs" was a caution,—sumac berries, white-oak bark, prickly ash, prickly alder, willow bark, dogwood bark, sassafras bark, sweet-gum bark, black cohash, blackberry roots, boneset, burdock, yellow dock, bayberries, snakeroot, golden seal, juni-

per berries, etc., being the ones in most general use. From these the attendants in the hospital made decoctions which they issued to the sick
"in quantities to suit." We had no vessels in which to prepare them at
the dispensary, nor bottles to put them in, and I am at a loss to know
how they prepared them inside the hospital to make them effective:

The hospital itself was a mere makeshift,—a simple enclosure containing five or six acres, enclosed with a tight board fence, and located
perhaps a quarter of a mile from the south end of the stockade and extending a very little east of its east line. It was situated contiguous to a
nice stream of water, called "sweet water," so that a canal was dug to
lead a portion of it through the enclosure from west to east on the south
side and discharge again into the same stream. This branch and the one
passing through the stockade united a short distance below the hospital
and flowed on to Flint River, a few miles below.

I found the hospital accommodations here in the worst possible condition for the treatment of the sick. Our preconceived ideas of a hospital
were such that we had accepted suitable buildings for shelters as a fore-
gone conclusion, and we were not prepared, even by our stockade experience, to expect to see such miserable substitutes as we found actually
existing. By far the larger percentage of the sick were lying on the ground,
with only a little straw under them, and temporary shelters overhead
sufficient only to keep out the little sunshine that might have benefitted
them. One side was open as an entrance, the rear side in most of them
being too low to stand up under. Some were large enough to hold a dozen
patients, and from that down to a capacity of two. The smaller tents were
low and usually occupied by convalescents; for, strange as it may appear
and sound, they did have some convalescents in there, though I think it
was not the intention of the Confederate government.

The dense pine growth overhead cast a deep shade which kept
the quarters in a mouldy, unhealthy condition, and fungi inside and
outside the shelters indicated a condition of things well calculated to
make a well man sick and a sick man die. I could only view the whole
place as one vast shade of death, and was not surprised that of the many
who went in there so few came out alive. Indeed, when we consider the
extreme point to which they had to be reduced before admission to hospital was granted, the unhealthy condition of the quarters, and the coarse
character of the food, the wonder is that any came out alive.

For the convenience of the surgeons they divided the enclosure
into wards of a certain number of sick, each surgeon taking care of a
separate lot of men, and each ward having its nurses, cooks, bottles, etc.
I had to get a pass from Wirz in order to get into the hospital enclosure,
so that I made a very close study of the condition of things and am thus
careful in noting it, as what I write may in course of years become history.

Occupying a wall-tent near our dispensary was a lady with a young child. I at first supposed that she was the wife of one of the officers in charge, but soon learned that she was a prisoner, having been captured in company with her husband, who was a steamboat captain and a civilian, though at the time of his capture he was engaged in transporting government troops or supplies somewhere on the coast of North Carolina. His name was Herbert Hunt, and their first child, who was named Frank, was born in that tent,—an experience that perhaps has not a parallel in all history. Born into an experience like that of Andersonville, not twenty steps from a Confederate battery, surrounded by earthworks, he ought to be proud of the beginning of his career, for I think he stands alone.

The mother bore her trials with considerable fortitude, though only a prisoner nominally, as she was permitted to go where she pleased and spent a great deal of time at Mr. Smith's, about a mile south of the prison. Mr. Hunt was acting as ward-master in the hospital, and was "hail fellow well met" with everyone. One of the Confederate attachés, a Mr. Robertson, had his wife with him, and the two ladies seemed to enjoy themselves together very much. We found them to be a cheerful part of our hospital association, and very estimable ladies, and we had the pleasure, when we became acquainted, of spending some very pleasant evenings at their quarters, after they had taken possession of two vacant shanties deserted by some of the batterymen. Such are some of the bright spots of our prison experience to which we turn with pleasant memories.

A day or so after I came out of the stockade we had one of the hardest rains I think I ever saw. In the midst of it we were surprised to see an unusual activity among the guards, who were hastening in the direction of the stockade. The battery near us fired a blank or two, punching a piece of clinking from between the logs toward the pen. We were surprised to see the little brook swollen into a mighty rushing torrent, which piled drift against the stockade so that it finally gave way, making a break of nearly fifty feet. The boys inside were having a jubilee. We could see them astride of logs, paddling around in the flood, gathering driftwood for fuel. A similar break was made on the lower side. It was quite exciting for a little time.

CHAPTER XXX

The Medical Staff

WE found the medical department pretty well represented by nine surgeons. Dr. R. R. Stevenson, who was in charge at that time, I was told, was practising in Indiana at the breaking out of the war, but, being in sympathy with the South, drifted into the Confederate army as surgeon and was detailed to Andersonville. One of our boys, who claimed to have known him in the North, vowed he had a family there; but he transferred his affections to a young Confederate lady and married her. As he was acting in the capacity of General Medical Director I know nothing of his medical ability. He accomplished little or nothing for the boys, though he had considerable to say of what he was going to do.

Dr. Karr, who seemed to be a kind of roustabout whose duty was to superintend the hospital attendants and enforce orders (I do not think he held any commission), was addicted to inhaling ether and chloroform and getting into a kind of drunken state, when he was full of "Old Nick." Taking him all in all, he was, as Schroeder expressed it, "any how a funny fellow." He took special delight in watching close to the hospital gate after night, trying to catch the guards and men trading. He was acting as hospital steward.

Dr. Thornburg was a man of fine feeling and medical ability, with a high sense of justice, that saw in the sick prisoner before him a human being who required medical attention and medical sympathy. His heart was with his patients, and he took pleasure in doing all he could to render them comfortable, carefully diagnosing his cases and noting

127

every change in order to meet the necessities of the case promptly. I frequently heard him lament the absence of requisites to render the men comfortable. More than that, he read me a paper he had prepared for transmission to the Surgeon-General at Richmond, in which he fairly portrayed the condition of the men and asked that means might be put at the disposal of the medical staff to ameliorate the condition of the prisoners, or that some arrangement might be made to have them sent North. He also reported the fearful mortality.

Dr. Mudd was a bitter, red-hot rebel from Kentucky, who suffered his prejudices to bias his judgment. In his eyes a Yankee was no better than a dog. He was a surgeon of no mean ability, of phlegmatic temperament and well-defined muscle. If there was a soft phase to his nature he left it at his quarters, and to the prisoners he was always distant and haughty. He took some pride in his profession and boasted of his relationship to President Lincoln's wife, who he thought was "no great shakes" after all.

Dr. Thompson was a South Carolinian, who, to use his own language, "fought the false idea of secession like a devil, stumping his State in favor of the Union, but drifted with the tide." He was a voluble talker, always ready to laugh at a good yarn, and to go one better, but never suffering himself to be outspun. He was attentive to his patients and kind withal, but too reckless to be trustworthy,—a true type of Southern *abandon*. He declared that rum, women, and tobacco had been his ruin, and that his love for them was his only fault. He did not have much confidence in the stability of the Confederacy, and often said that he was "only waiting until he could get back home,"—meaning under the old flag and government.

Dr. Johnson was an individual from upper Georgia, whose medical ability, if he had any, was known only to himself. His latent hatred of the Yankees was extremely bitter, and when his better judgment was warped by intoxication his maudlin abuse was irritating in the extreme and knew no bounds. On one occasion, when in this condition, he came into the dispensary and attempted to help himself to more whiskey from our supply. On being refused he broke out into an abusive tirade against us for daring to offer any objection. He became so loud in his talk as to attract the attention of Mr. Dance and Mr. Robertson, Confederate attachés, who came in and dragged him out on his back, heels foremost, into the rain. He was always fastidiously dressed, silk plug hat and all, but that dragging out gave him a very unpresentable appearance. Schroeder remarked, with an approving nod to the boys, "It is any vay schoost right; he vas so very madt as de debil, und lookedt as if he vouldt knock de headts off from us all. Py Gott! it vas too goot; he bumpdt over the step, schoost likt a sledt, and dot plug hat come down mit a plump-

plump!" The doctor left Andersonville a few days later for a visit home, and he never returned. After my return from prison I became acquainted with Dr. Boyd, the surgeon of an Ohio regiment. He asked me if I ever knew a Dr. Johnson at Andersonville. He said that he had come across a man of that name after the fall of Atlanta,—near Jonesboro, I think,— who said he was at one time in attendance at Andersonville. He told Boyd how inhumanly the men had been treated; how he had lain awake and wept nights thinking of their condition and trying to devise ways to render them even passably comfortable; and how he had spent a fortune of his own in trying to do something for them. He made himself out to be an immaculate saint, and for his great benevolence our officers had put a guard around his property and furnished him a great many supplies from our commissary. I described our Dr. Johnson to him, and the picture fitted his Dr. Johnson so well that we concluded the two were identical. We of Andersonville will always remember him in the ridiculous aspect of "Schroeder's sledt."

Dr. McVeigh, a Virginian, was a tall, easy specimen of "don't-care" activity, whose attenuated form required the support of a cane. He was easy in his manners and cordial in his intercourse with the boys. I knew several of his relations in Ohio, Alfred McVeigh, of Lancaster, a lawyer of some prominence, being one of them. He was as well posted, perhaps, in family history as he was in medicine.

Dr. Shepherd, Sr., was an old man in his dotage, who claimed to have been a surgeon in the United States Army or Navy, which I think likely, as it is a notorious fact that all the old wards of the government who found their way into the rebel army showed the meanest, most vindictive spirits we had to contend with. Like his Satanic Majesty when thrust out of Heaven for treason, they all seemed to want to get up a little realm of their own. The doctor was an imperious, arbitrary old fellow, who, for all I know, may have forgotten more medical lore than an ordinary faculty possesses, but the fact was patent that he had not so retained it as to make it available at Andersonville. He was one of the bitterest men I ever met, yet without any clear reason for being so, and he was the only surgeon in the "outfit" who dressed in out-and-out Confederate uniform.

Wherever you met the old veteran, you would always find him shadowed by his son, Dr. Shepherd, Jr., a man perhaps fifty years of age. A peculiarly marked trait of the younger doctor was his veneration for his father, whom he called "Pap-pay." Wheresoever you met them walking, the son's position was always about a rod in the rear of the old man, which peculiarity might have been accounted for by the fact that he was very deaf, and, lest he should lose the old fellow, as he could not keep his ear on him, it became necessary for him to drop behind, so that he might the more readily keep an eye on him. The old gentleman's solicitude for his son was equally great. My opinion of the younger fellow was that he was daft; but I might have been prejudiced: at any rate, he was an inoffensive person affably inclined, his deafness possibly rendering him a little diffident. He was a hobbyist as a doctor, his constant medical theme being the fine therapeutical effects he had seen in the use of "camphor water," from which we are led to believe that if he did the sick in his ward no particular good, he did them no particular harm. One day, when in a particularly good talking mood, he said to me, tapping a demijohn of camphor water with his cane, "There is one of the finest remedial agents in the world, 'Aqua Camphorate.'" After that we all knew the couple as Dr. Camphor Water and "Pap-pay." They disappeared from Andersonville before I left.

Dr. Roy was a dapper young man who carried with dignity and honor the medical lore of two continents without its seeming to hurt him in the least. He was a true gentleman, who bowed as low to the prisoner in his rags as he did to the officer in his tinsel. He lived about two miles north from Andersonville on a farm. Whether that was his home or not, I cannot say. His knowledge of medicine was theoretically good. I noticed that his opinion was sought after and respected by all the surgeons there. Practically he was a novice, having only taken his diploma some nine months before in Paris, and then run the blockade. He was justly proud of his profession and his professional attainments, and he sought every chance to investigate disease. Most of the diseases at Andersonville, however, though they assumed many forms, were the direct results of starvation and exposure.

There had been other surgeons connected with the prison of whom I have heard the boys speak; one, especially, whom they held in high repute because of his kindness and avowed Union sentiments, but I never met any of them, as they were gone before I was detailed. Several of those whose names I have given kept "bachelor's hall" nearly a mile south of the hospital. A negro who did their cooking told us he had frequently overheard them comparing notes to see which had helped the most Yankees off on any particular day,—meaning how many had died in their wards under their treatment.

Chapter XXXI

The Cemetery

THE manner in which the surgeons performed their duty was to visit their wards every morning, visiting each patient and writing their prescriptions in a book which was then turned over to a ward-master. This officer made a computation of the number of doses, if of roots, barks, or herbs, and we in the dispensary issued them in bulk. It was rather a unique way, but we could do no better, as we had no paper in which we could divide the doses. Every other day we made pills of various kinds, generally about seven thousand in number. This work generally kept us busy until the middle of the afternoon.

The mortality was very heavy during the months of August and September, 1864. The following tabulated record of twenty-four days in the month of September will give a clear idea of the inroads death was making in our ranks, and the skeptical reader may from this evidence incline to believe that my experience and record of life in Southern military prisons is not overdrawn.

SUN.	MON.	TUES.	WED.	THUR.*	FRI.	SAT.	
....	.....	.....	....	105	104	113	-322
94	98	105	98	111	76	96	-681
99	111	78	102	83	100	130	-703
90	95	99	81	60	77	79	-581
						Total....	2287

The record begins on Thursday the 1st of September and ends on the 24th.

131

These numbers were given to me each day by Dorence Atwater, the clerk who kept the death record, as he received them from Mr. Avery, who superintended the burying of the dead at the cemetery, and there can be no mistake as to the numbers and dates, as I have carefully preserved the figures. The greatest number of deaths in one day during the history of the place occurred on Saturday, September 17, when 130 were recorded. When a prisoner died, his name, if known, was written on a slip of paper and pinned to any article of clothing he might have on (which was very little, as the men generally took care of all that could be utilized), and the body was then carried to the dead-house.

From the dead-house the corpses were piled on a wagon like cordwood as long as one could be made to stick on, and were then driven to their last resting-place at a brisk trot. It was a ghastly sight: here an arm and there a leg dangling over the side, and sometimes a head rolling from side to side over the footboard,—twenty-five or thirty bodies in a pile, the skin and bones of what had once been "human forms divine." Each corpse told its own tale of suffering and starvation too plainly to need an interpreter.

"God is not mocked." Who, I wonder, in the Last Day, shall garner the fruits of this harvest of Death? Whose shall be the responsibility? God have mercy on their souls!

The cemetery was nearly half a mile north of the stockade in an abandoned field surrounded by pine woods. It was beautifully located on high ground, inclining, for the greater part, to the northeast, and contained by my actual measurement fourteen and a quarter acres. I also drew a plot of it, a copy of which I gave to Mr. Atwater, who laid it before the War Department at Washington, and who, after the war, was sent, in company with Miss Clara Barton, to superintend placing headstones at the graves and putting the ground in the shape it now is, as a government cemetery. The enclosure as finally arranged contains possibly twice the area that my measurement shows, as my figures cover only the actual space used up to the latter part of January, 1865.

The burying was under the immediate supervision of Alonzo Avery, of Rochester, Minnesota, who was a member of the Ninth Minnesota Volunteers and a prisoner. He had a squad of negro prisoners to assist in digging and filling up the trenches. Much credit is due to Mr. Avery for the masterly and careful manner in which he performed this sad rite for our martyred, heroic dead. His task was an onerous one. From morning till night, rain or shine, he was to be found at his post, using every care in his work that there might be no mistakes.

The manner of burying was to dig long trenches, six feet wide and four feet deep, with a six-foot space between trenches. The bodies were placed side by side without any coffin, and generally naked or nearly so. As each one was placed in position, the paper containing his name was inscribed with the number of his grave and the date of death. At the same time a stake was numbered to correspond, and laid on the ground opposite or above the body, and when the trench was filled this stake was driven in at the head. These papers were handed in each evening to Mr. Atwater, who copied them in the death register, name, number and date, so that if any one should ever wish to remove their friends they could do so. Many were removed after the war, but we believe it was a mistaken kindness to the memory of those noble martyrs to disturb their resting place. They died for their country, seemingly forgotten by her; left, in the hour of their extremity, to breathe their life away surrounded by horrors no pen can tell, themselves an embodiment of suffering even beyond the reach of thought. They were sacrificed upon the altar of their country for a glorious principle. That principle lives, and some subsequent age will erect to these men the monumental shaft their sacrifice demands. Let them rest *there* "on the field of their fame."

The cemetery was on the route to the enclosure where the cattle were slaughtered for the stockade, and the wagon that delivered the dead would run out to the slaughter-pen and bring a return load of beef to the cook-house, a practice not calculated to engender pleasant thoughts when we were eating the beef. The cattle were confined in what had been a cornfield, but they had eaten even the stalks until there was nothing but stubs left. Here they were kept without any other feed than they could grub from the stalks until all were slaughtered. The beef was blue and gluey. I have seen it so much so at times that I could not eat it, after I got outside where I could forage for myself. The butchers used to declare that they always killed those that could not step over a certain number of rails in the fence, because it showed that they could not last much longer. Of course that was only a facetious drive at the starved condition of the beeves, but there was more truth than poetry in it after all. I had the curiosity to go out to the pasture once, and found the "critters" to be but a few removes from the condition mentioned by the butchers.

There was a short time in August and September, 1864, that Captain Wirz was off duty and Lieutenant Davis was in command in Wirz's stead; but the change was not perceptible in any amelioration of the prisoners' condition. Davis was in no way an improvement. A Mr. George Howenstein, who was a prisoner at this time, and who was removed from Andersonville to Millen when Sherman threatened the former place, gave me an instance of Davis's meanness in his own experience in some stockade in which he was confined after leaving Andersonville. He was one day standing looking out at a crack in the fence, when Davis, who was passing along the opposite side of the street, drew his revolver and shot at him, the ball striking close to his head. Not long after this Davis was taken in Ohio playing the role of spy, but he missed his deserts and went free. Our quarters were moved, soon after my being taken out, to a log shanty nearer the hospital enclosure. I suppose it was not deemed wise policy to keep us inside their fortification, especially as their magazine was near our quarters. We liked the change, as we were not so much under the immediate eye of the guards.

Soon afterward Dr. Stevenson developed a very fine place for an extensive hospital. He laid off the grounds and had several wells dug. His plan was to erect a number of long, narrow buildings to extend north and south on each side of a wide street running east and west. At the west end of this street and immediately in front of it, was to be a large two-story building about twenty-five by eighty feet, to be used as dispensary, laundry, storeroom, office, etc., the upper story to be devoted to the use of Confederate attachés. But the work progressed so slowly that up to the time of my departure the main building only had been completed, and we made a second move of the dispensary. It was a very fair specimen of Stevenson's "go-aheadativeness" ; he planned well, but failed in the execution. As soon as I gained sufficient strength I began using the privileges of my parole, seeing pretty thoroughly all that was to be seen within its bounds, sometimes extending it considerably. I traveled around enough to convince me that they were very loose in their camp duties, inasmuch as I never saw a picket or guard on duty outside of the immediate requirements of the stockade and hospital, even when Sherman was making his march to the sea. When a raid seemed imminent there were no precautions taken to prevent a surprise, and a very small force of disciplined troops could have cleaned them out quickly.

Chapter XXXII

The Irishmen of Andersonville

THE news of the Chicago Convention of August 29, 1864, that nominated George B. McClellan for President, and George H. Pendleton for Vice-President, spread through the South like wildfire and was hailed as the harbinger of peace and the independence of the Confederate States. In their platform they declared "the war on the part of the North a failure," and their expression of opposition to its continuance in an aggressive warfare was a cause of general rejoicing through the South.

Often was I asked by officers at Andersonville if I did not think that power in the North (meaning a very heavy element that was organized into a secret society known as the "Knights of the Golden Circle," whose avowed purpose was to throw every obstacle in the way of the successful accomplishment of war measures by the North, and which unfortunately gained the ascendency in the Convention at Chicago and controlled the manufacturing of its platform) would not rise in armed opposition to a further prosecution of the war and prohibit the calling out of any more men or furnishing any further supplies. That that unfortunate expression of sympathy with or for the South may have been made in good faith and with good intentions may be possible; but that it was the means of prolonging the war several months admits of no possibility of doubt: it *did* do so beyond all controversy; for, being behind the scenes, I could see it. Like straws to drowning men it inspired them with new hope and zeal.

How many times did I have the resolution of that Convention regarding the "abandonment of the prisoners to their fate" thrown in my teeth by their ever ready eagerness to seize on anything to vindicate them in their treatment of us. Recruiting-officers would make strong appeals to us to retaliate by uniting with them; preaching the great revulsion that had taken place in the North as the result of Lincoln's tyranny, as instanced by the Chicago Convention. Drawing a picture of our sufferings in consequence of our abandonment by our government with the most brazen audacity, they seemed to forget that though our government had abandoned us, it was not responsible for the direct inhuman treatment we were receiving at their hands from day to day. To ask us to clasp hands across the dark chasm of death that yawned at our very feet was an insult of the basest kind,—an insult to our manhood as well as to our patriotism,—and was so looked upon and received by us and spurned with just indignation.

It was announced that on a certain day an Irish colonel (O'Neal, I think), who commanded an Irish brigade in the Confederate army, would dress his brother Irish in the hospital. True to the appointment he was on hand, and all the convalescent Irish were brought out to hear him orate. I had taken a position astride a pine log close by, to watch the proceeding and hear the speech.

The colonel and his staff presented a fine appearance in nice new suits of Confederate gray, elaborate with tinsel. But the squad that came out to be harangued—ghouls and hobgoblins!—what a magnificent lot to recruit an army from. There was not a man in the outfit that could stand erect without a support; some on crutches, some with walking sticks in each hand, some hopping on one leg, some crawling on hands and knees,—all dirty and ragged, some without hats, some shoeless.

Mounting a stump the colonel extended a cordial greeting to his "Brethren from Erin's Isle." He was a wily dog and had evidently kissed the Blarney stone. He led them away to Hibernia's sunny hills and moonlit lakes, her castle-tipped crags and peaceful vales; then, with his audience, bade adieu to her rocky coast and found an asylum in America. He followed them through the march, the camp, and the battle's din to their present condition, asking them, as brethren, to contrast that condition with his and to see how much better they would be in the Confederate army. He asked them to consider how they had been betrayed by their adopted country, quoting from the resolutions of the "Great Irishmen's Party," as he called it, at Chicago, to show how, in its judgment, their efforts against the South had been pronounced a failure. He begged them to understand that the South had ever been the Irishmen's friend, and that she then stood ready with open arms to receive them in fraternal relationship and to forgive the wrongs they had ignorantly committed against her in the name of Freedom. He offered them a place among their brethren in his brigade, which composed the "flower of the Confederate army"; told how he would give them a large bounty, a suit of clothes, and a month's furlough; and he closed his speech with an invitation for any who wished to avail himself of the opportunity to escape the privations of the prison to give him his name.

After giving a hideous groan, one of them, who appeared to be spokesman by previous appointment, said:

"Colonel, we thank you for the disinterested interest you take in our welfare, but before we'll turn our backs to the flag of our adopted country and enlist under the one you represent, we'll go back to the prison pen and starve to death if needs be; won't we, boys?"

"Yes, by God, we will!" was the response, and back they filed, leaving the colonel to his thoughts. He got one recruit from the prisoners, and he was an American, a keen, shrewd young man, who told me he made the venture as a "forlorn hope," believing he could reach his regiment quicker through the ranks of the Confederate army than through the walls and vigilance of a Confederate prison. Possibly he was right; the contingency was extreme in either case.

CHAPTER **XXXIII**

A Prison Dandy

ABOUT this time I became conscious of presenting an appearance of *abandon* in dress. My wardrobe would not bear inspection; in fact, it was a little the worse for wear, and I would have to spruce up a little before I dare venture to interview any of the families living within the circuit of my parole. I had discovered that there were several. My hat, which was a light-colored fur and low crowned, had reached the last stages of disintegration. The top bore some resemblance to the ill-fitting lid of a coffee-pot. My hair protruded all around, giving me something the appearance of a Comanche warrior. My blouse had long since ceased to be useful as a covering to nakedness; the holes in my shirt, unfortunately, corresponding with those in the blouse; and my trousers,— well, the least said about them the better; suffice it to say they did the best they could. But my good genius came to the rescue.

An old fellow who was choring around for the "Johnnies," while in a sleepy inebriated state one day, dropped a coal of fire from his pipe among some bedding, burning several white-duck ticks so as to spoil them for mattresses. I happened to be standing near when Mr. Dance took charge of them, and asked him if he would not let me have one to make a shirt and pair of trousers.

"Well," he said laughingly, taking a visual inventory of my outfit; "I think they would do as much good in that way as any other," and then he told me to take what would be sufficient.

We had a man helping us in the dispensary, named W. A. White, a tailor. He cut me out a shirt and pair of trousers and showed me how to put them together. With his assistance I soon had the ticks converted into an excellent outfit. I darned up the holes in my hat and drew the edges together, washed out the grease with a little aqua-ammonia, and then pressed it over the bottom of a crock until it dried. It made quite a respectable hat under the circumstances. Mr. Dance complimented me on my general improvement, saying he had no idea there were such possibilities in an old burnt straw tick.

Meantime Dr. Karr, in one of his predatory raids at the hospital, confiscated a part of a caddy of tobacco in the act of being transmitted through the lines. This he brought into our department and told us to take charge of it. Now, anything that came into our hands we felt at liberty to dispense for the needs of the sick; consequently, when we found a patient who we thought would be benefited by tobacco, we prescribed it for him, or allowed him to prescribe for himself, until it was all gone. I gave one of the boys at the cook-house a plug or two, which he appreciated so highly that he gave me an extra blouse he had. This completed my outfit and put me in quite a presentable shape—for a prisoner.

Our dispensary was the only place where medicines could be procured within a number of miles of Andersonville, and citizens sometimes came, with orders from headquarters, to draw from us for family use. One afternoon three ladies, having such an order, came up on horseback. As they had not sufficient bottles of their own, and we had none to spare, in order to supply them, it was necessary, when they all wanted the same thing, to put it all into one bottle. They were laughing about it and wondering what they could do in order to get all they wanted. I suggested that they would have to let the one who lived most convenient to the other two take all the medicine to her house. Then she could get up a quilting-bee some afternoon and invite the other two, who in the mean time could hunt up spare bottles and have them in readiness to divide the medicine and make a social visit too. They thought that a happy solution of the problem. They were very pleasant and sociably inclined, and we joked back and forth while I was getting the things ready. To use a phrase of the country, "we had a rale good time." Lady customers were a little out of the common order, and we brought our rusty social etiquette into use in the best manner possible, doing the agreeable the best we remembered how. Over three years as a soldier— and fifteen months of that in rebel prisons—made us a little awkward, I expect; but I got them off in good shape, with a merry "Good evening" and a "Call again, ladies!"

My friend Schroeder, who all this time had been complacently smoking his pipe at the back end of the room, now springing to his feet, and bringing his fist down on the board counter with such emphasis as to make everything rattle, exclaimed, "Py Gott, Hydte! Dat vas schust first-rate done. I've been sitting here schust vatching you schoaking mit dose ladies like old friendts, und helping dem out from dare difficulties mit dare division. You maked dem tink you vas any vay schust right, und you bowat dem oudt schust so good as any pody, mit your vite shirt und pandts. It vas any how goot done. Dose ladties remembers you for dat,—hey!—vhat?"

A few days after this I was called into the surgeon's office to assist in making out a requisition for more medicine, and was busily at work filling out a blank, when a small boy came bouncing into the room."

"Well, Bub," said Dr. Stevenson, "what will you have?"

"Nothin'; I'm looking for Mr.—*there he is*," —making for my desk without further explanation and coming down to business with, "Say, Mister, mother wants you to come out to our house to-morrow night."

"Why, my boy," I said, "I guess you've made a mistake in the person, haven't you?"

"No I hain't, neither; hain't you the man that stays over where the medicine is?"

"Yes."

"I thought yer was," he said gleefully.

By this time I could see quite a comical expression on the doctor's face, and a merry twinkle in his eye, as well as a look of expectation on the faces of the others present.

"Well," I said, laughing at the ludicrous outlook, "who is your mother, my boy?"

"Why, Mrs. Stubbs!"

"Stubbs," said I, more than ever puzzled. "Stubbs?—who's Mrs. Stubbs?"

"Why," said he, looking as though he doubted my veracity, "don't you know her?"

I could see the doctor shaking behind a paper he was holding before his face, and a broad smile diffusing itself over the countenances of the rest, as he said, in a kind of doubtful voice,—

"I thought you knowed her? Why," he continued, "don't you know them women you put up medicine for the other day, and told them to get up a quilting, so's they could divide the medicine?"

"Oh yes," I said.

"Well, that's mother—one of them women was; and she's going to have the quilting and says you must be sure and come out to it, will you?"

I sent the lady my compliments and told the boy to tell his mother I was a prisoner and not allowed such liberty,—it would be impossible for me to be present.

The little fellow really looked disappointed as he closed the door. I heard him say, "He can't come." Then I learned that there was a young lady on horseback at the door; she was to do the inviting, the boy having been sent in only to call me out. She rode off without my getting to see her. Finishing my work in a few moments, I went out and found Schroeder pacing back and forth in a kind of dog-trot, his hands clasped behind him. I knew something disturbed him.

"Py Gott!" he said, as soon as I appeared, "you schust madt a mistake dot time in not coming oudt to see dot young lady. Py shingo, she vas any vay—vot you calls dem—goot looks?" "Handsome?" I suggested.

"Dot's it, py Gott, Hydt; I almost did envy you, und vhen the boy saidt 'He can't come' she shakdt her headt und lookdt so madt as dunder. What for you not come oudt?"

"What for," I said, laughing, "you not calldt me oudt? The boy did not tell me she was on hand."

"Dot damndt poy, he any vay scheated you; dat is all—vhat!"

CHAPTER XXXIV

In Society

I MADE up my mind I would see that Stubbs family and apologize to the young lady for my seeming rudeness, and the opportunity came very soon. Mr. Hunt, having burst the soles of his boots, asked me to accompany him to a certain Widow Smith's, who lived in the area of our circle, and who, he had been informed, had some sole leather to sell (home-tanned leather was a very common thing through the South). We traveled through the pine woods and chinkapin bushes along foot or bridle paths, as they called them. There being few well-defined roads, more by good luck than by any skill in woodcraft, we came onto the clearing with its double log house. As we passed up to the porch the old lady came to meet us with a hearty "How do you do?" extending her hand with the salutation. I recognized one of my drug women, and after passing the courtesies of the hour and "taking cheers" I asked her if she got her medicines home all right.

"Oh, laws yes; after a spell and a heap of huntin' after bottles to put the stuff in. We was powerful glad to get them too, it 'pears like everything of that kind's gettin' so scarce in the country, it's hard to get hold of any mo'. The wah's done taken it all, 'pears like. We just had to laugh all the way home that day when we got to thinkin' about it. We thought you-all would think we was funny women, to come there with baskets to get turpentine and camphor and sich things in; but you know times is not what they was no way befo' the wah."

We found the old lady was true metal and had not taken kindly to the new order of things. Making the object of our visit known, she said she had sold all the leather she could spare, but that we could get all we wanted at Mrs. Stubbs's.

"You know her," she said, turning to me; "she was over to your place that day."

"Yes; how far does she live from here?"

"About two miles."

"In which direction?"

"Well, you just follow that path beyant the fence around to the left like. You'll cross one or two paths comin' into it, but you keep right on in that one till you sight the bridge across the creek onto the big road. She lives a sight from the bridge up in the timber like."

We did not expose our ignorance regarding the apparently matter-of-course distance, "a sight." After eating heartily from a bucketful of black haws which she placed before us, we bade the old lady good evening and hurried back to camp to be in time for roll-call. The last thing we heard as we crossed the fence was the old lady's invitation, for the fourth time repeated, to "call again."

We were in a dilemma regarding the leather, as to reach Stubbs's would require several extensions of our mile radius; and though we were not at all afraid of molestation by guards, we did not like to take the chances of a return to the stockade. I was not altogether a disinterested party on the leather question, as Hunt had promised me that if I could find the soles he would furnish me a part of the boot-tops to renovate my shoes and fit them for the winter. So next morning I went to Mr. Montgomery, chief clerk in Dr. Stevenson's office, an Alabamian and a very worthy gentleman, and called his attention to my shoes, the soles and tops of which were held together by thongs and held onto my feet by straps tied around under the hollow of the foot and over the instep.

"Now," I said, "Hunt has proposed that if I can get the sole leather he will share his boot-tops with me, and we will renew our understanding, which you can see for yourself is somewhat shattered and unstable, really needing a little patching up."

"Well, yes," he said, pointing to my big toe, which had wiggled out between the thongs, "that looks as though it needed housing, truly."

I told him I had found where I could get some leather to remedy the evil, but to reach it would necessitate my going beyond the limits of my parole, as it was nearly four miles out.

"Now," I said, "similarly situated and like shod, what would you do in the case?"

"Well," he said, "I don't know really, if put to the practical test; but I think I'd go for the leather."

"Then suppose I do so and am taken and put in the stockade for disobeying orders,—what then?"

"Well, send me word," he said, "and I'll get you out again. If you can find the leather and be back by night, go for it; I'll agree to be responsible for your actions."

Turning around to Mr. Dance, who attended to calling rolls and was listening to our conversation, I said, "You hear that, do you?"

"Yes," he replied; "all right; hope you'll succeed."

Hunt having sprained his ankle the evening before, he could not walk very well, and I found that I would have to go alone or get some one else to accompany me. Oyen, the Norwegian, said he would go after we attended to surgeon's call; which done, we started in search of Mrs. Stubbs. Following the path around the north side of the stockade, we struck the trail that led us by Mrs. Smith's, following it, according to the old lady's instructions, "around to the left like," paying no attention to the several paths that crossed or led off at right angles. We were not long in sighting the bridge through an open space among the trees.

We had rather a pleasant walk beneath "the whispering pines," which had already begun to drop their cones until our path was strewn with them. The soughing of the wind through the tops of the pines, the crisp snapping of the cones under our feet, the buoyancy of the pure December air, and the utter absence of any sound or object indicative of prison life, seemed to create a new life in us. Now and then we would stop and feast from a bush of winter huckleberries, or pick the nuts from the chinkapin burrs that grew near our pathway. Oyen, too, seemed to catch inspiration and buoyancy of spirits from our surroundings, and gave me an idea of his Norwegian home and life with a vividness peculiarly his own. He was a splendid fellow, finely developed physically and mentally, and had been educated at Christiana for the profession of druggist. His mind was well cultured and stored, and, so far as he could command the English language, he was an entertaining talker.

Thus occupied, we walked along until, as I said before, we sighted the bridge. We then took a survey of the country, so far as the nature of the roads would admit, to find a practical demonstration or solution of the old lady's measure of distance. "A sight from the bridge," "off to the left like," on the rising ground, we could see through the trees a neat, white, frame cottage, which we naturally concluded filled the bill, and toward this we made our way. We were met at the gate by one of the most formidable looking dogs I think I ever saw, who came bounding down to the gate to dispute our passage, dragging by his collar, and with apparent ease, a long chain of massive proportions. A lady came to the door and called him away. I recognized in her another of my drug women, but not the one of whom we were in quest. We had not properly estimated the distance of "a sight." Pointing us to a house visible through the trees, one we had not discovered before, she said, "That's the place you want to find." To reach it we crossed the "big road" the old lady had mentioned. The bridge was plainly visible from it, and so also was the house, and from this we inferred that the probable meaning of "a sight" was that the object to be sighted was in plain view of a given point.

We were not long in reaching the mansion, which we found to be an unpainted frame house with an "L" forming the almost ever-present open space through the middle, which on inquiry I found was used as the dining-room during the summer heat. We were met at the door by Mrs. Stubbs herself, the third, of course, of my visitors, who extended a cordial greeting and invited us in.

"Ah," she said, turning to me, "you should have been here Wednesday night. We were very much disappointed that you could not come. We got up the quilting as you suggested, and we wanted you to enjoy it so much,"—which I told her I certainly should have done under more favorable circumstances, but that I was so unfortunately situated that my time was not always at my disposal, nor my wishes to be gratified, though I assured her that her invitation met my approval and merited my sincerest thanks, which I hoped she would then and there accept.

"Possibly," I said, "you were not aware at the time that I was a prisoner."

"Oh yes," she said, "we knew you were a prisoner, but had no idea there would be any objections made to your attending our party. We never even thought of it, and supposed it would be pleasant for you and that you would come."

I then said that I owed an apology to her daughter, who came to give me the invitation, for not seeing her that morning, as I was not aware, until after she had gone, that she was there at all, the boy not having made it known to me. I found her very ready to lay aside all malice and to accept my explanation. We spent several hours very pleasantly with them. Oyen, I found, was very much abashed, so I managed to give Mrs. Stubbs a hint that he was a foreigner and his lack of knowledge of English embarrassed him somewhat. When she learned his nationality she took quite an interest in him and drew him out in such a way as to put him entirely at his ease.

We found that although Mr. Stubbs was a guard at Andersonville, his family were true to the old flag and very strong in their faith as to the ultimate triumph of the Northern army. This faith, I found, was based upon what she called her father's prophecy, which at my request she gave me. I will endeavor to give it as nearly as I can in the language she used, though there was a deep conviction of the supernatural evident in her mind, and a solemnity and pathos in her voice as she narrated it, that I cannot possibly transmit to paper, which will rob it of a great deal of its force and beauty.

The summer and fall of 1860 were remarkable for the brilliancy and long continuance of nightly displays of the aurora borealis, extending from the north and spreading over the whole heavens in crimson waves and brilliant flashes of electric light, grand and impressive in its constant variance, and well calculated to awaken awe in the minds of those who sought for "signs and wonders in the heavens." To these phenomena the lady referred, and her faith seized upon her old father's prophecy with a firmness that could not be shaken; and, as her faith seemed likely soon to end in fruition, I would not for the world question her right to view it in the light she did, especially as it threw around the memory of her father a beautiful sacredness.

"You remember," she said, "the summer before the war, what strange red lights used to appear of nights, spreading all over the sky like clouds of blood and haloes of glory. Down here they seemed to come from the north and south both, and to meet in mid-heaven, rolling and waving back and forth, sometimes long tongues of light shooting out like swords, sometimes bright clouds bursting out like smoke, sometimes like flags floating and waving in the air. We watched them night after night, and talked about them so much as to excite father, who was lying in that bed. He was very old and had lain there for months, not being able to get up at all unless assisted. One night we had all left the room to watch the clouds, which were unusually active. All of us were out in the yard, when who should we see standing in the door but father, intently gazing on them too. He astonished us as much as the clouds did. 'Ah,' he said, so solemn like, 'it is a warning from God, we are going to have war, a long bloody war. There will be hard fighting. For a long time it will be in doubt, but finally the North will overcome the South and all be right again, but it will end slavery and the South be like the North.' He then walked back to his bed and never got out of it again until he died, which was not long after. Yes," she said, "we knew there was going to be war, and it has come. We know, too, how it will end. The North will conquer."

We wished from the bottom of our hearts that Mrs. Stubbs's hopes might soon be realized. Her daughter I found to be all that Schroeder had pictured her. Vivacity marked her conversation, and her eyes fairly flashed as she dwelt on the manner in which the South had precipitated the war, rushing with blind madness into secession without waiting to see what Mr. Lincoln would do, just as if the North had not as much right to elect him President if they could as they had to elect Mr. Breckenridge if they could.

"There's South Carolina," she continued, "she always was a mean, stuck-up little State, more bother than she was worth. They are always too fast over there, it appears, as though they think they are just a little better than anybody else and all the rest of the country ought to bow to them and do just what they want them to. They have always been trying to kick up a fuss about something and trying to kick out of the traces. I often think the best thing the North could do with her, after the war is over, would be to get all the Irish in the country, with their carts and wheelbarrows, and dump the whole State out into the Atlantic Ocean, and it would not take them long to do it either. It's only a little three-sided fair any way."

I felt very much like giving her three rousing cheers. As it was, I thanked her, in behalf of the North, for her sound sense, good judgment, and sympathy. Her idea of the little Nullifier was very correct and her criticisms just, and her final disposition of the vexed triangle had the merit of originality at any rate.

There was sitting by, during our conversation, a lady who had refugeed from before Sherman's army. She was not so inclined to lay blame upon the South for secession, but she did not have much to say either way. She had vacated her place before the army reached her, and, not knowing whether she had a home remaining or not, the doubt was worrying her.

Having made the object of our visit known and secured the leather at eleven dollars a pound, Confederate money, we prepared to return to camp, but Mrs. Stubbs would have us remain to tea, which we were not loth to do. Long months had passed since I had had the pleasure of eating a lady's cooking from porcelain dishes, and served by a lady's hand. What a flood tide of home memories it awakened! We were delighted with our hostess and those surrounding the board, the pleasant prattle of little children, and all connected with the occasion. Certainly the freedom of the whole afternoon was calculated to make us feel as if we were under the influence of an enchantment as great as, and certainly more real than, ever characterized the city of the great caliphs in the "Arabian Nights." Such circumstances as this are the bright rays that occasionally penetrated the gloom of prison life, and we love to recall them, cast as they are upon the black background of Andersonville stockade.

CHAPTER XXXV

Captain Wirz

WE returned to camp by the route on the other (or south) side of Sweet Water Creek, in order that our whole afternoon's association might be one of new scenes and surprises. We reached camp just in time for roll-call, and in all our walk had not seen a rebel soldier to have hindered us from extending our walk to Sherman's army; but we knew the Andersonville idea of justice, when a Yankee was concerned, sufficiently to do no act that would bring us under condemnation or even suspicion.

We had rather an amusing instance of punishment under suspicion soon after I was taken out of the stockade. We had received an invoice of medicine, including a number of quart bottles of alcohol. These we had set on a shelf overhead, across one end of the shanty, and then had piled a number of boxes underneath for seats and bunks. On the day of the big rain I have mentioned before, the attendants from the hospital were storm-stayed and remained several hours. Next day, having occasion to use some of the alcohol, we found quite a number of bottles had been abstracted from the shelf,—whether by the boys the day before, or at what time, we could not tell; but as the boys occupied those boxes suspicion naturally rested on them, and on Mr. Reid, the druggist of whom I have spoken, and White the tailor. Reid had excited suspicion by being a little wandering in his talk, indicating "wit out and liquor in."

Wirz made things blue for a while, and then had them all put in the stocks until he had time to investigate more fully and find out who the really guilty ones were. He kept them in the stocks one whole day in the hot sun. The theft was traced to Reid and several of the nurses, who were sent to the stockade—or "hell," as they termed it. The others proved their innocence and went clear, but they had undergone a pretty severe punishment after all. White declared it was so hot in the stocks that he sweat until the sand was wet under him.

Not long after this circumstance we moved the drugs to a shanty nearer the hospital and outside the fortifications. The new location being in the timber, and nearer the creek, swarms of mosquitoes came out of the damp bottom to feast upon us. We used to burn sulphur to drive them out of the hut, which seemed a favorite rallying-place for them after dark, when the humming noise could be heard several rods away like bees swarming. The only way I could get any sleep was to take a bed sack and get into it feet foremost and let the open end fall over my head. In this way I could get the better of them and sleep quite comfortably.

The trees along the stream were festooned with long pendant moss, which gave them a weird appearance and formed lurking-places for myriads of insects, lizards, and small snakes. The vegetation was dense. Magnolias grew abundantly, and their deep green, shiny leaves, with a velvety brown under-surface, were handsome to see. There were also long creeping vines, reaching sometimes to the tops of the highest trees, with no perceptible variation in size and without a branch. Their wood resembled rattan; in fact the natives called it rattan. Briar roots were also abundant, as were laurel, cane reeds, and a species of palm with wide-spreading leaves like our palm fans. The laurel and sweet-briar roots were a bonanza to the boys, as from them they made pipes, rings, and other wooden trinkets. The roots of the cane reeds made handsome pipe-stems. These trinkets were in demand as relics and brought them tobacco and sometimes food. Some of the pipes were marvels of workmanship considering the implements with which they were wrought. Wild indigo grew in abundance. From this the natives manufactured their own indigo, by macerating the bruised leaves and plants and then evaporating the water. I have seen some very fine specimens of indigo made in this way.

Early in December they got the main building of Stevenson's plan completed, and we made another move with the drug department; one which gave us very good quarters, though we had to make a log heat outside to warm by. After Captain Wirz returned from his leave of absence, he made his headquarters near the station, but came over to Stevenson's quarters every few days. He was generally very communicative among his subordinates, and, being rather a loud talker with a peculiarly harsh voice, we could overhear his conversation. He and several of the attachés were one day in the supply-room enjoying some apples and other delicacies they had there, which seemed to open up the old fellow's humor, and he related the discovery, by his "gals," of a Yankee trick. He had married a widow in the South, and his "gals" were her two daughters,—his stepdaughters. It was a peculiarity of his nervous temperament to be always in motion, either walking back and forth with jerky steps, crossing and recrossing his legs, swinging his arms, or in some way keeping up a muscular motion. On this particular occasion he stopped suddenly in his walking, brought his fist down with considerable force, and exclaimed:

"Py Chesus Christ! one of my gals last night discovered one Got-damt Yankee trick."

"How so, Cap'n?"

"Vell, don'd you see, she was reading over from de letters out from the box of de prisoners, don'd you see, und pretty quick she comes to one what don'd be written on at all. 'Vhat the idea is?' she said to me, 'dat dis one don'd be written on no more. Dot Yankee makes one gread meestake mit dose.' But py und py, pretty quick, she goes to de candle mit it, to see off not de ink be poor, und py chance she looked it drough, and it vas shust so full mit writing as it could be. 'Ho, yo! vhat fer ting is dot for writing?' she says. From dot I takes holdt mit him, und looks, und vhat you dinks. Py Chesus Christ, it vas all over written mit one Got-damt paby's milk."

To the captain the discovery of the trick by the shrewdness of his stepdaughter was next to marvellous. To me, however, it was altogether marvellous as to how the poor fellow in the stockade procured breast-milk,—or "paby's milk" as he termed it. But Wirz did not seem to consider the absurdity of the thing in his admiration for the shrewd discovery.

He had some very bad ulcers on his limbs, of a character that required mercurial treatment, and he usually came to the dispensary after an ointment that we prepared from simple cerate and calomel rubbed together. As I was one day mixing him a portion he said,—

"Make him strong mit the calomel."

Being told it was already of more than officinal strength, he said,—

"Py Gott! I cares not for dat; I takes de law into my own handts. Make him two-three times as strong."

I then mixed it as stiff with mercury as I could, which seemed to please him, as he exclaimed:

"Hi-yi, dat is goot! Dat is right."

The next time he came, he said:

"Make him shust like dot last; it vas shust right."

As I have said, it was a mystery to me how those fellows secured so many luxuries to eat, unless it was in the way I have intimated—from boxes sent to the boys from home. They always seemed to have plenty for ordinary demands. Our men in the hospital were suffering from lack of vegetable food to combat scurvy. It would have been far more potent in arresting disease than any medical treatment that could have been used. The more I studied the nature of the diseases that were producing such sad mortuary results, the more I was convinced they were the direct result of scurvy, under an assumed garb, in four-fifths of the cases; but the fare issued was calculated to aggravate rather than to combat that disease, and was at no time really fit for a sick prisoner to eat.

One will frequently hear it asserted (as I have many times), in regard to the matter of food, that the authorities gave the best they had and did all they could for the men; that if vegetables could have been procured they would have been issued. This I know to be an utter falsehood. On one occasion four or five wagonloads of just such vegetable food was brought in by the citizens as a donation to the sick. But the authorities would not permit it to be sent inside under the supervision of the donors, but took charge of it themselves, and kept charge of it until it was all consumed by them; and, further, the citizens were informed that if they brought any more it would be confiscated, as they had food enough to feed the prisoners on and would attend to issuing it themselves.

Then, too, we who were on parole did not suffer for such things, if we could muster means to buy with from citizens. No; these are facts, coupled with the history of the place, that ought to be known and fairly represented to the world, from the fact that it lifts the responsibility of the brutality practiced from the South as a people, and places it upon the authorities, where it belongs. These evidences go to show that the citizens would have given us far different treatment and deplored the condition of things at Andersonville, and they should have their meed of praise. True, there were those among the citizens who would have preferred seeing us all starve to death, but they were a very small minority.

I remember an encounter with one of the latter class, which occurred in the case of myself and a Mr. Clark, who assisted for a short time at the dispensary. He and I arranged to go out one day and try to buy a chicken or two. We went around west of Wirz's quarters, west of the railroad, a direction in which we had never gone before (and I might add, nor since), striking a trail that led off through the brush. We finally brought up at a log shanty right in the woods. Clark being in the lead, I stopped on the fence, near the door, while he went up to make inquiries. A knock brought a woman of Amazonian aspect to the front, who, in answer to his question for chickens, said:

"No, we don't got no chickens hyer."

Then, surveying him from head to foot, she asked:

"Mister, ain't you-all Yanks?"

"Yes."

"Wall," she said, jerking an ugly-looking gun from the rack over the door, "you-all just git away from hyer in a hurry, will yer?"

We got. It was something like the story of Mark Twain's burglar: "You git?" "You bet!"

"Phew," said Clark, as we struck into the brush, "ain't she peppery, though!"

We struck better luck near by and secured chickens, eggs, and butter and went back rejoicing. We were getting these for Christmas. It was amusing and yet sad sometimes to hear the boys in the stockade tell how they would like to sit down and eat a dish of some particular kind their good old mother used to prepare for them when boys; or to hear them relate their dreams of sitting down to a meal of good things at home, with Mother pouring the coffee and Father asking questions about the war. How often have I myself been disappointed by waking up just as I was about to enjoy a feast of good things; and these dreams were so real apparently as to be really provoking and tantalizing. Their vanishing seemed like being torn from all the association of home,—every one rendered a thousand times dearer by contrast with our present surroundings.

I have seen fathers fast nearing the eternal home, upon whom the seal of death was fixed with actual certainty, in whose bosoms hope had died and death seemed welcome as a friendly release from torture. I have seen the silent tears coursing down their emaciated, dirt-grimed cheeks, as they gazed on the worn pictures of their little ones soon to be orphans. As I noted the fond, earnest, devouring, expectant look, as they held the picture in their trembling hands before them, their ears seeming to catch the sounds, "Papa!" "Father!"—I have been led to think that by some unseen psychological power the souls of both father and little ones were brought together in those extreme moments. While such a father fills a prisoner's grave at Andersonville, his place perhaps marked "Unknown," it is well that obscurity draws a veil over his suffering, and that his loved ones know not the cup he drank to the dregs, nor the tale that is told in the words: "Father died in Andersonville."

CHAPTER XXXVI

A Flogging

THERE were several negroes of both sexes employed around the hospital headquarters in various capacities, one of whom, an old negress whom they called "Aunt Sue," whose gray head and wrinkled features indicated an age not less than sixty years, had incurred the displeasure of one of the semi-officials, whose insulted dignity could be righted only by giving her a "strapping." As negro-whipping was an operation I had read of (with some doubts), but never witnessed, I managed to get a position to witness the ceremony without being seen myself. They took her into a cellar, under the south end of the building, where she was made to squat down and draw up her clothing so as to denude her person from the waist down. They then made her clasp her hands under her knees, and in this position she was tied with a cord so that she could not move. They then turned her down, with her face and knees on the ground, thus throwing her under parts up. One of the men then took the whip, which consisted of a leather strap about eighteen inches or two feet long, cut tapering from an inch to two inches in width and fastened by the narrow end to a handle about an inch in diameter and near twelve inches long. Taking a position behind her, the flogger raised the whip directly over his head as high as the ceiling of the cellar would admit. With the handle grasped in both his hands, he brought down the lash with all the power he could give it, in a direction parallel with the spinal column of the culprit. Limited as his efforts were by the height of the cellar, each blow made the old woman groan and her flesh

153

quiver. In this way she received thirteen lashes that I counted,—and I had seen enough; how many more they gave her, if any, I cannot say, but the old lady was off duty, confined to her quarters, for several days. The person who handled the lash was a young man dandily inclined, who said to me, in referring to the case,—

"I would rather whip a niggah than eat any time."

I told him I thought it a barbarous, uncalled-for mode of punishment.

"Well," he said, squirting out a mouthful of tobacco-juice, "I suppose it does look hard to you-all, with your Northern education and prejudice, but I tell you it's the only way we can get along with the cusses, and we are used to it; so we don't mind it down here, and if we don't strap them occasionally they become lazy and saucy and good for nothing. I've whipped lots of 'em; it's the only way to keep them under."

Chapter XXXVII

Prisons North and South

A CONFEDERATE officer who had but a short time before returned from Johnson's Island, where he had been a prisoner, made a visit to Andersonville and spent several days "doing" the place,—I suppose to satisfy a morbid curiosity, as he seemed to have no more particular business than to look around. In conversation with him one day I inquired as to the treatment they received at Johnson's Island.

"Well," he said, "we were treated very well there, aside from the knowledge that we were under guard and consequently confined against our will."

"Did you get plenty to eat, and food of good quality?"

"Oh yes; we had plenty of the substantials and of the best quality,—in fact had nothing to complain of except the bread."

"Bread!" I exclaimed in astonishment, "didn't they give you good bread and plenty of it?"

"Oh yes, enough,—too much; but they did not give us any but that damned flour bread, and I didn't like it; if they had only fed us on corn bread we would have been all right."

I told him I understood that they abused the prisoners there and practiced a great many cruelties toward them.

"That is a mistake," said he. "If we behaved ourselves I never heard of any one being mistreated. Our quarters were good, and accommodations ample for our comfort."

I suppose he was not aware that I was a Yankee and thus gave me his views without reserve.

I had a similar conversation with others who had been confined in Camp Chase and other places, and they told substantially the same story. They all looked in good condition, thus thoroughly evidencing their good treatment.

How different from our treatment in the South. To me it was a proud contrast, — heaven and hell in juxtaposition. Rats and mice were luxuries which our boys in the hospital were glad to get, and were sought after with eagerness. This is no fancy picture. Let me relate a circumstance in which I was particularly interested.

A dog that had followed a citizen into camp missed his master and begged quarters with us, which we extended to him. He stayed with us several days, seemingly so well pleased and contented that I was surprised to miss him one day very suddenly, but supposed that his master had returned and he had followed him away. Next morning, however, when Mr. Hunt returned from duty in his ward in hospital, he said to me:

"Hyde, where is your 'purp'?"

I told him I supposed Yankee fare was too much for his stomach and he had vamosed the ranch in search of something better.

"Not much vamosed," he said; "those fellows who took the medicine down yesterday coaxed him into the hospital, and he wasn't there long before they jerked his coat quicker than you could say Jack Robinson, and had his meat roasting, frying, boiling, and every other way; and not only that, but they dug up his entrails to-day, cleaned them up, and made soup out of them. Here," he said, "is what is left to tell the tale," — and he handed me a claw and a tooth. "There is your 'purp'; what do you think of him?"

Alas, poor dog, his love for the Yanks and their love for him proved his ruin. And now I will follow this with one more instance.

A Dr. Brown, who was taken out of the stockade some days after I was, told me of an instance in his experience while inside the enclosure. During the hard rain that caused a breach in the palisade he was standing near the break on the east side and saw something swim in from below. Seizing a piece of driftwood he plunged into the flood and succeeded in killing and securing it. He said its skin was like an eel's, but it had no fins and a suspiciously snakelike though blunt tail. Having nothing else to do he skinned it, and the flesh looked so tempting, and the pangs of hunger were so great, that he concluded to cook and eat it. So he dressed it nicely, cut it into thin slices, and fried it, eating heartily of it himself and giving part to his chums, telling them it was an eel. They praised it highly and soon cleared the platter. From his description I suppose it was a water-moccasin, a venomous snake abundant in the swamps and streams of the South. That, however, would not affect the flesh, and I doubt not it made them a royal feast à l'Africaine.

This Dr. Brown, by the way, deserves more than simple passing notice. He was what might justly be styled a peculiar person,—in fact, to me he was an enigma. Perhaps sixty years of age, of swarthy complexion, rather below medium height, with a high forehead and rather heavy brows overarching keen black eyes, he had a peculiar shuffling gait, generally walking with his hands clasped behind his back, and his eyes bent on the ground, which gave him a decidedly stoop-shouldered appearance. He claimed to belong to a New York regiment, but I had my doubts as to his belonging to the army unless it was as a correspondent.

We were together some four months, but with all my study of the man, our walks and talks together, I could not come to any satisfactory conclusion as to who or what he was. By birth he was an Englishman, no doubt, as he claimed. He gave his name as Walter John G. Brown, asserting also his claim to an hereditary title of which, by foul play, he had been deprived. Certain it was that the authorities at Andersonville stood in awe of him and held him in such respect that he had about his own way with them. They did not resent any slur he might hurl at them, and sometimes he scored them deeply.

"Blarst your bloody lies," I heard him say to some of them. "Do you remember the letter in the London 'Times' of [such a date], regarding your blarsted Confederacy; you'll get a worse showing up than that if you don't look out." He threatened to report them to the Court of St. James, or to appeal, as an Englishman, to the Minister at Washington. He certainly impressed his jailers with the idea that he was some one more than ordinary, and I confess to about the same impression.

He was a voluble talker, words dropping from his lips with the easy flow of waters from a fountain, and, though very cockneyed in expression, yet so full of melody that, once you heard, you were bound to listen to the end. He claimed to have been apothecary to Queen Victoria and on intimate terms with Prince Albert, who, with the Queen, used frequently to come to his apartment for an iced lemonade. He wore a diamond ring, the avowed gift of Jenny Lind, and claimed that he had once loaned the young Napoleon a crown as they were enjoying a friendly bout at billiards. "Blarst 'is bloody heyes," was the termination of this story; "'e never returned it."

He was with the British fleet when they bombarded Cape Town, Africa, as assistant to the surgeon-general accompanying the expedition,—Liston, I think. He had quite an extensive diary, closely written in phonetic characters, from which he would sometimes read me extracts couched in the most beautiful language, rich both in description and in logic. I loved to listen to his conversation. Dr. Thompson (himself, as I have said, an excellent talker), after sitting by and hearing him talk, said to him:

"Dr. Brown, I'll give you a thousand dollars a year to come and live with me in South Carolina, just to have you talk to me."

Even the keeper of the bloodhounds held him in reverence and promised to give him a "purp" as soon as it got old enough to wean. Having an invitation to tea with one of the attachés who had his family there, and from some cause not liking to go alone, he gave me a left-handed invitation to go along, which I accepted with pleasure, being always ready for something new and novel and not caring for consistency then. We had a very pleasant tea-party, plenty of fruit sauce and knickknacks, which I had the irreverence to suppose were donations from some poor prisoner's box drawn upon for the occasion. As we were returning to our quarters he said, "Mr. 'yde, the gift of language is one of the greatest gifts of God to man; by it man can be led captive and locks turned aside." I confess I could not tell whether the man was a magnificent lunatic, or what; but he was certainly a success at whatever he was. Unfortunately he had a weakness for "tincture of 'ops" and imbibed pretty freely at times, to "drive away blue devils," but even when intoxicated he was as immobile as the sphinx.

He came to me one day in the latter part of November with the intelligence that in a day or two a squad of sick were to be sent north, and if he had some money he could get away with them. I gave him the money Felix had given me, telling him to try it on, and, if he succeeded in making it, to write to my folks and let them know I was yet alive. He was full of gratitude and gave me his I.O.U. for fifteen dollars, payable at Orelia, Canada, where he claimed his wife was. But, like young Napoleon's crown, "he's got it yet." Next day he left Andersonville and I never saw him again.

To my surprise, after my return home, my brother asked me who that person was that wrote him regarding having left me in a very critical condition in Andersonville, advising my instant removal by special exchange, giving it as his opinion that I could not live three months, and that he would return to Charleston soon and have me released. I read the letter which my brother had preserved, and found it dated at Fortress Monroe, just one week from the time I bade him adieu at Andersonville. An effort was made, through the Congressman of the District, to get me out by special exchange, but it failed, owing to multiplicity of red tape.

CHAPTER XXXVIII

The Bottle of Turpentine

SUCCESSFUL escapes from Andersonville were few, so perfect was the training of the bloodhounds already referred to. The effort was made by several of those who were on parole. A cousin of mine, who was working at the cookhouse, came to the dispensary one day, wanting to get some turpentine. I asked him what need he had for it. He said be wanted it to rub his feet with. Then, calling me to one side, he said that several of the boys at the cook-house were going to make an effort to escape, and had been told by a darkey that by rubbing their feet with turpentine and onion broth they could baffle the bounds. I tried to dissuade him from the attempt, urging the chances against it; but I found that he had fully counted the cost, and nothing but the experiment would satisfy him. (He had been one of Walker's Nicaragua soldiers.) I told him that I would place myself in a position that might bring me into trouble in case they were recaptured, which in some way I felt would be the case, and that if they were pursued he must dispose of the bottle by all means. With this instruction and understanding I gave him a half-pint bottle. I told Oyen and Schroeder what I had done.

Next morning early we heard the horn calling the dogs to the hunt, and learned that four of the cook-house boys had made their escape during the night. I listened with considerable anxiety to the baying of the hounds as they circled around in search of the trail, but they seemed to be confused, and after several hours gave up the hunt, baffled. We were encouraged to hope that the boys might succeed, especially as the day wore away without any tidings, and the next also. We began to breathe easier, but on the fifth day Dr. Karr, who had charge of the paroled men at the hospital, came rushing into the shanty with the turpentine bottle. He asked Dr. Brown if he had given any one a bottle of turpentine, or if he knew anything about it, and received very truthful negative answers. He then came on to Oyen about it; but the latter swore that he had never seen the bottle to his knowledge, neither did he remember having filled one for any party outside of the hospital orders. Schroeder was next called to the stand, but he said that he never gave such a bottle of turpentine out— "sure and certain only to de hospital."

I happened to come in just then, and a glance was sufficient to place me on my guard, as I knew the ordeal was coming. Turning to me, the doctor demanded:

"Did *you* ever see that bottle," holding it in front of my face, "or know anything about it?"

"Why, yes," I said, taking it from his hand, and taking up another just like it, "it's one of our bottles, certainly, as you can see for yourself."

"Yes, I know it is!"

"Why," I asked, innocently, "is there anything remarkable about it, or connected with it, that you want its history or to identify it?"

"Yes, by God," foamed the doctor; "there is just this about it. Those fellows who escaped from the cook-house have been brought in this morning, and this bottle of turpentine was found on them, and they say they got it at the dispensary, but would not tell how or of whom. Now I want to know who they got it from."

"Well," I said, "I presume they got it from me, I gave one of the cook-house hands a bottle of cough-medicine in it several weeks since."

"That's a fact," said Brown; "I remember when you did it, and he needed it too."

"Well," said Karr, "that is a satisfactory accounting for the bottle, but how in hell are you going to account for the turpentine in it, when there is no place this side of Americus, except here, that they could get it filled. Explain that, will you?"

"Nothing astonishing about that," I said; "don't you remember the conversation you and I had about that barrel of turpentine when you blocked it up at the end of the shanty? I told you then you had better put it in the storehouse; that that was not a good place for it. They could go there and get a bottle of turpentine themselves as easily as we could get it for them, and they would be getting it at the dispensary too. Of course they wouldn't tell you how they got it."

"That's so, that's so," he said; "I never thought of that. You were right about it. I was mighty 'fraid some of you-uns had been getting yourselves into trouble. I must have Dance get that barrel into the storehouse so they can't come any more such games over us."

I tell you I breathed easier when I saw that his mind was satisfied on the turpentine question, for the old stockade rose up vividly before my mind. But if that barrel had been put under lock and key, as I suggested at first, I don't know just how the case might have ended.

Schroeder, who during the conversation had been sitting on his bunk sweating with anxiety, came up to me, saying, "Py gollies, dat vas bully done! I must any vay shake handts mit you. Py tunder, Hydt, I didt tremple in my poots vhen I saw dat Dr. Karr mit dat bottle of turpentine. How in tunder did you so quick tink of all dat so slick; you youst vas so cool; you trow him off the track so quick, und madt it youst so plain as anyting. It vas any vay lucky for you aboudt dat medicine for a cough, py gollies; it vas goot generalship and it vas any how lucky for dot barrel to be outsidt. It vas youst luck all through—Vhat!!!"

Chapter XXXIX

A Southern Family's Bereavement

AS the holidays approached, we of the dispensary thought we would have a feast on Christmas, so White and I started out to hunt up the necessary extras. Following the railroad about a mile south, we found a Mr. Hickox, who promised to bring us two chickens, a peck of sweet potatoes, and a couple pounds of butter, the day before Christmas. In order to get some extra bread we began a week before to increase our quantity of flour for pill mass, in this way secreting about two pounds daily, so that we had a sufficient quantity by the time we wanted it. A Mrs. Smith living nearly a mile south did our baking. Thus we had a big Christmas dinner and no thanks to the authorities for it. In fact, after we were taken out of the stockade we could find enough to add to our prison fare to make it passable enough, but we had to make it by trading with citizens and not letting the authorities find it out.

Mrs. Smith would take her horse and buggy and go six or eight miles into the interior and bring in things for us. She was a strong Union lady, though she had to keep both that fact and her work in our behalf a strict secret. I had won her favor by a chance though sad circumstance. They had four children, one of whom, a boy named Wyatt, six or eight years of age, was a remarkably bright child and a great favorite. I happened over at her house one afternoon and found Dr. Thornburgh and the mother bending over him as he lay unconscious, evidently suffering from inflammation of the brain. The mother was bathing the burning brow with cold water, herself almost wild with agony. The poor fellow's sufferings were so intensely felt by the remaining portion of the family that they could not remain in the room. I asked the Doctor if depletion would not give some relief, and he said he had no lancet or he should have resorted to it before. I told him I had a thumb lancet at camp and would get it, but before I returned the child died. He had only been sick three days.

They were a heart-broken family, and as there were none there to assist in this hour of their emergency I told the doctor if he would answer for me in camp I would remain and assist in preparing the corpse for burial. The poor woman begged very earnestly for me to stay. Oh, how tenderly and carefully she lifted her darling boy, as we washed and dressed him, no one else coming into the room. After we had done this I asked in regard to a coffin. "Ah," she said, "Oglethorpe is the nearest point where we can get one." I inquired if they had any lumber that would do, and she suggested the boards in the garret floor overhead. I selected such as I thought would do, and told her to send the black boy over to camp with them, and I would try to find a carpenter among the paroled men. I was fortunate enough to find one who had done such work, and he made the coffin for them. This done, I had gone as far as I could; it would not have done for me to appear in the funeral train, as it would have taken me past Wirz's office, and might have resulted unpleasantly for them as well as for myself.

It was several days before I saw the family again, but when I did call the bereaved mother burst into tears as she thanked me for my kind interest.

"If it had not been for you," she said, "I do not know what we would have done."

I always had a warm welcome when I called there after that, and when she learned that I was going to leave Andersonville she sent word to know what day I was going to start. On the morning that I left, her black man brought me the half of a boiled ham and nearly a peck of biscuit, begging me to accept them as a memento of her kind regards.

CHAPTER XL

Jeff Davis's Speech at Macon

IN September Jeff Davis made a tour through the South, inspecting the Confederate army confronting Sherman, and trying to create enthusiasm among the disheartened soldiers. It had already been hinted that Sherman contemplated cutting loose from Atlanta and making a march to the sea. The Confederates hooted at the idea and tried to convey the impression that it was not a strategic move, but, on the contrary, a military necessity, as Hood had taken charge of that department and bad cut off Sherman's supplies so that he was likely to lose his whole army if he could not get up a communication by the seaboard and establish a base in that direction. That all sounded pretty enough, and no doubt the people down there took stock in it; but we got hold of the Macon "Telegraph" nearly every day and knew pretty well how things were moving.

The army under Hood was fast becoming little more than an organized mob, great dissatisfaction existing among his soldiers, many of whom were taking furloughs without leave. It was this state of things that necessitated Davis's visit of encouragement to the west, and on the 23d of September he tried to pour oil on the troubled waters in a great speech at Macon City, a report of which we got in the "Telegraph."

Some of those who went from Andersonville to hear him reported the speech as being the greatest rhetorical effort they had ever heard (which might have been and no doubt was so). They came back ablaze with enthusiasm. They told how, if Sherman cut loose from Atlanta, dis-

164

aster worse than that which overwhelmed Napoleon at Moscow would meet him at every step, and how his army would be annihilated if he remained at Atlanta; in fact, they brought it down to so fine a point that annihilation awaited him, take which horn of the dilemma he might. However, we did not "scare worth a cent." But when we read the speech in the "Telegraph" we were astonished that any sane man, holding the position that Davis did, would make a speech showing up so clearly the true state and helpless condition of the western army, and the tottering condition of the whole structure of secession, at such a critical time. It sounded more like the unmethodical speech of a lunatic. I will give it as reported in the "Telegraph."

"LADIES AND GENTLEMEN, FRIENDS AND FELLOW CITIZENS: It would have gladdened my heart to have met you in prosperity instead of adversity, but friends are drawn together in adversity. The son of a Georgian who fought through the first Revolution, I would be untrue to myself if I should forget the State in her day of peril.

"What though misfortune has befallen our arms from Decatur to Jonesboro, our cause is not lost. Sherman cannot keep up his long line of communication, and retreat sooner or later he must; and when that day comes the fate that befell the army of the French Empire in its retreat from Moscow will be reacted. Our cavalry and our people will harass and destroy his army as did the Cossacks that of Napoleon; and the Yankee general, like him, will escape with only a bodyguard.

"How can this be the most speedily effected? By the absentees of Hood's army returning to their posts; and will they not? Can they see the banished exiles, can they hear the wail of their suffering countrywomen and children, and not come? By what influences they are made to stay away it is not necessary to speak. If there is one who will stay away at this hour, he is unworthy the name of Georgian.

"To the women no appeal is necessary; they are like the Spartan mothers of old. I know of one who has lost all her sons except one of eight years. She wrote that she wanted me to reserve a place for him in the ranks. The venerable General Polk, to whom I read the letter, knew that woman well, and said, 'It is characteristic of her.' But I will not weary you by turning aside to relate the various incidents of giving up the last son to the cause of our country known to me. Wherever we go we find the hearts and hands of our noble women enlisted. They are seen wherever the eye may fall or the step turn. They have one duty to perform,—to buoy up the hearts of our people.

"I know the deep disgrace felt by Georgia at our army falling back from Dalton to the interior of the State, but I was not of those who considered Atlanta lost when our army crossed the Chattahoochee. I resolved that it should not be, and I then put a man in command who I knew would strike a manly blow for the city, and many a Yankee's blood was made to nourish the soil before the prize was won. It does not become us to revert to disaster. Let the dead bury the dead. Let us with one arm and one effort endeavor to crush Sherman. I am going to the army to confer with our generals. The end must be the defeat of our enemy.

"It has been said that I abandoned Georgia to her fate. Shame on such a falsehood. Where could the author have been when Walker, when Polk, and when General Stephen D. Lee were sent to her assistance? Miserable man! The man who uttered this was a scoundrel. He was not a man to save our country. If I knew that a General did not possess the right qualities to command, would I not be wrong if he was not removed? Why, when our army was falling back from northern Georgia, I even heard that I had sent Bragg with pontoons to cross it to Cuba. But we must be charitable. The man who can speculate ought to be made to take up his musket.

"When the war is over and our independence won,—and we will establish our independence,—who will be our aristocracy? I hope the limping soldier. To the young ladies I would say that in choosing between the empty sleeve and the man who had remained at home and grown rich, always choose the empty sleeve. Let the old men remain at home and make bread; but, should they know of any young man keeping away from the service who cannot be made to go any other way, let them write to the Executive. I read all letters sent me from the people, but have not the time to reply to them. You have not many men between the ages of eighteen and forty-five left. The boys—God bless them — are, as rapidly as they become old enough, going to the field.

"The city of Macon is filled with stores, sick, and wounded. It must not be abandoned when threatened; but when the enemy comes, instead of calling upon Hood's army for defense, the old men must fight; and when the enemy is driven beyond Chattanooga they, too, can join in the general rejoicing.

"Your prisoners are kept as a sort of Yankee capital. I have heard that one of their Generals said their exchange would defeat Sherman. I have tried every means, conceded everything, to effect an exchange, but to no purpose. Butler, the beast, with whom no commissioner of exchange would hold intercourse, had published in the newspapers that if we would consent to the exchange of negroes all difficulties might be removed. This is reported as an effort of his to get himself whitewashed by holding intercourse with gentlemen. If an exchange could be effected I don't know but I might be induced to recognize Butler. But in the future every effort will be given, as far as possible, to effect the end. We want our soldiers in the field, and we want the sick and wounded to return home.

"It is not proper for me to speak of the number of men in the field, but this I will say, that two thirds of our men are absent; some sick, some wounded, but most of them absent without leave. The man who repents and goes back to his commander voluntarily appeals strongly to Executive clemency. But suppose he stays away until the war is over, and his comrades return home, and every man's history will be told, where will he shield himself? It is upon these reflections that I rely to make men return to their duty; but, after conferring with our Generals at headquarters, if there be any other remedy, it shall be applied. I love my friends and I forgive my enemies.

"I have been asked to send reinforcements from Virginia to Georgia. In Virginia the disparity in numbers is just as great as it is in Georgia. Then I have been asked why the army sent to the Shenandoah valley was not sent here. It was because an army of the enemy had penetrated that valley to the very gates of Lynchburg, and General Early was sent to drive them back. This he not only successfully did, but, crossing the Potomac, came well-nigh capturing Washington itself, and forced Grant to send two corps of his army to protect it. This the enemy denominated a raid. If so, Sherman's march into Georgia is a raid. What would prevent them now, if Early were withdrawn, from taking Lynchburg and putting a complete cordon of men around Richmond? I counselled with that great and grave soldier, General Lee, upon all these points. My mind roamed over the whole field.

"With this we can succeed. If one half the men now absent without leave will return to duty, we can defeat the enemy. With that hope I am going to the front. I may not realize this hope; but I know there are men there who have looked death in the face too often to despond now. Let no one despond, let no one distrust, and remember that if genius is the beau ideal, hope is the reality."

Chapter XLI

The Stockade Emptied

MEANWHILE the days rolled on, and Sherman still lay at Atlanta. Word came of a masterly flank movement made by Hood that would necessitate Sherman's retreat; still he stayed. I asked them why, if things were so dubious, the old fellow took it so easy; and I wondered, too, why it was that they were moving the prisoners from the stockade at the rate of a thousand a day until they were all removed, only the sick in the hospital remaining.

Then, too, one of the funny phases of the flank movement was that they lost sight of Hood's army; he seemed to have obliterated his tracks and severed his own communications, and for a number of days no tidings reached them of Hood's movements; yet still Sherman lay at Atlanta, seemingly indifferent as to Hood's army or flanking, and there he continued to lie until about the 16th of November.

The people reported Atlanta in flames and Sherman marching in two columns on central Georgia. Every available man was sent to oppose his advance. It was thought that Andersonville was to be one of the points aimed at, but when they bore to the east from Macon we knew better. Milledgeville was entered on the 23d of November, just two months from the day that Davis made his speech at Macon. General Howard was also reported at Gordon Junction. I asked them how that looked for a retreating army and a Moscow disaster. Oh, well; they were just getting him where they wanted him; they would soon have him surrounded, and then look out. I told them there was certainly the most system in that retreat of any I had ever read of; besides it was remarkable to witness such an army retreating on the offensive.

In a few days more we got the report that Sherman had entered Savannah, and had issued a proclamation from there, offering protection to any Confederate soldiers who would come in and lay down their arms, "which," I observed, "is the end of the most remarkable and masterly retreat the world ever saw."

While the stockade was empty they ploughed and harrowed it over. What the idea was I could not learn, but I suppose it was to obliterate the evidences of the makeshifts the boys had to make to get shelter. They also erected a row of sheds on the north end, but they were all put there after the stockade had been emptied, so that those who saw the place at the close of the war saw it in much better shape for comfort than it was when full of men. About the 1st of January, 1865, they returned from 4,000 to 5,000 prisoners, but they were treated better than the old occupants had been, though they were mostly of the old inhabitants. They issued wood to them occasionally, and they had the sheds mentioned to use for the sick. Otherwise they had to furnish their own shelters as formerly, and occupied the south side.

About this time General Winder ordered a druggist, clerk, butcher, several nurses, and fifteen negroes sent to Columbia, S.C., to our officers' hospital. We druggists drew cuts, and so did the clerks, Dorance Atwater and I being the lucky ones, a Mr. Smith drawing the butcher's lot. The 2d of February was the day set for our departure. The day before we left Mr. Smith and I concluded we would ask Captain Wirz for a pass to visit the old stockade. We wanted to see some of the boys there, and had a morbid curiosity to see where we had lain and endured the tortures of hunger and disease. We went over to his quarters, near the railroad, but had to wait awhile, as he had not yet put in his appearance. The clerk told us we might prepare for a general cursing and refusal. On his arrival we approached him politely, telling him we were under marching orders and would like to see some boys in the stockade if he would favor us with a pass.

"So!" he said, "you have to go to-morrow,—ha?"

"Yes, sir."

"Und got friendts in de stockade you vants to see,—ha?"

"Yes, sir."

"Vell, I guess I lets you go in to see de poys and bid dem goot py." He handed us a pass and went out without saying another word.

"Well," said the clerk; "what's come over the old man? That's the first pass he ever wrote, to my knowledge, without making things blue first."

Whether he remembered my ointment, and thereby felt kindly disposed, I cannot say, but we got our pass and were satisfied.

As that was my last interview with and sight of Captain Wirz, I will digress. I have frequently spoken of his profanity, and given some examples of his use of it in conversation, but they will give you but a vague idea of its extent. He was, beyond controversy, the most intensely and abusively profane man I ever met. Expressions of this character were of frequent use with him: "Py Schesus Christ, shust so sure as I am going to hell!" or "Shust so sure as I rill never get to heaven, I'll do so and so!" And his whole bearing was in keeping with his profanity. He ever carried the impression, to my mind, of a man lost to every good impulse, over whose door the "raven of despair" constantly sat, who had a foreboding of his fate and had heard his eternal doom in this life.

Armed with this pass we approached the south gate and were admitted within the enclosure. I confess to a shuddering sensation when I heard the gate creak behind me and found myself within, but there were only a few hundred men now on the south side. The north side was entirely empty. Commercial Row, with its motley crowd of a few weeks ago, had passed away and a barren tract of sand alone remained. Its site, even, could not be traced. On the south side we found the boys occupying quarters similar to those that had formerly marked the spot. The men, as a whole, were looking better; the scurvy cases had mostly died or gone to other prisons.

I found several of my old friends,—Coulson, the one to whom I gave the turpentine, among the rest. I told him how nearly it had come to getting me into trouble. He said they had been out several days without hearing anything of their pursuers; they supposed they were out of all danger, and under this impression they were sleeping during the day without a lookout, when a party came onto them with another pack of hounds, who were in search of runaway negroes. The dogs struck their trail and were on them before they had time to do anything.

I also found Carlisle, of my Danville escape, who had stood the racket fairly. They all crowded around us, anxious for news. We told them that everything indicated a near ending of the war, that the Confederacy was tottering on its last legs, and that everything pointed to their near release. We thought it was only a question of a few more months at farthest, until the gates would be opened never more to close. We gave them the latest news from Sherman. Their dull eyes brightened, and a spirit of new life seemed to enter into them.

I viewed the spot, as nearly as I could locate it in the changed condition of things, where Felix and I had shared our mutual woes. Oh, the feeling of intense horror that passed through me at this retrospect. I thought, with a shudder, of my helpless condition as I lay there that day when they called my name at the gate, and upon what a slender thread my life hung; it was all owing to the chance call reaching Felix's ear as he sat vending soup on Commercial Row. Oh, I thought, every grain of sand in that stockade, had it a voice, could tell a tale of suffering that would freeze the very blood in the veins,—a story of suffering that would shame Satan himself, and that would forever fix the names of the perpetrators on the black roll of infamy.

As it is, Andersonville has passed into history, and to the masses her horrors are fast becoming a myth. Yet there are living to-day thousands upon the tablets of whose memories their sufferings there are graven as with pointed steel. On the other hand, there are those living to-day, honored and emulated, upon whose souls hang the curses of the nearly fourteen thousand victims who fell under the weight of their cruelty at Andersonville, with those of many more who died at other prisons.

As the sun sank in the west we passed down to Providence Spring, quaffed again its sweet waters, bade the boys adieu, and passed for the last time from the old stockade, shaking the dust from our feet as its hinges grated behind us.

Chapter XLII

General Sherman's Footprints

A S we were to start early in the morning we spent our last evening in hunting up our friends and bidding them good-by. There are those whose acquaintance we formed there, whose faces we love to recall, though we have lost track of all of them personally and have seen none of them since we bade them adieu.

Early in the morning we gathered with the boys to eat our last meal together (the last even to this day), after which Schroeder and Hunt accompanied us to the depot. As I clambered into the box car Schroeder came up to bid me good-by; thrown together as we had been, under such adverse circumstances, ours had been no common friendship. He had been more intimately connected with me in my sufferings than any other of my prison companions, though fifteen years my senior. Our acquaintance began at Richmond and closed at Andersonville. His quivering chin spoke more than words as he grasped me by the hand, saying, "Goot py, Hydt, goot py!" Poor fellow!—he was one of the victims of the steamboat "Sultan" that blew up on the Mississippi.

We moved slowly away and intervening woods shut off every view of the prison. We were nothing loth to change, fully assured in our own minds that nothing worse could meet us in the future. For surely Andersonville must be the culmination of Southern diabolism, and every sign in the military prison was prognostic of the rapidly approaching dissolution of that child of hell, the Southern Confederacy. Hood's magnificent flank movement had ended in disaster at the hands of that sterling hero, General Thomas, at Nashville, and his army was dead to all usefulness; only a remnant remaining, and it not much more than a mob. Wheeler's cavalry was looked upon with as much dread by the citizens as were the Yankees. Wandering over the country in predatory bands, they were known as "Buttermilk Cavalry," and against them Governor Brown had issued a manifesto.

We were paroled for the trip to Columbia, and consequently were not under very strict watch, a company of the First Florida Battery being our escort. They were a very clever set of boys, with one or two exceptions, and were without any means to offer us any indignities, as they had not a gun in the whole outfit, having been ordered to Columbia to man a battery there. We had several hundred of the sick from the hospital who were being sent to Macon, at which point we arrived about daylight on the morning of the 3d.

The train was heavily loaded with freight, except one car for the guards; consequently we had to take our position on the top, where we made ourselves as comfortable as we could; yet an allnight ride in February, on the top of freight cars, in our scantily clad condition, even in that latitude, was very uncomfortable to say the least. While possibly most of us slept some, we were nearly benumbed with cold, especially the sick, and when we came to unload, about sun-up, we found that two of our number slept "the sleep that knows no waking," and several more had become unconscious.

Leaving the sick. we who were ordered to Columbia were put aboard another train and taken to Gordon Junction, where we were again delayed several hours. This was the third time, in the past seventeen months as a prisoner, that I had been at Gordon; yet, like the boy who had been absent from home a whole month and "hardly knew the place, things had changed so," I could hardly recognize it. It had verily undergone a change since I last saw it.

Where before had been a nicely laid railroad track, nothing but the bed remained; the irons could be seen lying around in every conceivable shape; in some places six or eight encircled one tree. They lay here and there, cork-screwed, twisted, linked, hooked, and distorted into shapes almost inconceivable for a thing of that nature. Pieces of charred ties and fence-rails, broken walls, standing chimneys, and "sich," looked as though pandemonium might have been holding high carnival at this point, and broken up with a kind of "hell-let-loose" recklessness. Yet we were told it was only *one* of the footprints of General Sherman,—the Howard end of the reptile. My conscience! I thought, if this is the effect of setting down only one foot, what a lively, rollicking old time there must have been when he came down with his whole heft and went to work in earnest.

It was wonderful, even after eight weeks had passed, to "view the landscape o'er," and we thought it no wonder that the home guard (Dr. Thigpen) who went out near Andersonville to be ready to "close in when they got Sherman in the right place," returned so soon, awed by the immenseness of his immensity.

"Why," he said, in speaking to me about it, "he moved with the irresistible impetuosity of the roaring, rushing avalanche, sweeping everything before it, desolation and ruin marking its track. Our little company of home guards didn't seem to attract his attention any more than a feather would the tornado, and I just thought the healthiest place for me was at home. I might as well be there as to be running ahead of Sherman, so I left, and here I am, glad to be here."

I must say I took a great deal of silent satisfaction from the thought that where we now stood an army of bluecoats, possibly my own regiment, had been camped but a few weeks before, and left their work so plainly inscribed. It was almost as good as a letter from the regiment, telling plainly that they were all well and full of their fun.

The track had been relaid up to within a mile of Milledgeville, where we left the train and went into quarters for the night. We had to camp as we could find room among a multitude of Confederate soldiers who were being transferred from Hood's army to the East. They were very free to talk, and expressed themselves as much discouraged. I asked one of them their destination; he said he did not know, but supposed they were for the Eastern army, adding:

"We've been badly whipped and cut up by General Thomas at Nashville, and I suppose they want to finish us up in front of Sherman or Grant. It looks as if running is our business now, and we are getting tired of it and want to go home to our families."

They were very kind to us, furnishing utensils for preparing our supper, and in some cases sharing their rations with us. As this was the end of the railroad we had to march across country to another line running from Atlanta to Augusta.

I was disappointed in Milledgeville; it presented a very dilapidated appearance that morning, whether owing to the recent Yankee invasion or to natural decay, I could not tell, but we expected more in the capital of a State like Georgia. We found that the bridge across the Oconee, owing to Yankee cussedness or the result of war, had passed into the list of things that were, and we had to cross on a pontoon bridge, following the direction of the road grade which had never been finished to Carnak.

We marched along very leisurely, our squad sometimes measuring a mile or more in length. Our escorts were mostly men of leisure and did not seem to care so long as we kept in motion. We enjoyed hugely the passing through the country in this way. The marches were so easy that we stood it better than we expected, and had as much freedom as the guards themselves. The citizens along the way took us all for Confederates guarding the little squad of negroes.

We only made ten miles on our first day's march, and then camped to await the captain of the battery, who came that evening. Next day, about eleven o'clock, we reached Sparta, and lay by for several hours, as it was Sunday. A number of the citizens came out to where we were stopping in a little grove, just at the edge of the town, apparently to talk up the situation. They had a great many questions to ask us regarding the negro prisoners, where they were captured, what we intended doing with them, etc. I was talking with a party one of whom, an old man, claiming to have been born in Massachusetts, was very bitter in his feeling against the North. He seemed to be spokesman for the crowd, and, supposing I was one in charge of the negroes, asked me:

"Where are you bringing those black fellows from?"

"From Andersonville," I replied.

"Not prisoners of war, are they?"

"Oh yes; regular soldiers captured in line of duty."

"Where are you going with them?" was the next question.

"Taking them to Columbia, S.C., under an order from General Winder; we suppose he wants them to do drudgery about the prison hospital at that place," was my reply.

"You'd better a damned sight send them back to their masters and let them take care of them," he rejoined.

"You are wrong there," I said, "'those fellows have never been slaves; they are free-born Northern darkeys; if you will converse with them you'll find they are much better informed than darkeys reared in slavery. Those fellows can all read and write." (I didn't know whether they could or not, but put that in on general principles.)

"The ———have no business down here fighting white men, then. You'd better a damned sight take them down into the timber and run them up or shoot them, than to be guarding them through the country here; don't you think so?" asked this Northern-born Southerner.

"What?" I exclaimed. "Would you have us hang or shoot a lot of defenseless prisoners, simply because they are black and have been so unfortunate as to fall into our hands?"

"No," said he; "I can't say that it would be right to do it now, after they have been taken once; but the great mistake is in our boys suffering them to become prisoners; they ought to shoot them down whenever they catch them bearing arms in battle."

"Ah, then you'd raise the black flag against the black man," said I. "You are opposed to giving them any quarter?"

"*Yes*, I am," he replied; "the ———, they ought to be shot down where they are caught, when found bearing arms."

"Well now," I said, "you had better take your musket and go right to the front to do that kind of work. You'll find plenty of them up there to shoot at. You ought not to be back here in the rear, talking of hanging defenseless prisoners whom somebody else has taken."

Exit the Confederate with a flea in his ear. The guards, several of whom had heard the conversation, enjoyed the fellow's discomfiture very much. Whether he ever found out that he was talking to a Yankee I do not know.

Chapter **XLIII**

Robert Toombs and Alexander H. Stephens

WE reached Warrenton, to which point the cars were running over a temporary track, a mere military make-shift. We remained at this point until next evening, reaching Carnak early next morning. Here we expected to take train for Augusta, but learned that there was an obstacle in the way of reaching Columbia by that route, General Sherman being reported at or in the vicinity of Branchville. So, to prevent running across our friends, it became necessary for us to perform a flank movement by running up to Washington, the terminus of another branch road.

It was a very chilly day, and I was suffering from the effects of a severe sprain in the small of my back, received about two months before I left Andersonville, caused by having the weight of a heavy box thrown onto me suddenly while unloading some drugs. It seemed to me at the time that my back cracked as loud as a pistol report; it "wilted" me, to use an army expression, and I could not walk a step for several weeks. The marching and the motion of cars had aggravated the trouble so that I was glad to lie by.

We remained here for two days, encamped in a grove close to town. This was the home of Robert Toombs, so, notwithstanding my lameness, I managed to get to town to take a view of his residence. He seemed to live in good style, judging from external signs. His house, set back from the street, and almost hidden in shrubbery and trees, must have been a pleasant retreat during hot weather. On the opposite or south side of the street was his brother's residence, also a fine building for those days.

We talked with several citizens, who expressed considerable dissatisfaction at the state of affairs in the South. The financial burdens of the Confederacy were beginning to be extremely oppressive, every town having its revenue collector, who made heavy demands upon all products of the land. The people were beginning to look upon the thing as being a grinding tyranny. Nearly all the able-bodied males were enrolled in some capacity, and yet Sherman could wander around and there were not enough people left to offer any opposition to him.

Near where we encamped was a saltpetre leach, there being a number of leaches of several tons capacity. These were filled with earth collected from beneath the houses in the town, after which it was leached in the same manner that ashes are leached for lye in making soap. The lixivium was then evaporated in large pans. The amount of saltpetre collected in this way was small, but it kept several wealthy men's sons in government employ out of reach of danger. The young man who seemed to have charge was communicative, and I asked him in regard to the work. He said it was attended with a great deal of labor and small results. It was very laborious work getting the dirt from under the houses, though of course it was done by negroes. Then it required several days to exhaust a stand. A run usually made from six to eight pounds of commercial saltpetre, so that the manufacture of rebel powder in all its details would be interesting to follow.

The citizens began to object to the Yankees having the freedom of the town, urging that we were liable to do some act of incendiarism that would endanger the whole place, or that we might inflame the minds of the negroes and cause trouble in that way. Consequently we were ordered to remain in camp unless accompanied by a guard. Brave Washingtonians! They patrolled the town the night before we left.

Being the home of a noted Southern leader, we had felt considerable interest in seeing all we could of the place. Perhaps no other man in the State of Georgia had more to do in shaping the destiny of the State and drawing it into the vortex of secession than had Robert Toombs. Reared in the doctrines of Calhoun, and full of Southern bigotry, he was an enemy to the broad principles of a republican government,—a government of the people by the people for the people; and he was well fitted to lead in an attempt to overthrow it. As one of the representatives of his State in Congress, he had solemnly pledged himself to support the Constitution of the United States; yet early in the struggle he was one of the most potent and vindictive in seeking its overthrow, bitterly opposing Alexander H. Stephens in debate at Milledgeville, when he so earnestly pleaded with his people to remain true to the old flag. His strong will so overcame the weaker one of Stephens, that he was finally made to succumb and go with the tide.

There is no question but that if Stephens had been possessed of the staunch patriotism and noble firmness of Parson Brownlow, he would have counterbalanced the damnable perfidy of Toombs (that being the mildest construction I can put upon his actions), and become a rallying-point around which the Union element of Georgia—and it was strong—would have gathered and become invincible as was the band of hardy mountaineers who, clustering around Brownlow, proved the salvation of east Tennessee. As it was, his vacillation was as dangerous, and I do not know but worse, to the whole South, than was Toombs's open hatred, as Toombs's influence was not felt beyond his State, while that of Stephens was national in its character. We find the perfidy of the one and the weakness of the other rewarded by high positions in the Confederate Assembly; Stephens being elected Vice-President and Toombs being appointed Secretary of State.

It was a most unfortunate thing for the South that the mass of her people were not capable of intelligently investigating the great questions that led to secession, because they could not read, and consequently could not study them in the quiet of home, but were compelled to receive instruction from these very leaders, and generally under the influence of strong political excitement, in which blind fanaticism loves to measure swords with better judgment. The whole history of secession, from its inception to its close, is the most unanswerable argument, practically demonstrated, that could possibly be given in affirmation of education being the cornerstone and bulwark of a republican form of government. It was the demonstration of the problem that reduced it to a fact. It should stand out as an everlasting memorial, warning us as a nation to frown down and treat as a national enemy any party, whether civil or ecclesiastic, that offers any discouragement to the free dissemination of knowledge in our public schools. Educate our children, and political demagogism will lose its power to sway. Legislate to circumscribe the free education of our youth, and we legislate to political death. Ignorance and error go hand in hand, and fanaticism is their legitimate offspring.

Perhaps the citizens of Toombs's native town were justified in their fears that some of us might apply the incendiary torch to his residence. They doubtless had observed our scrutiny of the buildings, a pertinent fact being that there are none so afraid of justice as those who feel they have not had their past deserts at her hands.

CHAPTER **XLIV**

John Calhoun and State Rights

A S Washington was the terminus of the road, we took up the line of
march in the direction of Abbeville, S.C. One of the peculiarly noticeable features of our march through the country was the ease with
which we could procure eatables from the negroes, while the guards
could not get anything either by money or by threats. The negroes were
very shrewd, in point of intelligence much beyond what was accorded
them by the South, and they seemed intuitively to know the Yankee
from the Rebel. While they were ready and quick in supplying us, if the
guards attempted to secure anything they would declare, "We don't got
nuffin' to give." Sometimes one would attempt to impersonate a Yankee, but it would not win. "You no Yankee," they would say. The guards
generally took it in pretty good part, but sometimes they would threaten
to kill "the damned woolly-heads."

The first day out from Washington, as we were marching along,
we came to a point from which we could see several miles ahead, and
wondered at the peculiar appearance of the trees, which in the distance
seemed covered with snow. As we advanced, however, we found ourselves in the track of a tornado that had passed a few days before, and,
in its course, had demolished a cotton-gin and spread its contents in
such a way as to give the peculiar appearance we had noted. Several
new houses had been turned or moved on their foundations; trees were
blown down or wrenched off; fences were demolished and cotton was
strung on everything erect for nearly a mile.

As we neared the Savannah River the way seemed to become more animated and lifelike. We encountered many refugees and white families fleeing from South Carolina with their effects, to save them from Sherman, seeking temporary refuge in Georgia. If it had not been that truth knocked all the poetry out of the situation, it would really have been laughable in many cases (not but what it was serious enough to those immediately interested), but the Yankee "cussed-ness" was so big in us that we could not but feel more amused than otherwise and more gratified than cast down. It made us feel as though we were "getting the moccasin on the other foot."

About noon, or soon after, on the second day, we came to the Savannah River at the confluence of the Broad. Crossing right at the fork we stood once more on the "sacred soil" of South Carolina. In the early evening we filed off onto a wood-covered hillside and camped for the night. Near by was an old fashioned hewed log house of considerable size, from the well of which we got our water for cooking purposes.

And now we found that we had in truth camped on "sacred" ground. That house was the hallowed shrine toward which all true Southerners of the old régime pray,—the Mecca, so to speak, of the Confederacy, the fountain of State rights. Beneath that roof a child had been born in years past, who developed into the original secessionist and nullifier, John Caldwell Calhoun, a man of remarkable ability in some respects and dwarfed in others. Reared in a hollow, the narrowness of his surroundings possibly left its impress on his character; at least he was not a man of such broad views as would make him a safe manipulator of public affairs pertaining to a republican form of government. He did not appear capable of those higher essentials, those expansive ideas, that would enable him to grasp and solve the problem of a united country composed of dissimilar elements bound together, as one and indivisible, in Federal compact; and, rather than such a bond should result, he would sacrifice the whole to a part. He sought to establish and perpetuate a slave oligarchy; for the whole question of the much-talked-of "Southern rights" simmers itself down to a desire in a few individuals to establish for themselves a limited monarchy based on an aristocracy fastened by that peculiarly Southern institution, African slavery, itself a source of licentious indolence and vice.

CHAPTER **XLV**

The End Approaching

EARLY in our next day's march we passed the really beautiful mansion of another and later Calhoun, beautifully embowered in a grove on a rising knoll. Its colonial verandas and projecting roof gave it a subdued grandeur that bespoke the home of a well-to-do planter, and it was the only one we had passed in all our march across country. It seemed to give a standing invitation to the weary traveller to stop in and rest. It had the really hospitable look so frequently spoken of by travellers through the South in days gone by.

A sharp turn in the road which follows the trend of the narrow valley, up a steep pitch, brought us into Abbeville, close under the walls of a church whose tapering spire and neatly proportioned vane carried our minds back to the village-dotted hills of our own beloved Ohio. We had passed, too, from the region of pines into forests of hard woods, which helped to carry out the association and brought to us new-born hopes. We camped in a grove near the southern part of the town, if simply enjoying the protection of the trees could be called camping. As I was still suffering severely with my sprained back, my friend Atwater collected me a bed of leaves, and spread an old piece of tent cloth over them, so I rested comparatively easy, though the marching had about played me out. I was glad to learn that we would probably remain here over Sunday, a rest somewhat necessitated by my condition, as I could not stand alone next day. The weather was all we could desire; even at

182

that early season we felt no inconvenience from being in the open air without fire save to cook by.

We had now been nearly two weeks on the way from Andersonville, and Columbia was still in the future. From the little news and vague rumors that reached us from the negroes who managed to get around, we learned that it was very doubtful if we would ever get there. We resembled a sailless and rudderless bark on the wide ocean, now drifting with the wind, and now becalmed. It was very evident that our whole march from Gordonville had been a series of flank movements to avoid meeting our friends, who, we were morally certain, were at no time more than fifty miles away. It was also certain, from the conduct of the guards, that adverse winds were blowing against the Confederate ship of State, though to what extent we could not tell. It was patent, however, from our manner of marching, that we were keeping just about parallel with Sherman's army, and exercising no little caution to keep out of his way. We learned also that General Winder, under whose orders we were moving, had died of apoplexy since we started. Our guards therefore determined to carry out their first instructions to take us as near to Columbia as prudence would permit.

On the morning of the third day, February 13, we took the train and ran several hours until we came to a washout in the road, when it became necessary for us again to take to the highway. We were nothing loth to do so, as we courted delay, and we generally made easy marches, our guards not feeling called upon to rush matters. It seemed to be a kind of holiday with all concerned. We were now travelling toward Columbia from the west and expected to meet a train at Alston that would carry us there that evening, provided our friends did not get there before us and necessitate another flank movement on our part. We passed squads of people hurrying into the "back country," in wagons and carts, on horseback, on muleback, and in every conceivable way; some carrying immense bundles on their backs, some driving cattle, sheep, hogs, turkeys, geese, and even goats. Occasionally we would see a fine carriage loaded with women and children, and with trunks, bedding, and light furniture piled on top,—like the rest, seemingly intent on reaching the back country. This of course was an evidence of something behind. As the long line of scum indicates the approach of the tidal swell, so this anxious hurrying away from Columbia indicated the near approach of a power as irresistible in its course as the waves of the sea.

"Whar you-all going, uncle?" asked one of the guards of an old, gray-headed negro who had an immense bundle of bedding on his head; "what's the matter with you-all?"

"Runnin' away from Sherman, sah; he's dun comin' sure, sah; speck dey'll be in Columbia befo'-night; dey's only fifteen miles away, sah, and comin' strait along's fast as dey can, sure."

"Well, but whar you going?"

"Don't know, sah, dat's sure!."

"Well, for God's sake, uncle, don't run too far, or you'll run out on the other side; you will as sure as you're born, it's getting small now."

Those negroes *looked* a deal more than they spoke. As eye telegraphed to eye we fully understood that there was no hope of our reaching Columbia that night, if ever. We reached Alston, some twelve miles west-by-north of Columbia, about noon, and stopped to let the company close up. The Confederates drew to one side to hold a consultation, and we were enjoying the rest afforded by the halt when the ominous boom of a cannon reached us from the direction of Columbia. Another and still another. Of course we knew not of what nature they were, but supposed they were signal guns, and we took it as an evidence that Sherman was not far away.

It became a question with us whether our guards would make any further advance in that direction,—a question which was soon answered by the order to fall in. We started in a direction to the left and at right angles to the road to Columbia. We were once more adrift, and navigation was becoming dangerous. We were executing another flank movement to avoid our friends, and moving on Winsboro. The booming cannon seemed to give fresh impetus to the flying citizens; all was bustle and confusion. Consternation seemed to seize on all. It was the first time in my army experience that I happened to be in position to observe the effect of an approaching victorious enemy upon the inhabitants of the country. There seemed to be no thought of resistance, but an uncontrollable desire to abandon everything. Taking the expression of the citizens as my criterion, I could have supposed we were in imminent danger of being captured by a band who would mercilessly trample us into the dust and wipe out every trace of our existence,—an invader as ruthless as the flood. Neighbor inspired neighbor with terror until the mental agony of women and children was piteous to see, as they sought safety in flight, loading themselves with whatever could be loosely gathered together in their hasty flight.

Ours was really a peculiar position. We were a squad of Yankees loose behind the scenes, yet no one seemed to notice us or think anything of our being there. Possibly they did not know we were not of them. The guards did not seem to care any more than the rest, and paid no attention to us when we reached Winsboro other than to find quarters for us and themselves in the court house. We passed the evening rather uproariously. There happened to be an old violin and a drunken

Irishman in the crowd, and between the two we had a loud time of it. The prisoners' squad was in excellent spirits, of course. The fact could be concealed no longer that the Confederate balloon had been punctured and was in a state of collapse. We had no longer Andersonville to dread, as they would not dare to retain us, and there was a possibility, if we remained in Winsboro long, "of falling into our own hands," as one of the party jocularly expressed it.

The confusion and hubbub on the streets, and the jam on the railroad, continued through the night, and by early dawn we were in the thick of it, seeing what was to be seen and enjoying the uproar. Trains were moving prisoners and valuables from Columbia with a recklessness indicative of haste. We went to the depot and watched the citizens hurrying their effects aboard the cars, and I thought Sherman's army would have been safer hands for furniture to fall into. The baggage-smasher was in his glory, and got his work in well. I got on top of a car on the side track, beside a Confederate officer who was in charge of the Yankee officers from Columbia prison. The jam was such that he could not get his trains out, and the Yankees would insist on poking their heads out of the freight car doors, which made him furious. He drew his sword and made a pass at one, and threatened to shoot another, yelling at the guards to shoot the first Yankee ———that showed his head.

Everybody was excited; the trains from below seemed to have the right of way,—they held it at least, and Winsboro could not get her cars attached to any of them. Consequently everyone was in a perfect fever of excitement and suspense lest Sherman's cavalry should come in on them and destroy everything. I presume it was well for us that we were not known as Yankees; but oh! how we enjoyed it, having nothing at stake! We felt—

"It must be now the Kingdom coming, the Year of Jubilee."

I saw one of the bankers roll a keg full of specie out of the bank along the pavement, and thought at the time that if Kilpatrick's cavalry should happen to drop in on him somebody would get a nice haul.

The court house had a very tall spire, in which was fixed a town clock. While all was confusion below, Mr. Atwater and myself found our way up into the tower and set the machinery of the old clock to running. We then went down into the street and mingled with the crowd. Pretty soon the "iron tongue of time" in the tower began to sound. Its first note had scarcely rung out before nearly every eye was turned in that direction. Heads were shaken ominously; the old clock had spoken; the old clock that had not been in running order since the war began had broken silence. What could it mean? Was it a warning? As we passed along the street we could hear them ask,—

"Did you hear the old clock strike? It struck three!"

I think if Gabriel had given a toot or two on his horn it would not have inspired more awe than did the clock in the steeple as it sounded that day over the doomed town. People's minds were in that state of extreme tension that anything unexpected seemed almost to overcome them. I'll venture to say that you will find parties in that country who will solemnly swear the old clock struck a warning; for three days from that time Winsboro was in Yankee hands and in flames. The old clock fell with the rest.

Mr. Atwater secured a relic from the desk in the court house, in the shape of the "town whip," such an instrument as I have described as used in the punishment of "Old Sue" at Andersonville. We supposed that it was used in the public chastisement of negroes. The handle was all notched up, indicative, perhaps, of the number of victims who had felt its weight. I think Mr. Atwater told me, after the war, that he had presented it to the National Museum at Washington as a relic of the days of darkness.

It was very evident from the railroad jam and the overcrowded condition of the cars from below that we would have to spend another night in the court house. We were much more crowded the second night, owing to straggling soldiers coming in to lodge, but we got along very well together. One young man, who was returning to his regiment from furlough, had a box filled with such luxuries as a loving mother would be apt to find for her boy when sending him away to the front. This regiment was with Lee at Richmond. After he had opened his box he asked if I would not come and eat with him, saying he could perhaps give me more generous fare than I would otherwise get, and as the roads were in such a crowded condition he would not be able to carry his box with him. Thanking him kindly I took a seat beside him on the floor, and "Yank" and "Confed" broke bread together.

We feasted and chatted together harmoniously, not a word passing between us indicative of the difference in our characters, and I did not know whether he knew me as a prisoner until after we had finished eating, when he remarked that he had seen an article in the paper regarding an exchange of prisoners that might interest me, and that if he could find a paper on the street he would secure it for me. I saw no more of him that night, but next morning he came hurrying in with the paper, wishing, as he waved an adieu, that I might soon have a happy realization of the article in question,—which was to the effect that in all probability an exchange of all prisoners held by either side would soon be effected.

As I went into the street I saw one of our squad engaged in an amicable discussion with a citizen and joined myself to the group in time to hear the stranger (whom I think they called Judge Reynolds) giving expression to an argument so original in part that I took it down, and here produce it as an example of the feeling of representative Southern men, for he said he had once represented his State in Congress. He was from Charleston. It seems they were discussing the capability of the Southern States to maintain an existence independent of the North, and the eternal fitness of slavery, giving the latter an attribute I had never before seen or heard accredited to it.

"Why," said the judge, "the South is dependent on the North for none of the necessaries of life. We have everything within our borders that is necessary for the building up of one of the greatest commercial countries in the world. We have fine harbors and navigable rivers, plenty of lumber for shipbuilding and all mechanical purposes, and an inexhaustible quantity of iron and coal. Gold is found in our mountains, also marble and building stone. We can raise plenty of cotton for factories, and have some of the finest unimproved waterpowers in the world, where factories can be run at small expense to work up the raw material. We raise the finest tobacco in the world outside of Cuba, which, with rice and sugar, the great commodities of the world, we can export as a source of revenue. Your great North depends upon us for all these things, and has to buy them from us as necessaries, while we are dependent on her for nothing but ice and whores. These are all we get from the North, and, as luxuries, we can dispense with them. By slavery we hold our females from becoming prostitutes; our slave women serve us as mistresses, thereby removing from our young women the temptations that would otherwise be urged upon them. Slavery is the great safety valve of the South."

A portion of the judge's argument, regarding the slave women, was evidently true, from the great number of almost white slaves that could be seen in any portion of the South. In fact I have seen many handsome women who were slaves, in whom not the slightest trace of negro blood could be discerned. What influence all this might have had in establishing a high standard of virtue among the fair daughters of Dixie I am not able to say, but it seemed to me an admission that should have been a cause for shame rather than an admitted argument in favor of slavery.

Chapter XLVI

The Prison Hell at Salisbury

THAT afternoon we bade adieu to Winsboro, boarding a train for the
North, and after an all-night ride we arrived at Charlotte, N.C. Here
there was a complete jam; the trains from Columbia stopped here, and
every available foot of track seemed occupied. The Treasury and Engrav-
ing Departments of the Confederacy occupied several trains. The attachés
of these departments were mostly women. The "promise to pay two years
after the ratification of a treaty of peace" could not stand the pressure of
Sherman's boys in blue, and rolled out of Columbia in a lively manner,
though what for I never could imagine. Certainly they had nothing our
boys would care for. Their miserable paper was then freely offered by the
citizens and soldiers at twenty dollars for one in greenbacks, the money
of the "Lincoln hirelings." I wondered how I would feel fighting for a
cause, and offering that amount of its medium for one of the medium of
my enemy, and that, too, to a prisoner in my hands. It was a kind of pseudo
confidence in the stability of the cause that bore a lie on its face. We taunted
them considerably regarding it. Southern business men would curse the
United States and tell how they were willing to die and rot in the "last
ditch" before they would consent to live again under such a despotic government, and how easily they could get along without any help from the
"damned Yankee," while at the same time a greenback dollar went much
farther with them toward feeding the hungry and clothing the naked than
did a Confederate "promise to pay." They did not stop to consider the
want of harmony between their actions and professions. It looked like

188

madness, though we had to confess that this discrimination in favor of greenbacks showed method.

I think I heard more profanity in those four days of railroad jamming than generally falls to an ordinary lifetime. The unsavory side of human nature seemed to be atop, and it is wonderful how man's selfishness reveals itself under such excitement. Demoralization ruled with a high hand, and respect for the gentler sex and tender youth was lost sight of. The blush of modesty availed not.

After another night's delay we boarded the train, and in due time, without further mishap, brought up at Salisbury, N.C. Here was located another of the prison hells, and it seemed for a time as though our evil star was in the ascendant, for after leaving the train we were marched to the prison stockade and once more we were surrounded by frowning guards and made the companions of misery and filth.

We found Salisbury some little improvement on Andersonville, though not much. There were several factory buildings inside the enclosure which were available for hospital use, and underneath the buildings quite a number of the boys found good comfortable quarters. Aside from these there were no shelters or accommodations provided, and the men fared similarly to those at Andersonville. The water here was drawn from wells, and the ground, being of a clayey nature, held the water so that the quarters were damp and the streets muddy during rainy weather. One of the factory buildings was a prison for Confederate military offenders, deserters, etc. Our two weeks' exercise in the open country and pure air had restored acuteness to our olfactory nerves, so that we were very sensible of the odor that pervaded the place, similar to the loathsome smell that attaches to a pest-house. We had considerable difficulty in finding an unimproved tract to file a claim upon, but succeeded finally, by dickering and squatting, in getting room to lie down. Of course that was all we needed, and with that we were satisfied and felt ourselves fortunate.

We found the place under the charge of Major Moffit, who was commanding at Danville during our sojourn there. Smith, who had been paroled as butcher under the Major at the former place, saw him the second day of our confinement and told him we had been paroled at Andersonville for the trip around to Columbia; that we had been faithful to our pledge all the time, though we had had ample opportunity of escaping, and he thought that it was not in good faith for them thus to confine us. Major Moffit claimed not to be aware of these facts, and told Smith to have all the whites of the party at the gate next morning, when he would take us out and send us north on the first train and have us exchanged at Wilmington.

When Smith came back we were busy in trying to improvise a shelter from our scant wardrobes. After standing by and watching our ingenuity for a time, he said, "Well, you needn't bother yourselves about a shelter. Why? Oh, we are going out of here in the morning!" Then he told us his conversation with the Major. We had him repeat it the second time, and then we made him sit down on the blanket and tell us once more, and what Moffit had said. It was hard for us to realize at one telling. We asked him if he thought Moffit meant it.

"Yes, I do," he said; "any way it won't be long to wait, so we'll just make ourselves as comfortable as we can and finish our improvements to-morrow."

"I vow," said Atwater, cutting a pigeon-wing, "that'll be bully!"

It was a ray of hope to say the least, a straw to grasp at, a theme for dreams through the night. It seemed almost too good to hope for, and yet why should we not be exchanged after nearly eighteen long weary months of privations, anxiety, and sufferings beyond the power of pen to describe. We had been looking for a rift in the cloud, through which a ray of light might penetrate, on which to base a hope of deliverance. And now would to-morrow come? Ah, yes; but would Moffit come with it, or was this a "delusive hope," an *ignis fatuus*, to lead us into the fastness of the swamp, that we might be swallowed in the quagmire of despair? No! something seemed to assure us that all would be well. We had marked the decadence of the Southern cause in marching through Georgia and South Carolina, and we felt that our tribulations were near an end. We spent the greater part of the night in talking about it. There was "no slumber for the eyes nor sleep for the eyelids" that night. To-morrow, we felt, would of a surety see the beginning of the end, and in accord with that belief early morning found us waiting by the gate.

The sun's first rays, as they shot across the pen, cast our shadows on the gate, waiting, trembling between hope and fear. Higher and higher the day-god climbed his accustomed way, until the half of his first quadrant had been accomplished, and still we stood within. We had almost given up, when the gate slowly turned back on its hinges and Major Moffit stood before us, paper in hand. As our names were called we passed out one at a time and were immediately taken to the depot. It would be impossible to tell what emotions filled our breasts as the gates closed behind us. We were glad, under the circumstances, that we had been placed in this stockade, being the fifth prison in which we had been confined. It gave us an opportunity of studying the character of each.

The prisoners at Salisbury told us how they had been shot at on the slightest provocation, and had been deprived of their rations for fancied misdemeanors, and how on one occasion even artillery had been brought to bear on them. This was some time in November, 1864, about three months before we were confined there. It appeared from their report that several of the squads had been deprived of rations for several days because of some offence committed by members belonging to those squads, and the authorities cut off the rations of the whole squad until the offenders were given up. Possibly they were known, possibly not; I did not learn as to that. The men were driven to desperation by such treatment, and declared they might as well die trying to make their escape as to die of starvation, so they organized, and when the relief guard came they overpowered them and seized their guns. In the *mêlée* two of the guards were killed and several wounded. The alarm of an outbreak was immediately sounded and the forces and citizens called to arms. It must be remembered that only a very small number of those confined there were engaged in the revolt. Yet the authorities ordered two field-pieces mounted on the walls to be double-shotted and discharged into the mass. The guards and citizens fired at the men indiscriminately, and notwithstanding that five or ten minutes of such work were sufficient to quell the disturbance and to drive every man to the shelter of his improvised tent, they continued for some time to shoot at any one who showed himself, thus wounding many and endangering the lives of all, whether guilty or not. There were fifteen killed and something over fifty wounded.

As Salisbury was our last prison I will say here, after a careful study and sad experience in so many of them, that to me the whole system of rebel prisons seemed to be a studied, systematized mode of torture intended to offset the arming of the negro by the North. As the Southern cause began to wane, and the conviction was brought home to the Confederates of how they had underrated the strength and valor of the North, and had equally overrated the prowess of the chivalric South, the vindictive spirit natural to the training they had received under the fostering influence of slavery manifested itself in their treatment of the prisoners. Note General Forrest's brutal, inhuman butchery of the negro soldiers and their white officers at Fort Pillow,—an act that should have given his name to infamy and his body as food to buzzards. This same vindictiveness ran through the whole system and history of rebel prisons. During my nearly eighteen months' experience I was (very fortunately for myself) at different times placed in position carefully to study and observe its workings. All the prison-keepers, so far as my observation extended, were men of strong Southern prejudices, in whom the animal nature was strongly marked, and the moral impulses were correspondingly weak. The faithfulness with which they followed the spirit of malice, and the implacable fidelity with which they pushed it to the bitter end, needs no further evidence than the many thousands of graves of Union soldiers in the prison cemeteries, while thousands yet alive show in their shattered constitutions the fruits of prison life. Why was it that the Northern prisons did not show similar results? Let any candid person contrast the results of the two systems, and they will find out that what I say cannot be gainsaid. The deliberate system of torture inaugurated and so faithfully executed in the prison pens of the South are historic facts so deeply graven that time can scarcely obliterate them.

Chapter XLVII

A Slaveholder's Dilemma

REACHING the depot we found that no provision had been made for sending us away, so that all we could do was to await further developments. We had been so long under prison discipline and whimsies that we did not try to look farther ahead than the present moment; so we made the best disposition we could of ourselves to secure personal comfort if we had to remain any time in the depot.

We had in our squad an Irishman from the Twenty-seventh Massachusetts, who, with that peculiar faculty known only to those initiated, managed to get enough tanglefoot to keep up a double head of steam, that kept us at our wits' ends to keep him in proper bounds. We hadn't been out of the pen an hour before Pat came around the corner of the depot singing an Irish bacchanalian song. Starting off with his body bent forward, he would spring suddenly erect and bring his hands down to his hips with a slap. Merging his steps into a double shuffle, he would wind up with "St. Patrick's Day" and cap the whole by springing in the air, cracking his feet together, and shouting "Hoorah for the bloody Twenty-Seventh and the shamrock of old Ireland!"—then coming to "attention" in front of a squad of negroes who had clustered around to watch his movements. He was irrepressible in his maudlin fun. One of his auditors, who had aspired to the dignity of a very fair plug hat and polished boots, attracted his attention finally, and, stepping up to him, he said: "Jabers, and that's a foine hat yees after wearing, my good mon, an maybe it's affther thrading with a por devil loike me, ye'd be at now,"—at the same time lifting the darkey's tile from his head and giving it an elegant poise on his own. "But the loife of me now, an thot's a fit loike the gintleman that I am,—an' it's a thrade, ye say is the same now, my good mon. Yees a gintlemon if yees is black." Then he pulled his greasy time-worn cap over the head of the darkey, who looked as though he failed to see that mutual consent of two usually necessary to make a bargain, though he acquiesced with a fair grace. Pat said, "Good, me foine man. The 1oike o'ye can afford to do that for the bloody Twenty-Seventh,"—and away he went on one of his comical rounds on a double shuffle while the darkey and his squad made themselves scarce. As the guards showed no disposition to interfere, Pat kept the hat. The last we saw of Cuffee he was the centre of a circling squad some distance down the track, where he stood cap in hand, looking very subdued, while Pat came up to us, lifting his hat with a stately bow, and saying, "Say, now, an didn't oiworrk that thrade foine on the black divel." There seemed to be no compunction in Pat's make-up.

While I was watching the Irishman's manoeuvres I noticed a citizen coming leisurely along through the depot, and stopping occasionally to pass a word with the boys. Finally, coming up to me, he said,

"I am told you are from Ohio; are you from any place near Lancaster County?"

I told him there was a county seat named Lancaster in Fairfield County, but no Lancaster County in the State.

"That is the place," he said.

I told him it was my county.

"Good," he said, "there will be a man here pretty soon to talk with you," and he passed out of the depot, going up the street.

It was not long before another man came in like manner directed to me. He asked me if I knew any one of the name of Richwine. I told him there was one of that name in my regiment.

"Well," he said, "that's my brother. I am glad to meet you; come up to my house, I want to talk with you."

I told him it would be impossible for me to do so without a guard.

"I'll arrange it," he replied. Taking me to the officer in charge he said, "I want to take this man to my house and give him something to eat, if you will allow it. I will vouch for his safe return."

"All right," said the officer, "take him along, but be back by sundown, as we expect to start by that time."

So I went with him to his house and had a sumptuous repast on bread and milk. He said he had not heard from any of his family since the breaking out of the war, which found him, through matrimonial alliances, with a farm near Salisbury and the consequent negro appliances, which put him in just such a condition that he could not get away without great sacrifice. So he concluded to remain and chance it there for a small sum, not anything to compare to old prices, but much better than to have to turn them loose. "Some parties advise me not to sell," said he, "but to hold on to them, and if they are liberated by the exigencies of war I can recover full value from the government. Now, do you think the government will remunerate the people of the South for her liberated slaves. What is your idea of it?"

"Well," I said, "you are placing me in a delicate position, and asking me a question difficult to answer, and at best I can only give you my convictions on the matter, as to what may be done in the adjustment of the negro problem, and in doing that I may clash swords with you, and possibly wound your feelings in your own house, which you might consider an unjust return for your hospitality."

"Not at all," he said, "a free, unbiased opinion is what I want,— the idea of a man who has no personal interest in slaves, as all the people here have. I want your advice and your opinion as a Northern man; it may decide me as to what I should do in the case."

"Very well, then," I said.

"You see," he continued, "where I stand, I've got to act quickly and make my answer in a day or two."

"My opinion then," said I, "is that the time has passed in which the South may indulge a hope or even the shadow of a hope for such reimbursement. If she had accepted the terms of the overtures made by Lincoln's first proclamation, by the terms of the proposition the government would be held. That was the probationary period. Those were the days in which mercy could have been found, and the South haughtily refused to accept the terms. In Divine law, a mercy rejected is damnation accepted. Now, let me ask you, does a conquering nation ever compensate her enemies for losses of property they may have incurred as a result of war?"

"No, certainly not," he said.

"Much less, then, would it become the duty of a government to reimburse a portion of her citizens for losses they may have sustained as a result of their rashness in attempting to overthrow that government. You see the absurdity of the position at once. No human eye in 1861 could have penetrated sufficiently far into the misty future as to know what great social changes would be wrought by the conflict. Certainly the South had not counted on the abolition of slavery as being one of the possible changes. In the first place she assumes the position of a total separation from the United States and appeals to arbitration by arms under the infatuation, if you please, of an exalted opinion of her own prowess. Discouraged by the outlook after three years of disastrous war, she now seeks to assume the position of non-liability for her actions, and hopes that the government which she sought to overthrow will in its magnanimity overlook the heavy cost already accrued and add more by paying her for the goats and bullocks she offered on the shrine of her idolatry, or, in other words, paying for her lost property. For what is your slave, more than your horse, your cow, your mule, your hog, or any other livestock you may possess; he is simply a chattel to be disposed of at your will."

"Very well," he said.

"Then why can you hope for remuneration for a slave more than for any of the rest?"

"That is just the view of it I have taken," he said. "But our big slaveholders are counting on some day getting pay for their freed slaves, if the North conquers, and the man who offers to buy mine seems to have no fears as to that, and he is a bitter rebel."

"Well," I said, "as you ask my advice, I think you will be foolish to hesitate a moment in making a transfer of your slaves to him."

"But then," he said, "you may not know the warm ties that exist between us and our slaves. I would hate to sell mine to him and have him sell them and separate them."

"Very true," I said, "under the old régime, but don't you understand that virtually they are free already, and Sherman is liable to drop in on you any day and then they are free indeed. If you can secure yourself by the sale, let him have them; it will be good enough for him. Sherman has probably taken Columbia by this time, and will soon be here."

"Yes," he replied; "word came here last Saturday evening that General Hampton had evacuated Columbia and set fire to the town. Winsboro had also been taken."

While I was prepared to hear of Hampton's evacuation, I was surprised to learn that he had applied the torch to the place, and asked what reasons were assigned for so doing, as there was certainly no military advantage to be gained by it, the city being of no particular advantage to Sherman.

"No," he said. "But when Hampton withdrew he left a regiment of cavalry, with orders, when all available stores were removed, to burn what remained, together with all the cotton, a considerable quantity of which had been collected there. This was done, and from this the fire extended to the city, urged on by a stiff breeze blowing at the time."

"Yes," I said, "and the Yankee will get the credit of it!"

"No," he said, "the report is that they did all in their power to put out the fire, and it was only through their exertions that the city was not entirely destroyed, and this report I heard confirmed by other parties soon afterwards."

Thus I passed the afternoon very pleasantly with Mr. Richwine, and when it became time to return he gave me a liberal supply of light biscuit and butter to take along, which my friends Atwater and Smith made rapid disposal of.

Sundown came, but no means were supplied for our journey, and sunrise found us still in the depot. We might possibly have felt easier if we had been a little farther removed from the prison, which was but a short distance away to our left. Yet some way I felt that we would not again be put under such severe restriction. My friend of the day before came to see if we got away. Finding us still there, with no provision, he told me to keep watch up the track for his negro boy, whom he would send with something to breakfast on. Soon after I saw a little darkey lugging a market basket, dodging back and forth among the cars. Coming up to where I was standing, he set the basket at my feet and passed out. I found a feast within that might have done justice to the stomach of an epicure, hot mashed potatoes, sauerkraut, chicken, and biscuit enough to last all day.

In the afternoon Mr. Richwine came down again and visited me for fully an hour. It seemed to do him good to have some one to freely express himself to. As he took me by the hand to bid me good-by he pressed a twenty-dollar Confederate bill into my palm, saying it might do me some good before I reached the lines. It was not much, very truly, but the spontaneity of the gift, and the spirit in which it was given, spoke a value for it far beyond its intrinsic worth, and for that value I still retain the bill, as a souvenir,—"the silver lining," if you please, to the dark cloud of surrounding circumstances.

Near the depot on the opposite side of the town, and on the same side as the prison, was a large building used as an armory. From the workmen there several came to talk with us. One especially, I remember, asked if I thought he would be conscripted and forced into the army if he went North. He said that that was the report circulated there, that all refugees were conscripted, but if he was sure there would be no danger he and several more fellow workmen at the armory would make their escape to the North. I assured him there would be no danger at all on that point, as the appearance of a stranger anywhere in the North would not even be a matter for comment, let alone for conscription, but I advised him, if he had any interests at stake, to remain where he was, if he was so situated by his mechanical skill that he would be exempt from conscription in the Southern army. I told him that if he had a position for two or three months, by all means to hold on to it, and I thought by that time there would be no need of his leaving Salisbury to get inside the Union lines, as probably the lines would come to him and he would have no principle to sacrifice that might make it unpleasant afterwards. He said he thought himself that the Confederacy was becoming unsteady and tottering. He told me substantially the same story regarding the evacuation and burning of Columbia that Mr. Richwine had.

The burden of the Confederacy had come to be truly onerous, and a system of tithing or military tax-collecting had been organized by which the tillers of the soil, and producers generally, were required to bring in a percentage of their products in kind. The collector at this point we found to be John Noles, the Danville Prison stuttering Englishman, whose office was near the depot. One of the boys, who had been a cook at Danville, recognizing him, made himself known. Noles asked him if I was in the crowd, and, learning that I was, he sent me word to call around some time in the afternoon to see him. I must confess to considerable astonishment at the delivery of such a message, and told the fellow he must have misunderstood him. "No," he said, "he asked particularly for you by name and wants to see you."

Really my only acquaintance with Noles was when he took me up to headquarters at Danville to identify my gold pens, etc., but my curiosity was excited and I went up toward evening to his office. He greeted me cordially, and had scarce passed the compliments of the day before he began to apologize for the false impression he made at Danville, saying "Hi th-th-thought you would b-b-be hexchanged sh-sh-shure th-th-that time." He had a great many questions to ask regarding my trials since I left Danville, and talked freely and feelingly of the sufferings of the prisoners and the outlook for Confederate success, which he thought dark and foreboding. He had prepared and in readiness for me a large piece of boiled ham (still hot) and some fresh bread, which he hoped would prove acceptable, as he had not had time to get anything better. He said he was very sorry he had not learned sooner of my being there. Certainly under these peculiar circumstances I dwell with pleasure on this meeting with John Noles, Military Collector at Salisbury., N.C.

Chapter **XLVIII**

Once More Under the Old Flag!

WE had now been thirty-five hours waiting at the depot and not a mouthful of rations had been issued to us during that time. True, circumstances had so wonderfully intervened that a portion of us had fared sumptuously, and all had by Yankee ingenuity and traffic secured something to eat. Still the authorities were none the less censurable for their negligence, as it would have been all the same with them if we had not received aid from outside sources. Darkness was again settling around us, and we were making preparations to spend another night in the depot, when a train came along on which we were fortunate enough to secure room, and were soon rolling onward in the direction of the North.

Sunrise found us at Greensboro. Here the train was delayed some time, and we were permitted to get off, but not to leave the train. The captain in command of the guard said,

"Keep them men together near the train, as we do not know how soon we may start."

"We have," was the answer made by one near me, "all but that fellow over there with the stovepipe hat, and the devil himself could not keep him together without shooting him."

He alluded to Pat, who had wandered off to one of the street corners, where he had taken up his position, his plug hat set on the forward part of his head, and was vigorously dancing a double shuffle, singing at the same time in stentorian voice, "St. Patrick's Day in the Morning," to the amusement of a dozen or more citizens whom his antics had drawn around him.

By the time they got Pat gathered in, the order came to mount, and we moved on to Raleigh. Here we again entered a scene of jam and confusion which seemed inextricable. An extra guard was thrown around us, composed of boys from fourteen to eighteen years of age and men from the workshops. The boys were under military training, Wore a uniform, and bore the chivalric name of cadets. A great many of them looked out of proportion to the guns they carried, and brought forcibly to my mind the time-worn verses:

"Oh, were you ne'er a schoolboy."

One of them came near having serious results to me. I was standing in the door of the car—a common box car—when one of the boys, in attempting to get in on the other side, tossed his gun in first, which struck in such a way as to discharge it, the ball striking me squarely on the heel of my right foot and bounding back several feet. I really thought my whole foot was gone. The force threw my foot out vertically. Smith, who was sitting near, cried out, "Hyde is shot," and sprang to my assistance. On examination it proved to be a severe contused wound, drawing but little blood, but most excruciatingly painful. It was certainly a most wonderful and providential circumstance. The cartridge was lightly charged, as at that distance a full cartridge would have blown my foot to atoms. As it was, it spoke well for the toughness of my *tendo Achillis,* proving me to be more invulnerable in that point than Achilles himself.

After rations had been issued to us in the raw state, we were taken a mile or so out of town and went into camp, or rather field, as we had no camp equipage of any kind, nor any cooking utensils outside of our prison make-shift. My foot pained me so that I could not walk, and two of the boys carried me on a pole, one at each end, while I sat on it with an arm around each of their necks. We had received accessions to our ranks at different points since leaving Salisbury, so that we now numbered several hundred as ragged, squalid-looking men as ever squadded together, though we were mostly in good spirits, in anticipation of near exchanges.

We remained at Raleigh until the next morning, when we again boarded the cars for Goldsboro, arriving there early next day. There we were to be paroled preparatory to being sent through the lines. As we were marching from the train to the camp, perhaps half a mile distant, one of the sick men lay down in the road exhausted, and died. Poor fellow, he was not able to travel, but the excitement produced by the hope of a near exchange had acted as a tonic for a time and nerved him to attempt the trip in hopes that he might reach his friends and find him "a grave in his childhood's home!" The tenacity with which he clung to life was really surprising, bearing up until he fell exhausted and died in a few seconds. No one seemed to know him, and a grave was hastily dug and he was buried where he fell at the side of the road. We passed the spot a few hours afterward on our return to the railroad. We were paroled and started toward Wilmington that evening, reaching neutral ground on the 27th of February, 1865, about ten o'clock in the morning.

As the train was brought to a halt right in the woods, and we were ordered to get out, we beheld on the left-hand side of the train an officer and company of United States soldiers standing ready to receive us. It was a glorious sight to our prison-wearied eyes. The Stars and Stripes proudly waved above them, emblem of the free. Fronting them was a company of Confederates with the contemptible rag floating over them under which we had seen so much misery. It seemed to me that the old flag and the boys in blue never looked so beautiful. Much as I wanted to give a hearty cheer, I could not utter a word. I was really too full for utterance. To be free again and to feel that we were breathing the air of freedom was enough.

For one year five months and seven days we had seen nothing but trouble under the shadow of the Confederate "Bars," and finding ourselves once more "within the lines" seemed the dawning of a new era. It hardly seemed possible that all the misery I had seen and suffered could be crowded into the memory of those months. Even now, as I look back and reflect upon the privations and exposures, the heavy drain upon the physical and mental system to which we were exposed, I am not surprised at the fearful results of the well matured and executed plan of the rebel prison system, but I am surprised that so many of us lived through it from its inception to its close and are still alive. What atrocities were committed in the name of Liberty and "Southern Rights." How applicable were the dying words of Madame Roland as she bowed her head to the guillotine: "O, Liberty, how many crimes are committed in thy name!" To that tattered, dirt-begrimed, disease-shattered crowd who shook the dust from their feet as they passed from beneath the Stars and Bars to the protection of the Stripes and Stars, the Old Flag had a newer and grander significance than it had ever borne before to us! It was the emblem of Life, of Light, of Home, and was rendered doubly dear to us by our long sojourn beneath the shadow of one whose reign was Terror!

THE END